Lecture Notes in Computer Science 10518

Commenced Publication in 1973
Founding and Former Series Editors:
Gerhard Goos, Juris Hartmanis, and Jan van Leeuwen

More information about this series at http://www.springer.com/series/7410

Erich Schweighofer · Herbert Leitold
Andreas Mitrakas · Kai Rannenberg (Eds.)

Privacy Technologies and Policy

5th Annual Privacy Forum, APF 2017
Vienna, Austria, June 7–8, 2017
Revised Selected Papers

 Springer

Editors
Erich Schweighofer
Centre for Legal Informatics
University of Vienna
Vienna
Austria

Herbert Leitold
A-SIT
Graz
Austria

Andreas Mitrakas
European Union Agency for Network
  and Information Security
Heraklion
Greece

Kai Rannenberg
Goethe University Frankfurt
Frankfurt, Hessen
Germany

ISSN 0302-9743   ISSN 1611-3349   (electronic)
Lecture Notes in Computer Science
ISBN 978-3-319-67279-3   ISBN 978-3-319-67280-9   (eBook)
DOI 10.1007/978-3-319-67280-9

Library of Congress Control Number: 2017955573

LNCS Sublibrary: SL4 – Security and Cryptology

Printed on acid-free paper

This Springer imprint is published by Springer Nature
The registered company is Springer International Publishing AG
The registered company address is: Gewerbestrasse 11, 6330 Cham, Switzerland

Preface

It is our great pleasure to present the proceedings of the 5th Annual Privacy Forum (APF), which took place in Vienna, Austria, during June 7–8, 2017, organized by the European Union Agency for Network and Information Security, the European Commission Directorate General for Communications Networks, Content and Technology, and University of Vienna, as host. The oldest German-speaking university is looking forward to the new challenges of the knowledge and network society, in particular to the right to privacy for a free and democratic society. The General Data Protection Regulation (GDPR) was published in the Official Journal on May 4, 2016, to enter into force on May 25, 2018. On January 10, 2017, the Commission submitted the proposal for the ePrivacy Regulation. The basic framework for the implementation of privacy in electronic services is established but technological solutions and a viable implementation framework has to be further developed. Like last year, we focus on the implementation aspects of a sustainable future data protection framework. APF continues striving to close the gap between research, policy, and industry in the field of privacy and data protection. This includes presentations on privacy impact assessment, data lifecycle, and privacy challenges of new technologies.

We received 41 submissions in response to our call for papers. Each paper was peer-reviewed by at least four members of the international Program Committee (PC). On the basis of significance, novelty, and scientific quality, we selected 12 full research papers. Thus, this book presents 12 papers organized in three different chapters corresponding to the conference sessions.

The first chapter, "Data Protection Regulation," discusses topics concerning big genetic data, a privacy-preserving European identity ecosystem, the right to be forgotten and the re-use of privacy risk analysis. The second chapter, "Neutralization and Anonymization," discusses neutralization of threat actors, privacy by design data exchange between CSIRTs, differential privacy, and database anonymization. Finally, the third chapter, "Privacy Policies in Practice," takes the user on board, discussing privacy by design, privacy scores, privacy data management in health-care, and the trade-offs between privacy and utility.

In addition, four panels were organized:

- "Privacy Regulation in a Global Context Considering New Challenges Like AI" – to examine privacy-friendly solutions for a global market with big data analytics allowing more personalized services
- "Towards a European Data Protection Certification Scheme" – to explore the state of the art of certification mechanisms and data protection seals and marks
- "Practical Implementation of GDPR in Mobile Applications" – to discuss the application of data protection obligations in the area of mobile applications
- "Lawful Interception and PETs" – to find practical solutions between privacy enhancing tools and crime prevention.

We thank Springer for publishing the proceedings of APF2017 in the LNCS series.

APF 2017 would not have been possible without the commitment of many people around the globe volunteering their competence and time. We would therefore like to express our sincere thanks to the members of the PC – and to the authors who entrusted us with their works. Many thanks also go to our sponsors, in particular Microsoft, and to all conference attendees, who honored the work of the authors and presenters. Last but not least, we would like to thank the Organizing Committee. Their excellent and tireless efforts made this event possible.

July 2017

Erich Schweighofer
Herbert Leitold
Andreas Mitrakas
Kai Rannenberg

APF 2017

Annual Privacy Forum
Vienna, Austria, June 7–8, 2017

Organized by

European Union Agency for Network and Information Security (ENISA)
European Commission Directorate for Communications Networks,
Content and Technology (DG CONNECT)
University of Vienna

Organization

Program Committee

Luis Antunes	University of Porto, Portugal
Bojana Bellamy	CIPL, UK
Bettina Berendt	KU Leuven, Belgium
Athena Bourka	ENISA
Pompeu Casanovas	Universitat Autònoma de Barcelona, Spain and La Trobe University, Australia
Valentina Casola	University of Naples Federico II, Italy
George Christou	University of Warwick, UK
Fanny Coudert	Centre for IT and IP Law (CiTiP), KU Leuven, Belgium
Malcolm Crompton	Information Integrity Solutions Pty Ltd. and CSIRO, Norway
José María De Fuentes	Universidad Carlos III de Madrid, Spain
Paul de Hert	LSTS, VUB Brussels, Belgium
Roberto Di Pietro	Bell Labs, France
Josep Domingo-Ferrer	Universitat Rovira i Virgili, Spain
Prokopios Drogkaris	ENISA
Hannes Federrath	University of Hamburg, Germany
Mathias Fischer	University of Hamburg, Germany
Lorena González Manzano	Universidad Carlos III de Madrid, Spain
Graham Greenleaf	UNSW, Australia
Marit Hansen	Unabhängiges Landeszentrum für Datenschutz Schleswig-Holstein, Germany
Dominik Herrmann	University of Hamburg, Germany
Marko Hölbl	University of Maribor, Faculty of Electrical Engineering and Computer Science, Slovenia
Walter Hötzendorfer	Research Institute AG & Co KG, Vienna, Austria
Sokratis Katsikas	Center for Cyber and Information Security, NTNU
Stefan Katzenbeisser	TU Darmstadt, Germany
Dogan Kesdogan	Universität Regensburg, Germany
Peter Kieseberg	Kibosec GmbH, Austria
Els Kindt	K.U. Leuven, ICRI, Belgium
Sabrina Kirrane	Vienna University of Economics and Business, Austria
Dariusz Kloza	Vrije Universitet Brussel, Belgium
Stefan Köpsell	TU Dresden, Germany
Gwendal Le Grand	CNIL, France
Daniel Le Métayer	Inria, Université de Lyon, France
Herbert Leitold	A-SIT, Austria

Fabio Martinelli	IIT-CNR, Italy
Vashek Matyas	Masaryk University and Red Hat Czech, Czech Republic
Chris Mitchell	Royal Holloway, University of London, UK
Andreas Mitrakas	ENISA
Gregory Neven	IBM Research, Zurich, Switzerland
Sebastian Pape	Goethe University Frankfurt, Germany
Peter Parycek	Danube University Krems, Austria
Aljosa Pasic	Atos, Spain
Hans-Juergen Pollirer	Secur-Data Betriebsberatungs-GmbH, Austria
Joachim Posegga	University of Passau, Germany
Charles Raab	University of Edinburgh, UK
Kai Rannenberg	Goethe University Frankfurt, Germany
Vincent Rijmen	KU Leuven, Belgium
Heiko Roßnagel	Fraunhofer IAO, Germany
Kazue Sako	NEC, Japan
Peter Schartner	Universität Klagenfurt, System Security Group, Germany
Ingrid Schaumueller-Bichl	University of Applied Sciences Upper Austria, Austria
Stefan Schiffner	ENISA
Erich Schweighofer	University of Vienna, Austria
Jetzabel Serna	Goethe University Frankfurt, Germany
Florian Skopik	AIT Austrian Institute of Technology, Austria
Christoph Sorge	Saarland University, Germany
Morton Swimmer	Trend Micro, Inc., Germany
Christof Tschohl	Research Institute AG & Co KG, Vienna, Austria
Patrick Van Eecke	University of Antwerp, Belgium
Jozef Vyskoc	VaF, Slovakia
Edgar Weippl	SBA Research, Austria
Stefan Weiss	Swiss Re, Switzerland
Diane Whitehouse	IFIP working group 9.2 on social accountability and ICT, Austria/UK
Bernhard C. Witt	it.sec GmbH & Co. KG, Germany
Harald Zwingelberg	Unabhängiges Landeszentrum für Datenschutz Schleswig-Holstein, Germany

General Co-chairs

Erich Schweighofer	University of Vienna, Austria
Kai Rannenberg	Goethe University Frankfurt, Germany

Program Co-chairs

Erich Schweighofer	University of Vienna, Austria
Herbert Leitold	A-SIT, Graz, Austria
Andreas Mitrakas	ENISA
Kai Rannenberg	Goethe University Frankfurt, Germany

Additional Reviewers

Christian Burkert	University of Hamburg, Germany
Maximilian Blochberger	University of Hamburg, Germany
Nicolas Fähnrich	Fraunhofer IAO, Germany
Ioannis Fragkiadakis	University of Piraeus, Greece
Majid Hatamian	University of Frankfurt, Germany
Katharina Issel	Universität Regensburg, Germany
Alina Khayretdinova	Fraunhofer IAO, Germany
Marek Klein	University of Passau, Germany
Sergio Martinez	Universitat Rovira i Virgili, Spain
Alexander Marsalek	IAIK, TU Graz, Austria
Sara Ricci	Universitat Rovira i Virgili, Spain
Erik Sy	University of Hamburg, Germany
Carles Angles-Tafalla	Universitat Rovira i Virgili, Spain
Stephanie Weinhardt	Fraunhofer IAO, Germany

Sponsors and Organizers

Contents

Data Protection Regulation

The GDPR and Big Data: Leading the Way for Big Genetic Data?

Kärt Pormeister[✉]

University of Tartu, Tartu, Estonia
kpormeister@gmail.com

Abstract. Genetic data as a category of personal data creates a number of challenges to the traditional understanding of personal data and the rules regarding personal data processing. Although the peculiarities of and heightened risks regarding genetic data processing were recognized long before the data protection reform in the EU, the General Data Protection Regulation (GDPR) seems to pay no regard to this. Furthermore, the GDPR will create more legal grounds for (sensitive) personal data (incl. genetic data) processing whilst restricting data subjects' means of control over their personal data. One of the reasons for this is that, amongst other aims, the personal data reform served to promote big data business in the EU. The substantive clauses of the GDPR concerning big data, however, do not differentiate between the types of personal data being processed. Hence, like all other categories of personal data, genetic data is subject to the big data clauses of the GDPR as well; thus leading to the question whether the GDPR is creating a pathway for 'big genetic data'. This paper aims to analyse the implications that the role of the GDPR as a big data enabler bears on genetic data processing and the respective rights of the data subject.

Keywords: General Data Protection Regulation · Genetic data · Big data · Right to object · Right to be forgotten · Sensitive big data · Genetic privacy · Control over personal data

1 Introduction

An intriguing clause can be found in the Estonian Human Gene Research Act[1] (hereinafter 'the EHGRA') in regard to genetic data and the rules for personal data processing. Namely, according to paragraph 7(2) of the EHGRA, personal data processing rules do not apply to coded (i.e. pseudonymised) genetic data processing if the genetic data is being processed as a set of data, and on the condition that the data set includes the genetic data of at least five donors. Seen as the exemption from personal data protection rules is conditional both on the data being coded and the size of the data set, this rule could be referred to as a sort of 'big genetic data' rule, which relieves the data controller/processor from having to adhere to personal data protection rules when it comes to pseudonymised genetic data processing in larger volumes (i.e. in this case a minimum of five donors).

---

[1] *Inimgeeniuuringute seadus* (Human Gene Research Act), RT I 2000, 104, 685.

© Springer International Publishing AG 2017
E. Schweighofer et al. (Eds.): APF 2017, LNCS 10518, pp. 3–18, 2017.
DOI: 10.1007/978-3-319-67280-9_1

From a personal data protection law perspective, the notion of 'big genetic data' is a thought provoking concept that raises a number of questions, concerns and counter-arguments, and calls for an analysis of the concept in the light of the new General Data Protection Regulation[2] (hereinafter 'the GDPR'). The GDPR is a product of the data protection reform in the EU, whereas the reform itself has been labelled as "an enabler for Big Data services in Europe"[3]. In this regard, there is no differentiation in the GDPR as to different types of personal data. This leads to the question whether the GDPR is creating a pathway for big genetic data, and if so, what implications this bears on genetic data processing and the rights of the data subject.

In order to analyse the challenges of big genetic data from a data protection law perspective, first the substantive implications of the reform of the personal data protection regulatory framework on the processing of genetic data will be explored. Second, the notion of big genetic data will be explored in the light of the GDPR to introduce some key issues that arise from this concept.

2 Genetic Data Under the Personal Data Protection Regulatory Framework

Before exploring the concept of big genetic data under the GDPR it is necessary to address the regulation of the use of genetic data under the EU personal data protection regulatory framework in general. The implications of the GDPR on genetic data processing will be analysed by, first, addressing genetic data under the current EU framework, and, second, comparing the latter with the substantive rules that govern genetic data processing under the GDPR. As a third step, the issue of identifiability in terms of the concept of genetic data as a category of personal data will be addressed.

2.1 Genetic Data as a Novel Category of Personal Data?

The reform of personal data protection rules in the EU has resulted in genetic data being expressly recognised as one of a number of special categories of personal data (i.e. sensitive personal data).[4] However, genetic data has not been incorporated into the regulatory framework of personal data protection just recently – it falls under the

---

[2] Regulation (EU) 2016/679 of the European Parliament and of the Council of 27 April 2016 on the protection of natural persons with regard to the processing of personal data and on the free movement of such data, and repealing Directive 95/46/EC (General Data Protection Regulation) [2016] OJ L119/1.

[3] European Commission, 'The European Data Protection Reform and Big Data', (*Factsheet* march, 2016) <http://ec.europa.eu/justice/data-protection/files/data-protection-big-data_factsheet_web_en.pdf> accessed 31 January 2017.

[4] Art. 9, GDPR.
Art. 10, Directive (EU) 2016/680 of the European Parliament and of the Council of 27 April 2016 on the protection of natural persons with regard to the processing of personal data by competent authorities for the purposes of the prevention, investigation, detection or prosecution of criminal offences or the execution of criminal penalties, and on the free movement of such data, and repealing Council Framework Decision 2008/977/JHA [2016] OJ L119/89.

special categories of personal data under Article 8 of the current, 1995 Data Protection Directive[5]; most notably as part of data concerning health. This was already concluded in 2004, in a working paper of the Data Protection Working Party (the DPWP), which referred to the definition of personal data in Article 2(a) of the 1995 Directive stating, "There is no doubt that genetic information content is covered by this definition."[6] The DPWP emphasised the particularity of genetic data by adding that genetic data should be subject to "reinforced protection".[7]

Taking into consideration the complexity and sensitivity of genetic data, the DPWP stressed that with genetic data there is a great risk of misuse and/or re-use for various purposes by the data controller or third parties.[8] To minimise this risk, the DPWP strongly suggested that in terms of genetic data, the purposes for processing must be clearly defined.[9]

Considering how much other (sensitive) personal data genetic information can or could potentially reveal about a person and their next of kin, the clear determination of the purpose(s) for the processing of genetic data should be an essential precondition for processing. Even more, adding to a very crucial point, the DPWP recognised that the informative and practical value of genetic data would increase over time with the emergence of new technologies.[10] In this regard, in the context of genetic databases for medical and scientific research, the DPWP stressed the notion that with genetic data collection and the further processing thereof there is a specific issue regarding the fact that already retrieved data can later be further processed "for purposes that may have not even been conceived at the time of their collection".[11]

From the above it can be concluded that genetic data was subject to the personal data protection regulatory framework of the EU already before the reform. Furthermore, the specific risks concerning the processing of genetic data were outlined by the DPWP in 2004. Thus, the explicit incorporation of genetic data into the GDPR is not necessarily a revolutionary step or an immediate cause for celebration; although some have celebrated this explicit recognition of the sensitivity of genetic data as a solid step forward in terms of protecting genetic data.[12] Based on the DPWP's working paper, it

---

[5] Art. 8, Directive 95/46/EC of the European Parliament and of the Council of 24 October 1995 on the protection of individuals with regard to the processing of personal data and on the free movement of such data [1995] OJ L281/131.

[6] Data Protection Working Party. Working document on genetic data. Adopted on 17 March 2004, 12178/03/EN WP 91, p. 5. Accessible online at http://ec.europa.eu/justice/data-protection/article-29/documentation/opinion-recommendation/files/2004/wp91_en.pdf [last accessed on May 25th 2016].

[7] Ibid.

[8] Ibid., p. 6.

[9] Ibid.

[10] When describing genetic data the DPWP refers to the fact that genetic data "are likely to provide, in the future, scientific, medical and personal information relevant throughout the life of an individual." Ibid., p. 4.

[11] Ibid., p. 11.

[12] See, e.g., D. Hallinen et al. "Genetic Data and the Data Protection Regulation: Anonymity, multiple subjects, sensitivity and a prohibitionary logic regarding genetic data?" *Computer Law & Security Review* 29 (2013) 317–329, at 318.

is evident that the heightened sensitivity of genetic data, and the respective need for heightened protection, was recognised long before the data protection reforms. However, it appears that the result of the reform might impact the substantive rules governing genetic data processing contrary to the suggestions made by the DPWP.

2.2   Genetic Data Under the GDPR

Genetic data is expressly listed as a special category of personal data under the GPDR and as such is subject to the general prohibition of processing under Article 9(1). Hence, when it comes to the substantive rules governing the processing of genetic data, the devil lies in the exceptions to the general prohibition. In this regard, the GDPR follows much the same logic as the 1995 Directive. Thus the substantive rules regarding the processing of genetic data might best be illustrated by comparison between the current directive and the upcoming regulation.

The exceptions to the general prohibition of processing sensitive personal data in the 1995 Directive and the GDPR have been briefly compared in Table 1 (See next page)[13]:

The simplified comparison in Table 1 illustrates that – contrary to what one might assume, considering that one of the alleged aims of the data protection reform was to give "citizens back control over their personal data"[14] – the GDPR introduces additional exceptions to the general prohibition, creating further grounds for legally processing sensitive personal data without the data subject's consent. In other aspects, Article 9 of the GDPR very much resembles the current framework in its language and does not seem to create more uniform rules than the 1995 Directive. In fact, in a 2010 study conducted for the European Commission, the use of "rather vague requirements" of "appropriate guarantees" and "suitable safeguards" in terms of the rules regarding processing of sensitive personal data has been criticised as giving "Member States considerable freedom to apply, restrict or extend the rules on sensitive data".[15] The same vague requirements and resulting considerable freedom can be detected in Article 9 of the GDPR.

In terms of processing genetic data specifically, under Article 9(4) of the GDPR, Member States "may maintain or introduce further conditions, including limitations". Hence, the GDPR recognises the (possible) need for more stringent requirements regarding the processing of genetic data. However, at a time when the EU is moving towards a single digital market, and genetic data is processed digitally, fragmented

---

[13] The table is drawn for purposes of offering a brief introductory comparative overview. For the full and exact wording of the exceptions please see respectively Art. 8(2) of the 1995 Directive, and Art. 9(2) of the GDPR.

[14] As stated on the official website of the European Commission: http://ec.europa.eu/justice/data-protection/ [last accessed on May 25th 2016].

[15] D. Korff. Working Paper No. 2: Data protection laws in the EU: The difficulties in meeting the challenges posed by global social and technical developments European Commission Directorate-General Justice, Freedom and Security. Center for Public Reform, 20 January 2010, p. 73; accessible online at http://ec.europa.eu/justice/data-protection/document/studies/files/new_privacy_challenges/final_report_working_paper_2_en.pdf [last accessed on 3 June 2016].

Table 1. Comparison of Sensitive Personal Data Processing Rules under the GDPR and the 1995 Directive (apparent differences underlined).

1995 personal data protection directive	2016 general data protection regulation
Explicit consent (Art. 8(2)(a))	Explicit consent (Art. 9(2)(a))
Certain purposes in the field of employment (Art. 8(2)(b))	Certain purposes in the field of employment and social security and social protection law (Art. 9(2)(b))
To protect the vital interests of the data subject or of another person where the data subject is physically or legally incapable of giving his consent (Art. 8(2)(c))	To protect the vital interests of the data subject or of another natural person where the data subject is physically or legally incapable of giving consent (Art. 9(2)(c))
Processing relates to data which are manifestly made public by the data subject or is necessary for the establishment, exercise or defence of legal claims (Art. 8(2)(e))	Processing relates to personal data which are manifestly made public by the data subject or necessary for the establishment, exercise or defence of legal claims or whenever courts are acting in their judicial capacity (Art. 9(2) (e) and (f))
Purposes of preventive medicine, medical diagnosis, the provision of care or treatment or the management of health-care services, and where those data are processed by a HCP subject to a secrecy obligation (Art. 8(3))	Purposes of preventive or occupational medicine, for the assessment of the working capacity of the employee, medical diagnosis, the provision of health or social care or treatment or the management of health or social care systems and services, subject to safeguards, and under supervision of a HCP subject to a secrecy obligation (Art. 9(2)(h) and 9(3))
Reasons of substantial public interest subject to suitable safeguards (Art. 8(4))	reasons of substantial public interest, upon the condition that it is proportionate to the aim pursued, respects the essence of the right to data protection and provides for suitable and specific safeguards (Art. 9(2)(g))
–	Reasons of public interest in the area of public health subject to suitable safeguards, in particular professional secrecy (Art. 9(2) (i))
–	Archiving purposes in the public interest, scientific or historical research purposes or statistical purposes in accordance with Art. 89(1) (Art. 9(2)(j))

rules amongst Member States might not suffice and are likely to create a forum-shopping effect. Furthermore, this leads to the conclusion that the GDPR does not truly harmonise substantive rules concerning the processing of genetic data, nor does it strengthen them in comparison to the 1995 Directive.

Thus, as genetic data is subject to the 1995 Directive as a special category of personal data, and the personal data reform has had little impact on the substantive rules regarding the processing of sensitive personal data on the EU level[16], it appears that the *expressis verbis* inclusion of genetic data into the GDPR has a rather modest effect of progress in terms of safeguarding genetic data. To the contrary, the GDPR introduces further exceptions to the general prohibition of processing sensitive personal data, thereby adding to the legal grounds for processing genetic data without the data subject's consent.

To conclude, regardless of the heightened sensitivity of genetic data already recognised by the DPWP in 2004, the GDPR does not introduce a more stringent regulatory framework for the protection of genetic data in comparison to other types of sensitive personal data. Conceding, as D. Hallinan et al. point out, the general mechanisms of the GDPR that strengthen the transparency of the processing of personal data and add to the accountability of the processors/controllers will be applicable to genetic data as well[17] – which is certainly commendable. However, the GDPR does not add to the substantive safeguards of processing sensitive personal data; nor does it reinforce an individual's control over their genetic data.

2.3   Genetic Data as Personal Data

The GDPR defines personal data as data that can (directly or indirectly) be linked to a specific individual.[18] The identifying attributes of data are the key question when determining the applicability of the GDPR. Whether data is deemed as identifiable depends on what measures are available either to the data controller or others persons to link the data at hand to a specific individual; when determining available measures, factors like the state and developments of technology, and the cost of such technologies must be taken into account.[19] As such, the GDPR draws a line between pseudonymised and anonymised data, categorising the former as identifying data and the latter as data that falls outside the scope of the GDPR.[20] In the pseudonymisation process the personal data is stripped of identifying attributes, which can be linked back to the data subject. Once this link is disabled, and the data is permanently (i.e. irreversibly) stripped of identifying attributes, it ceases to be personal data and falls outside the

---

[16] This conclusion is based merely on the rules and requirements of the 1995 Directive and does not take into account the practical implementation by Member States, which might have not met such minimum requirements. Thus, making the minimum requirements directly applicable in all Member States via a regulation is certainly a step forward in the general protection of personal data.

[17] See supra note 12, at 325. D. Hallinen *et al.* bring as examples of these strengthening mechanisms, amongst others, the obligation of the controller to carry out a data protection impact assessment as prescribed in Art. 35 of the GDPR (at 324) and the introduction of administrative fines up to 10 000 000 EUR under Art. 83 (at 325).

[18] Art. 4(1): "[P]ersonal data' means any information relating to an identified or identifiable natural person ('data subject'); an identifiable natural person is one who can be identified, directly or indirectly, in particular by reference to an identifier such as a name, an identification number, location data, an online identifier or to one or more factors specific to the physical, physiological, genetic, mental, economic, cultural or social identity of that natural person[.]".

[19] See Recital 26 of the GDPR.

[20] Ibid.

scope of the GDPR. By this logic pseudonymised data becomes anonymous once the key code used for pseudonymisation has been terminated.

Unlike most other types of personal data, genetic data is identifying as such. This means that it can never truly be rendered anonymous. As D. Hallinan et al. have put it, "Genetic data also challenge the assumption that anonymity can ever be an enduring status."[21] This argument holds up both scientifically, and legally.

On the scientific side, it has been shown that an individual's membership in a specific cohort can be determined based on their DNA profile and cohort allele frequencies alone.[22] Furthermore, the possibilities of identification based on genetic data will increase over time in correlation with developments in science and technology.

On the legal side, the definition of 'identifiable' established in case-law further supports the argument that genetic data is in itself identifying (i.e. even without any further links to the data subject). The Court of Justice of the European Union (CJEU) ruled in 2013 that, "Fingerprints constitute personal data, as they objectively contain unique information about individuals which allows those individuals to be identified with precision",[23] referring to a prior ruling of the European Court of Human Rights (ECHR) in 2008[24]. Addressing an argument made by the UK government that fingerprints as a data source are "unintelligible to the untutored eye and without a comparator fingerprint", – a counter-argument that could *mutatis mutandis* be applied in terms of genetic data – the ECHR emphasised that "this consideration cannot alter the fact that fingerprints objectively contain unique information about the individual concerned, allowing his or her identification with precision in a wide range of circumstances."[25] Furthermore, the ECHR emphasised that due to the information they contain, "the retention of cellular samples and DNA has a more important impact on private life than the retention of fingerprints".[26]

Additionally, it is noteworthy that in the United States, in a proposal for revising the Common Rule (governing human subject research) it was recognised that, "New methods, more powerful computers, and easy access to large administrative datasets produced by local, state, and federal governments have meant that some types of data

---

[21] See supra note 12, at 322.

[22] See, e.g., A.J. Pakstis et al. "SNPs for a universal individual identification panel", *Human Genetics*, Vol. 127, 2010, pp. 315–324. See also R. Wang et al. "Learning Your Identity and Disease from Research Papers: Information Leaks in Genome Wide Association Study", *16th ACM Conference on Computer and Communications Security*, ACM 2009, pp. 534–544. See also N. Homer et al. "Resolving Individuals Contributing Trace Amounts of DNA to Highly Complex Mixtures Using High-Density SNP Genotyping Microarrays", *PLOS Genetics*, Vol. 4(8), 2008.

[23] C-291/12 *Schwarz v. Bochum* [2013] ECLI:EU:C:2013:670, para 27.

[24] *S. and Marper v. United Kingdom* (2008) ECLI:CE:ECHR:2008:1204JUD003056204, paras 68 and 84.

[25] Ibid. para 84.

[26] Ibid., para 86.

that formerly were treated as non-identified can now be re-identified through combining large amounts of information from multiple sources."[27]

Thus the proposal aimed to shift the qualification of genetic data from non-identified to identifying as far as to afford research subjects certain control over their biospecimen and data derived therefrom in cases in which there are no additional identifiers. In terms of genetic data, the proposal expressed recognition on a federal level to the fact that genetic data cannot be treated as anonymous even when there are no further informational links to the individual. However, on 19 January 2017, the final version of the revised Common Rule was published, revealing that the proposed changes described above had been omitted from the revised regulation.[28]

Hence, unlike other types of personal data, genetic data cannot seize to be 'personal' as a result of stripping off other identifiers; as such, rules for operating with genetic data cannot follow the same logic as those designed for traditional categories of personal data. Given the informative scope of genetic data in comparison to fingerprints, based on the referred case law of the CJEU and ECHR, it can be asserted that in legal terms genetic data should be regarded as *per se* identifying. Furthermore, unlike fingerprints and other biometric data, genetic data can be retrieved from almost every cell of a human's body, and cannot be altered. This means that genetic data can easily be retrieved from a person even without their knowledge, making it much more vulnerable to retention and misuse in comparison to other personal data. Which, again, leads to the conclusion that compared to other types of personal data, genetic data constitutes a uniquely vulnerable category of its own, in need of additional safeguards.

To conclude the above, both legal and scientific arguments support the assertion that genetic data should be regarded as identifying data regardless of any additional

---

[27] Federal Policy for the Protection of Human Subjects. A Proposed Rule by the Homeland Security Department, the Agriculture Department, the Energy Department, the National Aeronautics and Space Administration, the Commerce Department, the Social Security Administration, the Agency for International Development, the Justice Department, the Labor Department, the Defense Department, the Education Department, the Veterans Affairs Department, the Environmental Protection Agency, the Health and Human Services Department, the National Science Foundation, and the Transportation Department on 09/08/2015. Accessible online at https://www.federalregister.gov/documents/2015/09/08/2015-21756/federal-policy-for-the-protection-of-human-subjects [last accessed 21 October 2016].

[28] Federal Policy for the Protection of Human Subjects. A Rule by the Homeland Security Department, the Agriculture Department, the Energy Department, the National Aeronautics and Space Administration, the Commerce Department, the Social Security Administration, the Agency for International Development, the Housing and Urban Development Department, the Labor Department, the Defense Department, the Education Department, the Veterans Affairs Department, the Environmental Protection Agency, the Health and Human Services Department, the National Science Foundation, and the Transportation Department on 01/19/2017. Accessible online at https://www.federalregister.gov/documents/2017/01/19/2017-01058/federal-policy-for-the-protection-of-human-subjects [last accessed 23 January 2017].

links to the individual. This means that genetic data stands out amongst other categories of (sensitive) personal data in terms of vulnerability and possible implications to privacy.[29]

3   The GDPR and Big Data

As laid out above, albeit its exceptionality genetic data is not expressly subject to any special regulations under the GDPR aside from Article 9(4) which grants Member States discretion to adopt more stringent rules when it comes to genetic, health, and biometric data. Thus it seems that the role of the GDPR as a big data enabler will affect genetic data in the same manner as other personal data. To analyse the implications of the concept of big genetic data under the GDPR, first, the concept of big data and its relationship with the notion of personal data will be explored. Second, the particular issues and possible implications in regard to genetic data as part of a big data set (i.e. big genetic data) under the GDPR will be analysed.

3.1   Big Data vs Personal Data

There is no one single universally agreed upon definition for big data.[30] The Oxford English online dictionary defines it as "extremely large data sets that may be analysed computationally to reveal patterns, trends, and associations, especially relating to human behaviour and interactions".[31] The Merriem-Webster online dictionary defines big data as "an accumulation of data that is too large and complex for processing by traditional database management tools".[32]

The term "big data" has not been defined in any legal instruments of the EU, however the DPWP has offered the following definition:

> "Big data refers to the exponential growth both in the availability and in the automated use of information: it refers to gigantic digital datasets held by corporations, governments and other large organisations, which are then extensively analysed [...] using computer algorithms. Big data can be used to identify more general trends and correlations but it can also be processed in order to directly affect individuals."[33]

---

[29] For an in-depth analysis on the privacy implications regarding the use of genetic data, see M. Taylor. Genetic Data and the Law: A Critical Perspective on Privacy Protection. Cambridge University Press, 2012.

[30] E. Vayena and U. Gasser. "Strictly Biomedical? Sketching the Ethics of the Big Data Ecosystem in Biomedicine". The Ethics of Biomedical Big Data. B.D Mittelstadt and L. Floridi (eds.). Springer, 2016, p. 18.

[31] See in the online English dictionary *Oxford Living Dictionaries* of Oxford University Press at https://en.oxforddictionaries.com/definition/big_data [last accessed 12 April 2017].

[32] See *Merriem-Webster* online dictionary at https://www.merriam-webster.com/dictionary/big% 20data [last accessed 12 April 2017].

[33] Article 29 Data Protection Working Party. Opinion 03/2013 on purpose limitation. Adopted on 2 April 2013, 00569/13/EN WP 203, p. 35. Accessible online at http://ec.europa.eu/justice/data-protection/article-29/documentation/opinion-recommendation/files/2013/wp203_en.pdf [last accessed 12 April 2017].

Thus, data being 'big' does not merely refer to quantity but also complexity. As Mittelstadt and Florini (2016) put it, big data can be defined as either referring to the breadth or quantity of the dataset, or data itself; with the latter approach defining 'big' "in procedural rather than quantitative terms, by connecting the size of the dataset to its complexity".[34]

In comparison, personal data – as defined in the personal data protection regulatory framework – comprises of pieces of data regarding a specific individual, constituting thereby "small data"[35].

In a report on big data in February 2017, the Committee on Civil Liberties, Justice and Home Affairs of the European Parliament linked the concept of personal data to that of big data by explaining that the latter "refers to the collection, analysis and the recurring accumulation of large amounts of data, including personal data, from a variety of sources, which are subject to automatic processing by computer algorithms and advanced data-processing techniques using both stored and streamed data in order to generate certain correlations, trends and patterns (big data analytics)."[36]

Thus essentially, big data is an accumulation of small data. However, the small data that makes up big data, might not necessarily be personal data. Furthermore, even if the accumulated data was personal data, big data analytics does not necessarily require processing of *personal* data in every stage.

M. Oostveen has argued that due to the definition of personal data and its focus on the concept of *identifiability*, big data might not be entirely covered by the personal data protection regulatory framework.[37] Oostveen distinguishes the three phases of the big data process as acquisition, analysis and application phase, arguing that whilst the acquisition phase comprises of collection of personal data, in the second phase (analysis) big data is often anonymised as it is concerned with "trends, models, and correlations, and not [..] specific individuals."[38] The third phase – application – might require identification of an individual, depending on the purpose of application, which might be of a general nature, but might also target individuals.[39]

Thus, generally, big data analytics presupposes personal data processing most definitely in the acquisition phase, most likely not in the analysis phases, and might

---

[34] B.D. Mittelstadt and L. Floridi (eds.). The Ethics of Biomedical Big Data. Springer, 2016, p. 2.

[35] The phrase "small data" has been used in regard to "conventional health care data" by N.P. Terry. "Big Data Proxies and Health Privacy Exceptionalism", *Health Matrix: Journal of Law-Medicine*, 24 (2014), 65–108, at 66. The phrase has also been used as referring to personal data by M.M. Hansen. "Big Data in Science and Healthcare: A Review of Recent Literature and Perspectives", IMIA Yearbook 9 (2014), 21–26. Accessible online at https://works.bepress.com/margaret_hansen/22/ [last accessed 13 April 2017].

[36] European Parliament, Committee on Civil Liberties, Justice and Home Affairs. Report on fundamental rights implications of big data: privacy, data protection, nondiscrimination, security and law-enforcement (2016/2225(INI)). 17.02.2017, A8-0044/2017, p. 4.

[37] M. Oostveen. "Identifiability and the applicability of data protection to big data", *International Data Privacy Law* 6(4) (2016), 299–309.

[38] Ibid., pp. 300–301.

[39] Ibid.

presuppose it in the application phase (depending on the specific purpose(s) of the application).

As demonstrated above (See Sect. 2.3 above), genetic data should always be considered personal data, regardless of any further links to the individual. Following this rhetoric, big data analysis of genetic data should always be subject to personal data protection rules since anonymisation is not possible when it comes to genetic data. Even if genetic data were not considered as personal data without further links to the individual, it would most likely not be anonymised, but pseudonymised, since the true value of genetic data lies in its correlation with health outcomes.[40] Pseudonymisation would not, however, affect the application of personal data protection rules as clearly stated in the GDPR.[41]

3.2   Issues with Big Genetic Under the GDPR

To begin, three points in regard to the interaction of the terms 'big data' and 'genetic data' must be made. First, it should be pointed out that genomics in itself is considered a big data science.[42] Second, a full genome sequence of one person could be considered big data, since 'big' refers to complex data that are "difficult to sort and analyse with existing computing technologies"[43]. J. Frizzo-Barker et al. have noted that, "The file size of a single genome can range from about 700 MB of raw data to 200 GB of annotated variant and metadata."[44] Hence, the whole genetic code of even one single person could technically be referred to as big data. Third, relying on the argument that genetic data always remains *personal* data despite any efforts of de-identification (e.g. pseudonymisation), big genetic data should always be subject to personal data protection rules.

Keeping in mind the three points outlined above, the question addressed here is not one of whether genetic data accumulation could or should be considered as big data, but whether the GDPR as "an enabler for big data science in Europe"[45] has adequately addressed the peculiarities of big genetic data, and how personal data protection rules should tackle the specific needs of big genetic data in comparison to other categories of personal data in terms of big data analytics.

In its opinion issued in 2015, the European Data Protection Supervisor stated that in their opinion the "responsible and sustainable development of big data must rely on four essential elements", amongst which they listed affording "users a higher degree of

---

[40] This is arguably the case for any biomedical data, not just genetic data. See G.M. Weber et al. "Finding the Missing Link for Biomedical Data", *JAMA* 311(24) (2014), 2479-2480.

[41] See Recital 26 of the GDPR, which states that, "Personal data which have undergone pseudonymisation, which could be attributed to a natural person by the use of additional information should be considered to be information on an identifiable natural person.".

[42] Z.D. Stephens *et al.* "Big Data: Astronomical or Genomical?" *PLoS Biol 13(7)*: e1002195.

[43] B.D. Mittelstadt and L. Floridi (eds), supra note 34, p. 2.

[44] J. Frizzo-Barker et al. "Genomic Big Data and Privacy: Challenges and Opportunities for Precision Medicine". *Computer Supported Cooperative Work (CSCW)* 25(2) (2016), 115–136, at 118.

[45] Supra note 3, p. 2.

control over how their data is used".[46] The data subject's control over their sensitive personal data is expressed in the personal data protection framework through the notion of explicit consent for specified purposes, and withdrawal thereof.[47] The GDPR lays out strict rules in regard to consent in Article 7, which are more stringent in regard to sensitive personal data under Article 9(2)(a). The latter stipulates that consent for the processing of sensitive data (incl. genetic data) must, in addition to the criteria laid out in Article 7, be explicit and set out one or more specified purposes for the processing.

In addition to consent, control is also expressed in the data subject's rights to object (Article 21) and to be forgotten (Article 17). The latter two become especially crucial in scenarios in which sensitive data processing is not based on consent of the data subject according to Article 9(2)(a), but on one of the grounds of processing independent of the data subject's consent.

The means of control in the form of consent is followed by a long list of exceptions to the general prohibition in Article 9(1) and the requirement of consent in Article 9(2)(a). The exceptions laid out in Article 9(2)(b)–(j) create legal grounds for sensitive personal data processing without the consent of the data subject, unless some form of consent is required under Member State law in terms of the exceptions that are subject to further regulation by Member States, such as Article 9(2)(b) and Article 9(2)(g)–(j); consent might also be required by other applicable EU law. Once any of these legal grounds for genetic data processing arise – aside from processing based on the data subject's explicit control – the question becomes one of opt-out possibilities of the data subject other than withdrawal of consent. However, in order to opt-out, the data subject must be aware and informed of the fact that their genetic data is being processed.

Big Genetic Data and the Duty to Inform. Genetic data can be obtained from sources other than the data subject (e.g. from an e-health database or biobank). In cases in which personal data has been obtained from sources other than the data subject, the data controller generally has a duty to inform the data subject of the processing as laid out in Article 14 of the GDPR. However, it seems that Article 14 contains an exception to the duty to inform that might be particularly relevant in regard to big data processing.

Under Article 14(5)(b), the data controller can be exempted from the obligation to provide information to the data subject when it comes to the processing of data of a large number of data subjects. The core of the exception in Article 14(5)(b) is whether informing the data subjects would involve a disproportionate effort on behalf of the controller. When assessing whether the effort of informing data subjects on behalf of the data controller could be deemed disproportionate, three factors should be taken into account according to Recital 62 of the GDPR: (1) the number of data subjects; (2) the

---

[46] European Data Protection Supervisor. Opinion 7/2015, "Meeting the Challenges of Big Data: A call for transparency, user control, data protection by design and accountability", 19 November 2015, p. 4. Accessible online at https://edps.europa.eu/sites/edp/files/publication/15-11-19_big_data_en.pdf [last accessed 12 April 2017].

[47] It can be argued that in terms of personal data that is not sensible, i.e. not listed in Article 9(1) of the GDPR, consent does not constitute a true means of control since the grounds for personal data processing laid out in Article 6(1) are so broad that consent effectively no longer plays a relevant role. Most notably, Article 6(1)(f) allows personal data processing for the "legitimate interests pursued by the controlled or a tird party".

age of the data; (3) the appropriate safeguards adopted by the controller. Due to the nature of genetic data, the age of the data cannot serve as an argument of the necessary effort being disproportionate (unlike, i.e. travel or shopping information, the relevance of which is likely to decline in time). To the contrary, the informative potential of genetic data depends on advances in science and technology, and as such is likely to increase over time.

It is difficult to assert what could be deemed as 'appropriate safeguards' specifically in terms of big data (one example of safeguards under the GDPR in, e.g. Art. 89, is pseudonymisation, which is likely to be applicable for big genetic data analytics; another safeguard could be encryption techniques[48]).

As to the number of data subjects, the argument speaks for the effort required by the controller being disproportionate, since big genetic data would presume the processing of the data of a large number of data subjects. Hence the sheer volume of data subjects whose genetic data is being processed, along with applicable safeguards (e.g. pseudonymisation, encryption or other such cyber security measures) might tip the determination of whether the effort required by the data controller is disproportionate in the favour of the data controller.

If the data controller could successfully claim the exemption under Article 14(5)(b) it would mean that there is no obligation to inform the data subject of the processing of their data. Although the referred article particularly emphasises processing for purposes of public interest, scientific or historical research or statistical purposes, it does not exclude other purposes either. As one of the three determinants of the application of Article 14(5)(b) is the size of the data set – i.e. size in the meaning of the number of data subject's whose genetic data is being processed – Article 14(5)(b) could thus be referred to as the 'big data exception' to the obligation to inform. Furthermore, as far as the emphasis on particular processing purposes goes in Article 14(5)(b), it is unclear how broadly the scientific research exemption will have to be applied by Member States.[49]

It stems from the above that unless the data subject has donated their DNA and signed a respective consent form, i.e. if the genetic data has been obtained from sources other than the data subject, and if the genetic data is included in a large enough data set, the data controller might be able to claim that informing the data subjects would involve a disproportionate effort on behalf of the controller. This, in turn, would render the data subject's rights to object (Article 21) and right to be forgotten (Article 17) practically ineffective. Although Article 14(5)(b) does call for the data controller to take 'appropriate measures' to protect the rights and freedoms and legitimate interests of data subjects, including making information regarding the processing publicly available, the latter might not suffice to ensure that the data subject is actually aware or informed of the fact of the processing of their data. This outcome of uncertainty cannot be accepted when it comes to data as vulnerable and with as serious privacy risks and implications as genetic data.

---

[48] Supra n 36, p 5.

[49] For an in-depth analysis of the Article 9(2)(j) and the research exemption in regard to genetic data, see K. Pormeister. "Genetic Data and the Research Exemption: Is the GDPR going too far?", *International Data Privacy Law* (2017) 7(2): 137–146.

Furthermore, invoking Article 21(1) requires the existence of "grounds relating to [the data subject's] particular situation". Hence, the mere wish of the data subject for their genetic data not to be included in a set of big data might not suffice in order to successfully invoke the right to object under Article 21(1).

It is not possible to determine a specific number of data subjects whose data needs to be included in a data set in order to trigger the exception in Article 14(5)(b) from the obligation to inform the data subject of the processing. It is doubtful that this would be a data set comprised of the genetic data of five people, as provided in the Estonian example laid out in the introductory part of this paper. It is impossible to draw a line and determine a number that would definitely relieve the data controller from the obligation to inform the data subject of the processing. However, when talking about big data in terms of the quantity of the dataset (i.e. and not the complexity of the data), one could assert that Article 14(5)(b) does create an exception for big data controllers from the obligation to inform the data subjects of the processing.

However, when it comes to data with heightened privacy risks and implications, the exception in Article 14(5)(b) should not be applicable.[50] Given the privacy implications of genetic data processing[51] (due to its heightened vulnerability and exceptionality as a category of personal data), the digitalisation of data storage and transfer, and advancements of e-solutions (incl. technical means for providing notice), notification of data subjects – at least in the case of data as vulnerable as genetic data – is an obligation that should be provided no exemptions from in order to make sure that data subjects have actual control over their genetic data, and can effectively exercise their right to object and to be forgotten.

Big Genetic Data and Article 11. In addition to the exemption in Article 14(5)(b) to the duty to inform, implications of big genetic data might arise from Article 11 of the GDPR. The latter applies to de-identified data and terminates the need for the data controller to collect, maintain or process additional data for the sole purpose of complying with the obligations in Article 15 to 20 of the GDPR. Article 11 applies if the purposes for which a controller processes personal data do not or do no longer require the identification of a data subject by the controller. The applicability of Article 11 to big genetic data would depend on two key questions. First, if one were to accept the argument made in Sect. 2.3. regarding the *per se* identifiable nature of genetic data, Article 11 might not be applicable to big genetic data at all, depending whether (although not anonymous) genetic data with no additional links to the individual should be considered de-identified within the meaning of Article 11.[52]

---

[50] See, e.g., J. Kühling and B. Buchner (eds.). Datenschutz-Grundverordnung: DS-GVO. Kommentar. C.H. Beck (2017), p 383.

[51] For a thorough overview on the privacy implications regarding the use of genetic data, see M. Taylor (2012), supra note 29.

[52] For an analysis regarding de-identification within the meaning of Article 11 of the GDPR, see M. Hintze. Viewing the GDPR Through a De-Identification Lens: A Tool for Clarification and Compliance; accessible online at https://fpf.org/wp-content/uploads/2016/11/M-Hintze-GDPR-Through-the-De-Identification-Lens-31-Oct-2016-002.pdf [last accessed on June 29th 2017].

Second, if genetic data with no additional links to the individual could be considered de-identified data within the meaning of Article 11 of the GDPR, the applicability of Article 11 would depend on the nature of the operations of the data controller. For example, if genetic data were used for more specific purposes, e.g. correlation between certain genetic characteristics and geographical location, the researcher would not necessarily have the need to identify data subjects as long as there is a connection between the two referred categories of data. In this case Article 11 could potentially be applicable. Although, under Article 11(2) the data controller should still provide notice to data subjects, if possible, the rights of the data subject under Articles 15–20 (including the right to be forgotten in terms of prospective processing) would not apply (except where the data subject, for the purpose of exercising his or her rights under those articles, provides additional information enabling his or her identification). However, if the data controller is engaged in a wider spectrum of genetic data processing activities, which would require, e.g., data to be updated or additional data to be linked back to a certain individual, identification of data subjects would remain necessary and Article 11 would not be applicable. The latter is more likely in terms of genetic data due to its various, virtually unlimited, potential different uses for analysis and research. Thus, the applicability of Article 11 for big genetic data – and its resulting implications on the rights of the data subject – would depend on a case by case assessment.

Whilst under Article 9(4) of the GDPR Member States have the right to adopt stricter rules when it comes to the processing of health related, biometric or genetic data, in a single digital market stricter rules enacted by single Member States will not suffice for granting individuals effective control over their genetic data. Discretionary safeguards per country will be of little use considering that genetic data can easily be digitally transferred to and processed in other countries. Furthermore, Recital 53 of the GDPR emphasises that enacting further restrictions "should not hamper the free flow of personal data within the Union when [these additional restrictions] apply to cross-border processing of such data". Hence, the lengths that Member States could go to under Article 9(4) in establishing additional safeguards for the processing of genetic data might be limited in practice; not to mention that fragmented regulations are likely to lead to forum-shopping. Hence, the uniform interpretation and application of the vaguely worded clauses in the GDPR is crucial when it comes to the protection of individuals' rights to self-determination and autonomy in terms of their genetic data and exercising control over it, regardless of whether their genetic data is being processed as part of a big data set or not.

4 Conclusion

Although genetic data is incorporated into the personal data protection regulatory framework (being governed by both the current directive and the upcoming regulation), it is not comparable to other categories of (sensitive) personal data. Genetic data stands out from the rest, because it contains unique information about an individual, has informative potential to yet unknown extents and has the potential to identify a person without any further links to the individual at hand. Although the same could be said about biometric data (e.g. fingerprints), unlike biometric data, genetic data cannot be altered and remains constant throughout a person's life and beyond. Furthermore, genetic data becomes truly valuable (both scientifically and commercially) when combined with other personal data (e.g. with health outcomes, but also personal preferences, etc.). The informative potential of genetic data has not been fully realised, and it is impossible to determine what conclusions could be drawn based on genetic data five, ten or fifty years from now. Given the identifying and informative potential of genetic data not just in regard to one individual, but also their next of kin, the processing of one person's genetic data will have privacy implications for generations to come.

In this light, the data subject's control over their genetic data becomes crucial. Although giving back control to citizen's over their personal data was advertised as one of the aims of the personal data protection reform in the EU, this remains questionable when comparing the current directive and the upcoming regulation.

When it comes to large data sets, i.e. big data, the GDPR has been claimed to be an enabler for big data science in Europe. The ways in which the GDPR acts as an enabler for big data, however, pay no explicit regard to the specific categories of personal data at hand. In this context control over (sensitive) personal data use becomes uncertain since crucial questions are subject to interpretation. This is even more problematic in terms of data as exceptional and sensitive as genetic data. It is one thing to have one's shopping preferences be forever part of an aggregated data set, but an entirely different matter in regard to genetic data.

It appears that when it comes to big data, the GDPR has an exception from the data controller's obligation to inform the data subject of the processing where data has been obtained from sources other than the data subject. However, if the data subject has no knowledge of their genetic data being processed, the rights to object and be forgotten are rendered meaningless. When it comes to personal data as vulnerable and with as serious privacy implications as genetic data, the exception to the duty to inform should be negated. However, this is not expressly clear from the GDPR, but a matter of interpretation by both data controllers and Member States. Furthermore, data controllers might find further relief from obligations under the GDPR by relying on Article 11. This leaves the rights and interests of data subjects in a questionable and uncertain position even with data as vulnerable as genetic data.

To sum up, the GDPR as an enabler for big data has not paid any regard to the specific aspects of different types of personal data that big data might comprise of. Thereby leading to a practical outcome that under the GDPR big genetic data seems to be equal to any other type or category of big data, without concern for the fact that genetic data remains identifying regardless of additional links, is constant through the data subject's lifetime and beyond, and bears immense informative and privacy implications not just for the data subject, but also for the next of kin of the data subject. The particularity and exceptionality of genetic data, and big genetic data in particular, under the GDPR will have to be addressed when interpreting and implementing the GDPR.

Towards a Privacy-Preserving Reliable European Identity Ecosystem

Jorge Bernal Bernabe[1]([✉]), Antonio Skarmeta[1], Nicolás Notario[2]([✉]),
Julien Bringer[3], and Martin David[4]

[1] Department of Information and Communications Engineering,
Computer Science Faculty, University of Murcia, Murcia, Spain
{jorgebernal,skarmeta}@um.es
[2] Atos Research & Innovation Identity & Privacy Lab, Madrid, Spain
nicolas.notario@atos.net
[3] Safran Identity & Security, Paris, France
julien.bringer@safrangroup.com
[4] Gemalto, Integration & Consulting Services, Prague, Czech Republic
martin.david@gemalto.com

Abstract. This paper introduces the ARIES identity ecosystem aimed at setting up a reliable identity framework comprising new technologies, processes and security features that ensure highest levels of quality in secure credentials for highly secure and privacy-respecting physical and digital identity management processes. The identity ecosystem is being devised in the scope of ARIES European project and aspires to tangibly achieve a reduction in levels of identity fraud, theft, wrong identity and associated crimes and to create a decisive competitive advantage for Europe at a global level.

Keywords: Identity management · Privacy · Biometrics · Digital identities · Identity derivation · Secure wallet

1 Introduction

Personal data and, in particular, individual identities are getting more and more vulnerable in a digital world with European stakeholders interacting in globalized scenarios. This on-going and increasing lack of trust derives from the current deficiency of solutions, including consistently applied technologies and processes for trusted enrolment, identification and authentication processes, in particular the use of online credentials with low levels of authentication assurance. Furthermore, there is a lack of a coherent joint approach in Europe (in terms of legislation, cross-border cooperation and policy) to address identity-related crimes which costs companies, countries and citizens billions of Euros in fraud and theft, and which are quickly growing and serious crimes.

In this context, the ReliAble euRopean Identity EcoSystem (ARIES) H2020 European research project aims to provide means for stronger and more trusted

© Springer International Publishing AG 2017
E. Schweighofer et al. (Eds.): APF 2017, LNCS 10518, pp. 19–33, 2017.
DOI: 10.1007/978-3-319-67280-9_2

authentication, in a user-friendly and efficient manner and with full respect to data subject's rights for personal data protection and privacy. For that, it will include means to present a proof of identity without need to disclose more personal data than actually needed in a given interaction (data minimization and proportionality). The ecosystem will allow the citizen to generate a digital identity linked to the physical one using biometrics and at the same time to store enrolment information in a secure vault only accessible for law enforcement authorities in case of cybersecurity incidents [10]. This will allow linking proofs of identity based on the combination of biometric traits and citizen eID/ePassport with the administrative processes involved in the issuance of breeder documents (like birth/civil certificates).

Users will be also empowered with mechanisms that allow them to derive additional digital identities from the ones linked with their eIDs/ePassports, but with different levels of assurance and with different degrees of privacy about their attributes. These digital identities will be usable in administrative exchanges where it is required by the government according to eIDAS Regulation [16] and be stored in software or hardware secure environment their mobile or smart devices.

The rest of this paper is structured as follows. Section 2 describes identity theft and fraud and some of its challenges. Section 3 provides an overview of the ARIES ecosystem, including main components, features and interactions. Section 4 describes the main use cases addressed in ARIES, which allow to assess the feasibility and reliability of ARIES ecosystem. Finally, Sect. 5 concludes the paper.

2   Identify Fraud

Identity theft, according to sources such as the UK Home Office Identity Fraud Steering Committee or CIFAS, a fraud prevention organisation in the UK, is the obtention of information about an identity (e.g. name, date of birth, addresses) of another person. Furthermore, the usage of false or someone else's identity details for personal gain is what's considered **identity fraud**, which is one of the challenges to be addressed by the ARIES Identity Ecosystem.

Addressing identity theft is multi-dimensional problem and hence must be considered from different perspectives and involving multiple stakeholders. As an example, identity fraud can be prevented by improving user and document authentication technologies and processes making them more resilient. E.g. biometric checks could be included for high-risk transactions or for documents with high level of assurance. As biometrics are harder to fake, impostures will be limited. On the other hand, remediation mechanisms could focus on limiting the impact of such frauds by applying early-detection techniques or by facilitating the identification of fraudsters or impostors. It should also be considered a distinction between the legal or policy-related dimensions as opposed to the technological one. In the case of legal or policy, strong fines, identify theft reporting mechanisms can be established in order to discourage fraudsters.

A different perspective for identity fraud is related to the exact process of the identity management lifecycle where the fraud is targeted. Addressing identity fraud in the enrolment phase for the issuance of breeder documents requires strong biometric controls (e.g. fingerprint) and checking the authenticity of physical source documents. Meanwhile, the authentication phase may have different set of requirements such as detecting the user presence or to have multiple-factor authentication (e.g. eID and PIN number).

All these perspectives and dimensions must be considered in order to properly address more effectively the challenges posed by wrong identity, identity fraud and associated types of cyber and other forms of organized crime. One of the most challenging aspects of identity fraud is to somehow find the right balance of the three pillars of trust in physical and digital worlds: identity, security and privacy. Whenever stricter identity requirements are added, in general, more secure the system will be but, in exchange, privacy is usually diminished as additional personal data has to be disclosed. On the other hand, privacy-preserving (i.e. anonymous) systems, while fully legitimate, usually allows secondary malicious uses that are very challenging to avoid (e.g. bitcoins used to pay ransomware operators or anonymous social media accounts to make offensive comments).

ARIES will demonstrate how its ecosystem, based on eID digitizing, can avoid a trade-off between privacy and security and support both, in ways that enables the development of ethical apps acceptable to society. ARIES ecosystem's novel technical capabilities and procedures will relate breed documents with digital identities through citizen's biometrics, enabling the usage of strong mobile identities through a convenient and secure mobile identity wallet.

3   Related Work

Identity management is commonly addressed by using well-known technologies, such as the *Security Assertion Markup Languaje* (SAML) [9], OpenID [2], OAuth [8] or WS-Federation [17]. These technologies, are, in turn, used as baseline by most of the European research projects related with the ARIES EU project.

The STORK (2.0) [3] EU project establishes a European eID Interoperability Platform that will allow citizens to establish new e-relations across borders, just by presenting their national eID/STORKs QAA model will shape the mobile identity derivation process. STORK's interoperability infrastructure is expected to be leveraged by ARIES components, which will might rely on STORK for certain kinds of eID authentications.

On the other hand, *Anonymous Credential systems* (ACS) [5] allow a selective disclosure of identity attributes to achieve a privacy-preserving identity management approach. A crucial aspect of privacy-preserving mechanisms is related to the design of mitigation strategies to avoid anonymity abuse, by considering *traceability* or *accountability* aspects. In this regard, ABC4Trust [14] EU project has provided advances for the federation and interchangeability of technologies supporting trustworthy and at the same time privacy-preserving Attribute-based Credentials. Nonetheless, ACS are still tacking off, mainly because of their complexity and lack of user-friendly tools. In ARIES, privacy Attribute Based Credentials are being considered as a mechanism to support privacy-preserving identity management operations through user-friendly apps.

The FutureID [1] EU project built a comprehensive, flexible, privacy-aware and ubiquitously usable identity management infrastructure for Europe. It is a holistic IdM that is able to interoperate with both, Abc4Trust and Stork technologies. Some FutureID outcomes are expected to be reused in ARIES to accomplish the goal of establishing a privacy-preserving and reliable European Identity ecosystem, which unlike in FutureID, it will support digital identity derivation.

The aforementioned EU projects do not allow to tie together trustworthy source documents with biometrical traits and derived mobile digital ID. ARIES will define a identity lifecycle processes to allow the linkage of physical identities and source breeder documents with new digital identities that can be derived from the physical ones, in order to maintain high levels of privacy preservation.

4   ARIES Identity Ecosystem

The main goal of the ARIES Identity Ecosystem is to provide new technologies, processes and security features that ensure highest levels of quality in secure credentials for highly secure and privacy-respecting physical and digital identity management with the specific aim to tangibly achieve a reduction in levels of identity fraud, theft, wrong identity and associated crimes and to create a decisive competitive advantage for Europe at a global level.

4.1   ARIES Ecosystem Overview

The process of authentication will be ensured with the use of a smart device allowing the acquisition of all required biometric (especially face) and electronic (using NFC) data. This process should ensure a high level of quality for biometrics acquisition, while assuring data integrity and delivering the derived identities required attributes to the adequate relying party (service provider). These features will be obtained by functionality deployed either locally (on the smart device) or centrally (back-end). Digital identities will be generated with privacy preserving technologies and will allow citizens just to prove to be in possession of some attributes without exposing the rest of their data, i.e. being over 18 years of age. Given that different levels of assurance are possible a biometric mechanism could also be used as a proof of digital identity possession where appropriate [12].

Figure 1 shows an overview of the ARIES ecosystem, where interactions between the entities are depicted. The user manages several identities and credentials, which are issued by Identity Providers (IdP) and presented to the Service Providers (SP) to access the services offered by them.

The ARIES approach considers a multi-domain interaction for eID management in order to achieve a distributed but unified eID ecosystem. Each domain

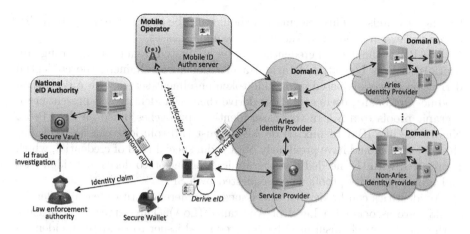

Fig. 1. Aries ecosystem

usually contains one or more IdPs and one or more SPs. The common use case is that a SP redirects user requests to the IdP within its own domain, although exceptions are also considered: a SP can directly authenticate the identity of the user (e.g. validating a certificate) and a SP could redirect to an IdP of another domain in which it trusts, including a mobile operator, a bank or a Government for Mobile eID authentication. IdPs can be interconnected relying on federated interoperability, thereby allowing delegation of authentication (e.g. using STORK) and also attribute aggregation (e.g. to create a derived credential which includes both governmental and academic information). User consent will be obtained prior to transferring any personal information. Interaction with legacy non-ARIES IdPs can be also achieved by contacting those IdPs via standard protocols such as SAML [9], OAuth2 [8], etc.

Users interact with the system through several devices, including computers and smart devices such as mobile phones or smart wearables. Such devices will require a secure element in order to securely protect digital identities with biometric features. Alternative, although less secure, storage and execution environments might be foreseen for larger adoption of the ecosystem, but with limited capabilities to manage the resulting risk. A secure electronic wallet will be provided to users for them to securely handle and manage their digital identities and their related data.

Users can request a new derived credential to an ARIES IdP after authenticating using its eID. These credentials may contain different identity attributes and/or pseudonyms, according to the user needs and required level of privacy and security. For an IdP to issue a new identity credential, it should previously authenticate the user by requesting another credential that the user may already have and that should have been issued by a trusted IdP. Generation of derived credentials shall be logged to assure traceability to the real identity for law enforcement purposes. This could be achieved by an encrypted and signed logging mechanism. This information should also be kept secured and only disclosed to law enforcement authorities in regulated cases.

In ARIES, the derived credential will be originated from existing strong credentials such as biometric data and a eID document. Namely, the credential derivation process is based on mobile token enrolment server with a derivation module. Optionally, users could also derive their own identity and present cryptograpic proofs to a SP. In this case, identity approaches based on Zero Proof Knowledge like IBM Idemix [7] or ABC4Trust [14] solutions can be used. For this, the user should have previously obtained a special kind of credential, which is prepared with the needed cryptographic information to derive new identities and provide identity proofs when requested by a SP.

As identities can be derived and issued by different entities, each credential would have associated a Level of Assurance (LoA). This serves as a measure of the security mechanism used by the credential issuer to validate the identity of the user. ARIES aims to keep the LoA or to avoid significant differences when using derived credentials. Similarly, ARIES will try ensuring that Level of Trust (LoT) among different entities is also maintained after adopting derived credentials in the ecosystem.

Accessing a service supplied by a SP will impose some requirements for the credential to be presented, including providing attributes about user identity and trust requirements. The user can choose the mechanism and credential he want to present according to his preferences and the information and trust required by the SP. This includes the usage of a derived credential with less identity information and/or a pseudonym; a proof of identity in which no credential is actually sent to the SP, but a proof that the user owns some identity or attribute; or a Mobile ID credential stored in a secure element, which makes use of the Trusted Execution Environment for authentication and can optionally involve mobile operator as party involved in circle of trust [11].

From the perspective of data protection, it is essential to take into account privacy by design principles, particularly when identifying which and how biometric data are going to be used. Indeed, the requirements of proportionality have to be analysed bearing in mind the demands of technical security measures, determining what is certainly essential to avoid identity thefts based on the access to biometric information (e.g. a photo in the case of face or a latent in the case of fingerprints) [15].

Likewise, the possibility of using several derived identity credentials demands a concrete assessment from the perspective of data protection. Therefore, it will be necessary to build up identification services prioritizing those technical and organizational solutions that minimize access to personal data to the absolute essential. To this aim, ARIES is devising means to comply with the minimal disclosure of information principle. In this sense, the principle of proportionality will play a key role in order to face this challenge, since it will be necessary to justify in each case by the service providers the personal data really required for authentication or authorization.

Moreover, the identity ecosystem will provide unlinkability at the relying party level through polymorphic user identifiers (when compatible with relying parties' authentication policies). These identifiers will be different for each authentication or for specified periods of time and will be a random identifier, so it will disclose no information. Likewise, unlikability at the Aries IdP will be also ensured, as the ecosystem will indeed hide the accessed service from the enrolment and authentication services. Unobservability will be ensured by the system architecture, the Identity Providers will have no information which SP the user wants to log into.

Following, the most important individual concepts and actors that will conform the ecosystem are detailed.

4.2 Identity and Attribute Providers

Identity and attributes are not always differentiated in identity federation systems, however, for the purposes of ARIES and specially for its secure-and-privacy enhancing approach it is crucial to make a clear distinction between these two relying parties and their roles.

1. **Identity Providers** are a kind of service provider that provides subject authentication to other stakeholders within an identity ecosystem, such as service or attribute providers.
2. **Attribute Providers** are responsible for the processes related to the establishment and maintenance of the attributes associated to a subject. Attribute providers provides assertions of attributes to the individuals and other stakeholders, specially to service providers.

While in some standards, such as SAML [9], Identity Providers are responsible for provisioning the authentication and the attributes, there are two main reasons within the ARIES project for the separation of both concepts: (i) to support anonymous and pseudonyms interactions, in which the identity providers can provide an identifier which does not divulge any other personal data. (ii) Empower the user to choose different attribute sources that provide different sets of attributes with different levels of assurance. One of the requirements of ARIES project is to avoid the unnecessary linkage of attribute and identity providers with service providers, for which an identity wallet managed in the data subject's smartphone will mediate in between identity, attribute and service providers.

In any case, jointly, identity and attribute providers must establish and prove to relying parties who the subject is and to provide required information about the subject.

4.3 Secure Vault

The ARIES ecosystem relies particularly on the storage of identity evidence for ensuring the integrity of the identity digitalization, derivation and authentication processes and for potential future investigation. This is implemented using a secure vault.

Secure vault technology is not new by itself and several products on the market are able to provide integrity, confidentiality, auditability and compliance with various security standards and legal requirements, to ensure that the content is safely stored, non-repudiation is enforced, and its authenticity can be legally assessed.

Nevertheless, ARIES emphasizes specific needs for securing e-ID documents and digital identities issuing process that justify the use of a secure identity vault at different stages of the architecture. The main motivation is storing the identity evidences used while proofing or authenticating an identity to generate a new digital ID. Following a privacy by design principle, the subject shall remain under control of his data. However, we foresee also the need for a legal authority to be able to access part of the content in case of identity fraud or cybercrime investigation.

ARIES will add additional features to modern secure vault technology to fully support the ecosystem processes. In particular, specific measures will be studied, such as proxy re-encryption [4], to avoid to handle cleartext data on the vault side, even when the requester of data is not the original provider. Some of the data will be accessible only to the subject. Some will be provided in case of legal investigation. And some non-sensitive attributes might be accessible to the system, where the vault will be able to play the bonus role of attributes provider (for instance to retrieve some attributes collected during the eID check, but not stored directly with the digital ID). Consent of the subject will be explicitly required for each attribute reading operation, except under legal authorization of authority investigation.

4.4 Digital Identity Derivation

New patented concept of identity and credential derivation is one of the starting points of ARIES ecosystem. The concept is based on creation of new anonymous credentials derived from existing strong credentials such as biometric data and a eID document. Newly created credentials, the ARIES token, should provide strong authentication means while preserving end user privacy. This credential derivation process is based on mobile token enrolment server with a derivation module.

4.5 Biometric Enrolment

The subject enrolment for issuing a digital identity relies on two important steps: validating he owns an established identity materialized with an eID document (more precisely an ePassport, a national eID or any kind of biometric electronic document issued by an authoritative source), and proving that he is the legitimate owner through biometrics authentication.

The main requirement is being able to ensure a good level of assurance while allowing self-registration on a smartphone. A mobile application will manage digital and physical security checks of the eID: it will capture a biometric data of the subject, and while connected to a dedicated service, check both, authenticity of the chip inside the eID, consistency with the physical part of the document and the comparison of the biometric data with the reference biometric data in the chip will be verified. Thanks to the security features of the eID document and the additional use of anti-spoofing technology for biometric recognition, the process will provide high level of assurance.

Moreover, part of the validated data will be stored either on the secure vault or locally within a mobile wallet. Particularly, biometric data will be tied to some credentials in order to enable biometric authentication when using a digital identity (generated after the initial enrolment). To cope with privacy and security constraints, the biometric data will always be stored protected to avoid risk of leakage within non-secure places like the subject's smartphone or a web server, and comparison will be made exclusively on a secure environment.

4.6 Anonymous Credential Systems

Anonymous Credential Systems (ACS) [5], such as Idemix [7] or U-Prove [13] allow users to present Zero Knowledge cryptographic Proofs in order to prove possessing certain attributes in the credential. These systems enable a selective disclosure of identity attributes to achieve a privacy-preserving identity management approach. Indeed, a user can prove different predicates associated to a subset of identity attributes without disclosing the content of such attributes.

In ACS the credential *issuance* process allows a *Recipient* to obtain a credential from the Issuer. This credential consists of a set of attribute values, as well as cryptographic information that will allow credential's owner to create a proof of possession. The user acting as a *Prover* can demonstrate the possession of a certain credential to a SP (acting as a *Verifier*). Concretely, taking the example of Idemix, several zero-knowledge proofs are performed to convince the SP about the possession of such credential by making use of the CL signature scheme [6].

ARIES will try to introduce simple versions and adaptations of the ACS concept, deriving different digital partial identities over the whole original credential obtained from the ARIES IdP. The credentials will be maintained securely in the smartphone wallet to be used afterwards in certain scenarios that require different level of assurance. In addition, ARIES will try to provide user-friendly and privacy-preserving app for smartphones that will allow selective disclosure of attributes in an intuitive way.

5 Fraud Prevention

5.1 ARIES Enrolment and Authentication

After reviewing the current state of the art technologies, ARIES ecosystems incorporates a new flow of biometric enrolment of users and creation of ARIES tokens that would provide basic implementation of security and privacy requirements. The main goal is to create anonymous credential that may be used for strong authentication and preserve a strong link between the new credential and biometric data that would allow examination of authorized parties for fraud investigation while preserving privacy.

The main use case of the ARIES project is user authentication. In the end, users should be able to use ARIES credentials to access online services or to be granted access to physical spaces. In order to acquire a new credential, users must enrol in the ecosystem using their smartphone.

In the first iteration of the ecosystem the privacy would be ensured by usage of anonymous identifiers and split of the data among many components so there would be no single point of failure that would allow disclosure of any personal data. While the first version of the ecosystem considers classical cryptographic schemes such as PKI and privacy based on process and deployment model, the second iteration is envisaged to be enriched by new schemes based on adaptations of Anonymous Credential Systems. In order to minimize privacy risks, ARIES ecosystem considers usage of ARIES Identity Provider for authentication of the tokens and a separate biometric Identity Provider for biometric enrolment and authentication. This would ensure the separation of ARIES data from the biometric information, improving privacy guarantees.

Enrolment. ARIES ecosystem enrolment process would with biometric enrolment; user's biometric data would be read and stored for future reference and his electronic document would be read to acquire his real identity. Note that the data would be stored in the secure vault that would enforce strong authorization process. At the end, the user would be given anonymous proofing ID that would be used for future reference to his biometric data.

After acquiring the proofing ID the user would be prompted to initiate creation of new ARIES token by scanning a QR code. During the enrolment, a new credential would be created in his ARIES application with anonymous ARIES ID that would be linked to his proofing ID in the ARIES Identity provider. At this step, the user may select which attributes would be provisioned to the token and provided to any relying party after successful ARIES authentication.

Authentication. The authentication use case is more similar to current state of the art cases because one of our goals is to provide smooth on-boarding of relying parties that use current SAML and OpenID Connect protocols. The main change will be in management of user information when the classical model will be replaced by privacy friendly scheme that would allow anonymous authentication while providing required attributes or proofs such as user age or state he comes from. The authentication would be managed by ARIES Identity provider application that would contact user's ARIES application and perform basic authentication. The result would be an anonymous ID and attributes provisioned with the credential. As an optional step, biometric authentication may be required.

5.2   e-Commerce Scenario

This use case aims to assess the specific challenges and difficulties in securing eCommerce transactions from identity fraud by including the technical robustness and security features of ARIES digital mobile identities in a realistic setting for provisioning eCommerce services. It also aims to assess the usability and convenience for customers of using ARIES digital mobile identities for both registration and authentication at the eCommerce online site. In addition, it will showcase more trustworthy interactions for citizens and customers with involvement of law enforcement stakeholders in the case of identity-related incident (using features of ARIES identity vault). This use case will compare the results with a 'control' environment in which the ARIES solution is not used in order to measure the positive impact of ARIES in reducing impact and levels of theft.

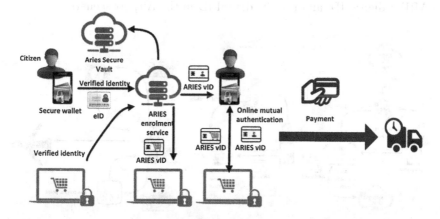

Fig. 2. Identity derivation components in the e-Commerce Use case

In order to address or prevent different identified identity theft use cases identified by law enforcement agencies, a typical eCommerce scenario has been re-designed to include ARIES technology (see Fig. 2):

1. Both, merchants and users must be enrolled in ARIES ecosystem by using digital certificates and eIDs which will provide them a digital identity;
2. Merchants will express through ARIES the minimum attributes, including required level of assurance, they require for customers' purchases. Customers will select the digital identity of their choice that meets merchants' requirements.
3. ARIES components at the eCommerce provider will check the validity of the digital identity and, if necessary, perform a biometric authentication (local or remote) using mobile device sensors (i.e. camera, microphone...).
4. Finally, and at the delivery stage, the recipient of the goods is also required to authenticate to the distributor, avoiding misappropriation of the delivered goods.

ARIES solutions are currently being developed. A first implementation of the ARIES ecosystem is expected to be validated for the e-Commerce scenario at the end of the first year of the project (September 2017), in Sonae, a multinational company with a diversified portfolio of businesses in retail, financial services, technology, shopping centers, telecommunications.

5.3 Identity Digitalization for Secure Travel Scenario

This use case shows under realistic near-operational conditions how ARIES technologies can be used to prevent and reduce the risk of identity fraudsters to physically impersonate victims and to take advantage of identity issuance procedures provided to legitimate citizens, to commit identity crime and fraud bypassing physical access control measures.

As it is shown in Fig. 3, this use case contains two main process; obtaining the ARIES digital ID, and use the digital ID in the Airport scenario.

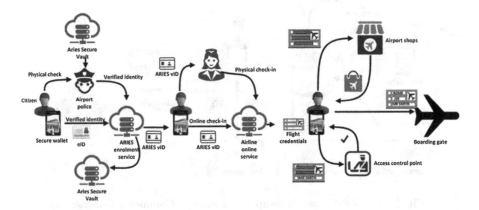

Fig. 3. Identity derivation components in the Airport Use case

Obtaining the ARIES digital ID:

1. The passenger self-enrols in the ARIES ecosystem by using her smartphone and eID/ePassport obtaining an ARIES vID linked to his eDocument.
2. Immediately, the passenger can present her mobile vID to obtain a boarding pass, linked to her mobile vID and to her biometric features and from which attributes can be disclosed in a privacy-preserving way. This credential will allow the passenger to go through airport's access control and board her flight.

Using the digital ID in the Airport scenario:

1. The passenger can demonstrate to the access control officers that she is allowed to go through the control by using her smart device and the recently issued digital identity to present a valid credential. No other information is disclosed except the minimum needed to compare with passengers list.

2. At the airport shop, the passenger can present an ARIES derived credential to provide a proof of ownership for a boarding pass to a flight outside the EU, without disclosing any additional information. This entitles the passenger to a VAT exemption.
3. The passenger at the boarding gate presents her smartphone and biometrically "unlocks" its ARIES derived boarding pass to access the plane.

The airport scenario is envisaged to be evaluated and validated during the second iteration of the project development (October 2018). In this sense, the ARIES ecosystem will be deployed and tested in a real airport (like the Brussels airport) and tested by a Law Agency Enforcement such as the Belgian Federal Police.

5.4   Supporting Law Enforcement Agencies

Law Enforcement Agencies (LEA) can be benefited from the ARIES technology as they might be granted to play the Inspector role in the ecosystem. The Inspector role is in charge of de-anonymize the user and access part of the data stored in the ARIES Security Vault, in case of identity fraud, misuse, liability or cybercrime investigation. To this aim, the Inspector should satisfy a policy that specifies which information should be recoverable as well as the inspection grounds describing the circumstances under the data can be inspected.

Notice that this authorization privilege is, in the end, materialized by endowing LEAs with specific cryptographic credentials that allow them decrypting such an information. Depending on the underneath technology, it might mean providing proxy re-encryption keys or anonymous credentials in case the LEAs need to access to Zero knowledge crypto proofs.

In ARIES scenarios LEAs can be granted to play the Inspector role in order to deal with identity fraud and identity tracking during the Airport Access Control. In the eCommerce scenario LEAs can take advantage of the ARIES capabilities to inspect payment transactions, thereby preventing refund fraud or fraudulent merchants.

6   Conclusions

ARIES European project is identifying, researching and testing the technological, organizational and societal means necessary to eventually establish the European electronic identity framework capable of addressing the challenges posed by wrong identity, identity fraud and associated types of cyber and other forms of organized crime. In this sense, this paper has introduced the identity ecosystem that is being currently devised and developed in the scope of ARIES European project. The ecosystem strives to safeguard the fundamental parameters of identity management: security, efficiency, user friendliness, trust, privacy and data protection. In the near future, ARIES will come out with an IdM architecture that will allow different kinds of credentials and mutual authentication mechanisms to provide the Level of Assurance required in each situation, enabling to link the physical and digital identities in a secure and trustworthy way, while supporting data minimization techniques and anonymous credential solutions.

Acknowledgments. The project leading to this application has received funding from the European Union's Horizon 2020 research and innovation programme under grant agreement No 700085 (ARIES project).

References

1. Future-id, shaping the future of electronic identity. http://www.futureid.eu/
2. OpenID. http://openid.net/
3. Stork, Secure idenTity acrOss boRders linKed 2.0. https://www.eid-stork2.eu
4. Blaze, M., Bleumer, G., Strauss, M.: Divertible protocols and atomic proxy cryptography. In: Nyberg, K. (ed.) EUROCRYPT 1998. LNCS, vol. 1403, pp. 127–144. Springer, Heidelberg (1998). doi:10.1007/BFb0054122
5. Camenisch, J., Lysyanskaya, A.: An efficient system for non-transferable anonymous credentials with optional anonymity revocation. In: Pfitzmann, B. (ed.) EUROCRYPT 2001. LNCS, vol. 2045, pp. 93–118. Springer, Heidelberg (2001). doi:10.1007/3-540-44987-6_7
6. Camenisch, J., Lysyanskaya, A.: A signature scheme with efficient protocols. In: Cimato, S., Persiano, G., Galdi, C. (eds.) SCN 2002. LNCS, vol. 2576, pp. 268–289. Springer, Heidelberg (2003). doi:10.1007/3-540-36413-7_20
7. Camenisch, J., Van Herreweghen, E.: Design and implementation of the idemix anonymous credential system. In: Proceedings of the 9th ACM Conference on Computer and Communications Security, CCS 2002, pp. 21–30. ACM, New York (2002)
8. Hardt, D. (ed.): The oauth 2.0 authorization framework (2012)
9. Hughes, J., Maler, E.: Security assertion markup language (saml) v2.0. Technical report, Organization for the Advancement of Structured Information Standards (2005)
10. Naumann, I., Hogben, G., et al.: Privacy features of european eid card specifications. Technical report, The European Union Agency for Network and Information Security (ENISA) (2009)
11. Kortuem, G., Kawsar, F., Fitton, D., Sundramoorthy, V.: Smart objects as building blocks for the internet of things. IEEE Internet Comput. **14**(1), 44–51 (2010)
12. Li, S., Kot, A.C.: Fingerprint combination for privacy protection. IEEE Trans. Inform. Forensics Secur. **8**(2), 350–360 (2013)
13. Paquin, C., Zaverucha, G.: U-prove cryptographic specification v1. 1. Technical report, Microsoft Technical report (2011). http://connect.microsoft.com/site1188
14. Sabouri, A., Krontiris, I., Rannenberg, K.: Attribute-based credentials for trust (ABC4Trust). In: Fischer-Hübner, S., Katsikas, S., Quirchmayr, G. (eds.) TrustBus 2012. LNCS, vol. 7449, pp. 218–219. Springer, Heidelberg (2012). doi:10.1007/978-3-642-32287-7_21

15. Schaffers, H., Komninos, N., Pallot, M., Trousse, B., Nilsson, M., Oliveira, A.: Smart cities and the future internet: towards cooperation frameworks for open innovation. In: Domingue, J., et al. (eds.) FIA 2011. LNCS, vol. 6656, pp. 431–446. Springer, Heidelberg (2011). doi:10.1007/978-3-642-20898-0_31
16. The European Parliament, the Council of the European Union: Regulation (EU) no 910/2014 of the European parliament and of the council (2014)
17. Weerawarana, S., Curbera, F., Leymann, F., Storey, T., Ferguson, D.F.: Web services platform architecture: SOAP, WSDL, WS-policy, WS-addressing, WS-BPEL. WS-reliable messaging and more, Prentice Hall PTR (2005)

Forget Me, Forget Me Not - Redefining the Boundaries of the Right to Be Forgotten to Address Current Problems and Areas of Criticism

Beata Sobkow[(✉)]

Queen Mary University of London, London, UK
b.sobkow@outlook.com

Abstract. In the landmark decision *Google Spain v AEPD and Mario Costeja González,* the Court of Justice of the European Union has declared that individuals have a so-called 'right to be forgotten', that is, the right to demand search engines to erase search results obtained through searches for their names. The ruling has been praised by many and seen as a welcome relief for individuals who were gradually losing all control over the private information stored about them online. However, because the court has failed to provide proper guidance as to the application and scope of the new right, the ruling has opened risks to freedom of expression and the right to receive and impart information as well as introduced questions as to the legitimacy, fairness and international scope of the delisting process. Taking a closer look at the problems currently surrounding the right to be forgotten, this paper will attempt to narrow down and define the scope of the application of the new right. In order to do so, it will first argue that personal information should be predominantly protected by reliance on existing laws rather than through the creation of an ambiguous right to delist search results. It will then advocate for a rejection of the court's broad formulation of the right to be forgotten and suggest that, in order to attain a fairer balance between the fundamental rights at stake, the right should be only permitted to apply in three, clearly defined and limited circumstances.

Keywords: Data protection · Right to be forgotten · General Data Protection Regulation · EU law · Privacy · Freedom of expression · Search engines

1 Introduction

Each day there are 3.5 billion Internet searches being performed, 4.8 billion pieces of content shared and 500 million tweets posted [1]. While having access to such enormous pool of information offers a range of benefits, it may also carry significant risks to individuals whose personal data is stored and processed online.

In its landmark decision in *Google Spain v AEPD and Mario Costeja González* ('*Google Spain*') [2], the Court of Justice of the European Union ('CJEU') acknowledged the role Google, and other search engines, play in providing access to personal data and declared that individuals have a so-called 'right to be forgotten' ('RtbF'), that

© Springer International Publishing AG 2017
E. Schweighofer et al. (Eds.): APF 2017, LNCS 10518, pp. 34–51, 2017.
DOI: 10.1007/978-3-319-67280-9_3

is, the right to demand the erasure of search results obtained through searches for their names.

The ruling has been welcomed by many as, at a time when individuals readily share private information about themselves online, it has opened up the discussion on the importance of protecting such data. However, 'because it addressed the rights involved in such a careless way, it opened risks to freedom of speech' [3] and even raised fears of starting 'a Dark Age of the Internet, where information mysteriously disappears and the past is deleted with a click of the mouse' [4].

These and other problems surrounding the RtbF will be explored in part 1 of this article. Part 2 will then argue that, considering the flaws of the current regime, personal information should be primarily protected by reliance on existing laws rather than through the creation of an ambiguous right to remove search results. Finally, part 3 will reject CJEU's broad formulation of the RtbF and suggest that, in order to attain a fairer balance between the data subject's right to privacy and data protection and the general public's, web publishers', and search engines' rights to freedom of expression and to receive and impart information, the right should be only permitted to apply in three, clearly defined and limited circumstances.

2 The Existing RtbF Regime[1]

2.1 Google Spain Decision

In *Google Spain*, the CJEU held that search engine providers fall within the scope of the EU data protection regime as they engage in the processing of personal data[2] and act as controllers[3] in respect of personal data stored in their indexes. Accordingly, individuals have a right to request search engines to de-list search results obtained through searches for their names where these relate to inadequate, irrelevant, no longer relevant or excessive personal data [2].

Whilst the CJEU has asserted that this so-called RtbF was firmly grounded in Arts. 12(b) and 14 of Directive 95/46/EC ('Directive') [5], many commentators argued that the right formulated by the court provided more extensive rights than those actually set out in the Directive [6]. As Arts. 12(b) and 14 provide data subjects with rights to request the rectification or deletion of certain personal data only in limited and defined circumstances, the provisions of the Directive would not assist individuals like Mr. Costeja who would want to hide certain search results and challenge the processing of their personal data 'merely because they consider that that processing may be prejudicial to them' [2] or 'would prefer not to be easily available through a link to [their] name on a search engine' [7].

---

[1] The most relevant (for the purposes of this paper) provisions of Directive 95/46/EC and Regulation 2016/679 as well as an excerpt from the decision in *Google Spain v AEPD and Mario Costeja González* are set out the Appendix.

[2] 'Personal data' is defined in Directive, Art. 2(a) and GDPR, Art. 4(1). 'Processing' is defined in Directive, Art. 2(b) and GDPR, Art. 4(2).

[3] 'Controller' is defined in Directive, Art. 2(d) and GDPR, Art. 4(7).

Whist some have praised the ruling on the basis that it would repair 'the damage to privacy the Internet—and especially Google—has wrought' [8], others have cautioned against any attempts to control the Internet and its content arguing that this created a risk of emergence of a 'black market' Google[4] and 'a new digital divide, between those who have the skills and expertise to locate data [...] and those that don't' [9].

2.2   General Data Protection Regulation ('GDPR')

Whereas the CJEU has formulated a very broad definition of the RtbF, the wording of the GDPR [10] might, on the other hand, suggest a return to the more limited pre-*Google Spain* position. Looking at the title of Art. 17 of the GDPR (Right to erasure ('right to be forgotten')), one might understandably expect Art. 17 to expressly codify and define CJEU's RtbF. However, rather surprisingly, the GDPR does not only fail to define this right but may, in fact, be seen as having whittled it down to mirror the already existing right to erasure.

Art. 17(1) closely mirrors the current provisions of Arts. 12(b) and 14 of the Directive and grants data subjects a right to erase personal data where its processing infringes the GDPR, EU or member states' law (Art. 17(1)(d)–(e)); when there is no legitimate ground for its processing or the controller does not fulfil the prescribed data quality requirements (Art. 17(1)(a)); or where data subjects withdrew their consent (Art. 17(1)(b)) or exercised their right to object (Art. 17(1)(c)). As such, Art. 17(1) does not provide a definition for CJEU's RtbF but largely re-states and clarifies the erasure rights previously recognised under the Directive [11].

Whilst Recital 66 and Art. 17(2) do refer to the new obligations of controllers to notify certain third-parties of erasure requests and request that these parties also erase their links to such personal data, nowhere does the GDPR explicitly mention the right of data subjects to request a mere *de-listing*. Neither does the GDPR extend data subjects' existing right to erasure to *Google Spain* situations where the data in question is accurate albeit embarrassing for the data subject.

Arguably, due to these inconsistent approaches to the RtbF in the *Google Spain* decision and the GDPR, it is currently not entirely clear whether there are two RtbFs with two definitions and two sets of criteria; whether the GDPR departs from CJEU's broad construction of the RtbF and therefore limits it to a mere right to erasure; or whether Art. 17 of the GDPR, although not expressly defining the RtbF, should be interpreted as incorporating CJEU's RtbF by reference.

Unfortunately, this is not the only problem surrounding the RtbF. The following section will examine the other key areas of criticism.

---

[4] See, e.g. the website http://hiddenfromgoogle.afaqtariq.com/ which archives deleted links and displays them together with the relevant search term and the source that revealed the de-listed information.

3   Problems Surrounding the RtbF

3.1   The Conflict with Freedom of Speech

Ever since the CJEU's decision in *Google Spain*, the idea of a RtbF has been the subject of a significant amount of controversy. Academics and advocates of the freedom of expression have been highly critical of this right, warning that it will be 'the biggest threat to free speech on the Internet in the coming decade' [11]. Whilst some have dismissed these concerns and argued that the RtbF is working exactly as intended [12], the examination of previous de-listing decisions shows that the assessments made by courts, national Data Protection Authorities ('DPAs') and search engines are often in conflict with each other [13], thereby demonstrating that the application of the RtbF and the making of de-listing decisions is far from straightforward.

Each request to de-list search results will, typically, bring into conflict a range of fundamental rights and interests: on one hand, the data subject's rights to privacy and data protection and, on the other, the rights of Internet users to search for, find and obtain information,[5] the right of web publishers to generate content and disseminate ideas [2], the rights of other third parties who may also be related to the content requested to be de-listed and thus may have a valid interest in seeing that the results are not removed or the rights of search engines to communicate meaning from crawling and indexing websites [2]. Therefore, each decision to de-list will require a careful evaluation of these rights to strike a fair balance between them [14]. Whilst both the CJEU [15, 16] and the European Court of Human Rights ('ECHR') [17, 18] have recognised that personal data processing may be restrained to protect privacy, the ECHR has repeatedly declared that 'as a matter of principle [the right to privacy and the right to freedom of expression] deserve equal respect' and that neither of these rights is absolute [19].[6] Therefore, as there is no formal hierarchy between these rights, the required balance must be struck on a case-by-case basis.

Unfortunately, the CJEU appears to have taken a different approach to the ECHR and, arguably, even the EU Justice Commissioner.[7] Declaring that the RtbF takes precedence 'as a rule' [2], the CJEU appears to suggest that the relatively new EU data protection rights are in a way 'more fundamental' than, for example, the long-established and 'recognised in nearly every national constitution and in most international human rights treaties' [21] right to freedom of expression.

Conversely, Art. 17(3) of the GDPR recognises the importance of the right to freedom of expression and information and provides that the rights set out in Art. 17(1), including the RtbF, 'shall not apply to the extent [the] processing is necessary for exercising' the two rights.[8]

---

[5] Charter of Fundamental Rights of the European Union, Art. 11(1); European Convention on Human Rights, Art. 10.

[6] Note that the European Convention on Human Rights does not contain a right to data protection but the ECHR largely includes such right in the Art. 8 right to respect for private life.

[7] The EU Justice Commissioner stated that the RtbF must not 'take precedence over freedom of expression or freedom of the media' [20].

[8] See also GDPR, Recital 65.

These inconsistent approaches to the resolution of the conflict between the various interests at stake not only contribute further to the uncertainty as to the application of the RtbF but may also create serious negative consequences for individuals and the public at large [14].

3.2 Lack of Criteria for Application

The uncertainty surrounding the application of, and weight assigned to, the RtbF is further exacerbated by the fact that there exists no universal list of criteria for assessing de-listing requests. As noted above, given that each decision to de-list may bring four fundamental rights into conflict, it is regrettable that the CJEU has failed to set out clear criteria which should be applicable to de-listing decisions. As one commentator has rightly observed:

> the criteria provided by the CJEU [are] scarce and difficult to apply, leaving national authorities and courts, not to mention search engines, wrestling in search of a proportionate and balanced outcome that fully takes into account all the rights and interests at stake [13].

Whilst the Article 29 Data Protection Working Party has proposed a list of generally-applicable criteria which should inform the evaluation of de-listing requests, these are tainted with vagueness and subjectivity.[9] Moreover, these criteria are, confusingly, stated to be addressed to national DPAs and their handling of de-listing complaints when, first and foremost, search engines, and not DPAs, will be responsible for the approval or rejection of de-listing requests.

The GDPR also fails to provide any criteria apart from setting out a list of situations where the Art. 17 rights will not apply (Art. 17(3))[10] and the matter becomes further complicated by the fact that search engines have produced their own set of criteria which will sometimes follow,[11] but at other times will come into direct conflict with, the Article 29 Data Protection Working Party guidelines.[12]

Considering that the de-listing decisions will be made, and fundamental rights of numerous parties will be evaluated, by commercial bodies with no democratic oversight or experience in balancing fundamental human rights, this lack of a clear and definite list of criteria becomes highly worrying.

---

[9] See [22–24] for a discussion of the problems associated with criterion 2 set out by the Article 29 Data Protection Working Party in its guidelines on the Google Spain decision [25].

[10] The further retention of the personal data will be lawful where it is necessary, for exercising the right of freedom of expression and information, for compliance with a legal obligation, for the performance of a task carried out in the public interest or in the exercise of official authority vested in the controller, on the grounds of public interest in the area of public health, for archiving purposes in the public interest, scientific or historical research purposes or statistical purposes, or for the establishment, exercise or defence of legal claims.

[11] See, e.g. criterion 9 set out by the Article 29 Data Protection Working Party [25] and criterion 4.2.1.6 set out in the report prepared by The Advisory Council to Google on the Right to be Forgotten [26].

[12] See, e.g. criterion 8 of Article 29 Data Protection Working Party [25] and criterion 4.2.2.6 of The Advisory Council to Google [26].

3.3 Google as Judge and Jury

The problems surrounding the RtbF are further aggravated due to the fact that the CJEU has charged commercial entities with the task of enforcing the RtbF. The Advocate General has, in his *Google Spain* opinion, cautioned against leaving these kinds of judgement to search engines [2] and many commentators have further expressed the view that they felt deeply uncomfortable about entrusting commercial bodies with such important decision-making powers [7]. Essentially, as Fraser rightly observes [27]:

> 'the search engine does not know the complainant, does not know the context, does not know if the individual is a public figure and does not know whether the individual has genuinely "moved on with his life". There may be some scenarios that are relatively easy to deal with [...] but for most cases the search engine will only have the complainant's submissions to rely upon'.

Academics have also warned that commercial entities will normally choose to err on the side of caution [28] and immediately comply with a de-listing request in order to avoid any potential legal liability or penalties for non-compliance [29].

The risk of such 'over-compliance' may increase further once the GDPR becomes applicable. Considering that certain infringements will be subject to a fine amounting to the higher of EUR20 million and 4% of annual worldwide turnover (Art. 83) (not a trivial amount for Google, Bing, Yahoo or other search engines) and that even personal liability might be imposed on company directors if the proposals of the Information Commissioner's Office are implemented [30], there is a real risk that search engines will choose to become censors [31]. Moreover, the GDPR imposes a very high burden on controllers as it no longer qualifies the right of erasure and rectification by the words 'as appropriate' as the Directive did in Art. 12(b) instead requiring personal data to be rectified or erased 'without undue delay' (Arts. 16 and 17(1)). Giving controllers little (if no) time to consider each request arguably leaves them with little scope to refuse such de-listing, even if it is inappropriate. Search engines are also required to provide 'sufficient explanation to the data subject about the reasons for the refusal [to de-list]' [25] which may further disincentivise them from rejecting de-listing requests. Consequently, search engines may refuse to engage in any time-consuming and difficult balancing of rights and choose to approve de-listing requests rather than risk a finding of non-compliance. After all, these search engines are businesses established with the purpose of generating returns for their investors rather than protecting human rights.

Some commentators [32], whilst noting the above concerns, have argued that there is no better alternative than entrusting search engines with the task of assessing de-listing requests on the basis that no country in the world would have sufficient resources to handle the sheer amount[13] of such requests. However, the quantity of requests should in no way entitle the EU or the individual member states to disclaim responsibility for the protection of fundamental rights and delegate their powers to commercial entities. Rather, as will be argued in Part III below, the scope of the RtbF should be limited to very specific and clearly defined situations and individuals should

---

[13] Since *Google Spain*, Google has evaluated over 1,835,005 URLs [34].

instead be expected to primarily rely on currently existing and court-controlled remedies to control their personal information.

4 Redefining the RtbF

4.1 Terminology

In order to address the confusion surrounding the RtbF, the first, and simplest, step would be to change the misleading name given to the right [7] and adopt a more suitable terminology. Whilst the current name easily captures the imagination of the media and the wider public, it is precisely this ill-conceived choice of terminology which some commentators have quoted as the reason leading to 'largely unfounded fears of critics and overblown hopes among enthusiasts' [11].

In fact, the right formulated in *Google Spain* is not a 'right to be forgotten' per se [26], as it does not result in the removal of the personal data itself, but merely a suppression of the link to it [33].[14] As such, the information is still available at the source site; it is only more difficult to be found. Consequently, the Article 29 Data Protection Working Party has rightly abandoned the troublesome 'RtbF' terminology in favour of a 'right to de-listing' [25].[15]

Moreover, whilst Art. 17 of the GDPR refers again to the old name, this should, arguably,[16] be understood as limiting the RtbF to a mere right of erasure thereby correctly recognising that only erased data can be truly forgotten.

4.2 Current Legal Framework

Whilst the adoption of proper terminology would be a highly recommended first step towards addressing some of the existing uncertainty, changes on a more fundamental level are required in order to address the potentially limitless scope of CJEU's RtbF as well as the concerns surrounding the designation of commercial bodies as arbiters of fundamental rights in RtbF cases. One such change would be achieved through limiting the scope of the RtbF by recognising that the current legal framework in the UK (and in the other member states through similar or equivalent laws and remedies [35][17]) already provides individuals with a right to control their personal information through laws protecting privacy and reputation; laws restricting the use or dissemination of certain types of information; data protection laws as well as tools made available by website providers and search engines.

As the application of these laws could lead to the removal of the relevant personal information at source or from search results based on the individual's name, this may expose these rights to the same freedom-of-speech-based criticisms raised against the

---

[14] See also [7, 21].

[15] Note that the term 'RtbF' is not used, even once, in that document.

[16] See Sect. 2.2.

[17] See also Shoor [26]; Code Civil (French Civil Code), arts. 9-10 and Grundgesetz für die Bundesrepublik Deutschland (Basic Law for the Federal Republic of Germany), §1–2.

RtbF. However, it is important to appreciate that these laws, contrary to the RtbF, only apply in defined circumstances; are subject to pre-set criteria; and are (with the exception of website tools) decided by courts or other administrative bodies which have adequate experience and expertise in evaluating removal requests and balancing fundamental rights and are also supported by valid claims of legitimacy and accountability.

Privacy and reputation. A range of remedies is available to individuals wishing to protect their privacy and reputation. Laws governing privacy [36–38], misuse of private information [39–42], and breach of confidence [43] protect individuals against those who disclose and use information about their private lives. False statements and allegations which would lead others to think worse of the individuals can be addressed via defamation [44], whilst passing off [45] may provide protection against false claims of association and unauthorised use of an individual's name, likeness or attributes. Where maliciously published false statements have caused financial loss, a claim for malicious falsehood may provide redress [46].

In addition, the Protection from Harassment Act 1997 and the Crime and Disorder Act 1998 may be relied upon in cases of cyberbullying to protect individuals whose personal data is used in connection with harassing or threatening behaviour and the Regulation of Investigatory Powers Act 2000 can be invoked where personal data has been obtained through interceptions of postal or electronic communications.

Special categories of speech and information. Inspired by the same ideas of forgiveness and right to self-determination as the CJEU when formulating the RtbF [47], European governments have expressly restricted the publication and circulation of certain types of personal information [21]. Accordingly, the law limits, for example, the publication and use of criminal records[18] or requires records of bankruptcies to be removed once specific periods of time have passed [49, 50], thereby allowing individuals to extricate themselves from their past and move on to fully reintegrate into society

Moreover, the law also limits the context within which certain personal information can be used. As certain types of speech have been refused protection due to their low value [51], the use of personal information in relation to, for example, threatening words and hate-speech [52], obscene and pornographic speech [53–55] or words glorifying terrorism [56] will not be allowed irrespective of any right to freedom of expression the person making such statements may claim to have.

Data protection. In addition to the above, existing data protection laws already provide individuals with a range of additional rights to control the collection and processing of their personal data, leading some commentators to conclude that the RtbF 'can more or less be reflected through the current obligations in data-protection legislation' [57]. The Directive gives individuals a right to consent to the collection and processing of their personal data and the right to withdraw such consent (Art. 7(a)). Individuals may also request their personal data to be deleted when it is no longer

---

[18] See, e.g. the Rehabilitation of Offenders Act 1974. Note also the existence of the so-called 'Mary Bell injunctions' protecting the identity of offenders discussed, e.g. by Whitehead [48].

relevant to its original purpose or upon their justified objection (Arts. 12(b) and 14).[19] Moreover, data subjects may also ask that their personal data be rectified, completed or erased when it is inaccurate or incomplete (Art. 12(b)).

Apart from merely supplementing the remedies discussed above, data protection laws may also assist individuals who wish to rely on such remedies to restrict the further processing of their personal data but are struggling to convince courts to order the removal or non-publication of such data. In cases where the personal data in question is already in the public domain, courts often refuse to grant injunctions, awarding, instead, only damages which rarely provide satisfactory redress to individuals whose personal data has been, or may be, shared on the Internet [59]. In these situations, individuals may be able to rely on data protection laws to object to the publication and use of their personal data as the conditions for their lawful processing will not be met [23].

Search engine and website tools. EU and member states' laws are not the sole sources of rights individuals can rely upon in typical RtbF scenarios. Most social media platforms permit their users to permanently delete information and content they have posted or uploaded themselves [60]. Certain jurisdictions have considered the various interests at stake in such situations and, recognising the merits of such right, have adopted it either through soft-law (in the form of best practices or guidelines, as, for example, in Korea [61]) or hard law. For instance, recognising the need to protect minors who often may not understand the long-term consequences of a simple act like posting a tweet or photograph online, a number of U.S. States have introduced so-called 'eraser button' legislation which requires web sites and social media platforms to allow children to erase information and content they themselves have shared [62, 63]. Interestingly, Art. 17(1) of the proposal for the GDPR expressly referred to such 'eraser button' right [64]. Whilst this has been removed from the final wording of the article, it is now contained in Recital 65, meaning that, arguably, this right will still become available to data subjects once the GDPR becomes directly applicable.

4.3 Accurate Information

The problem of the seemingly limitless scope of the RtbF could also be addressed by expressly recognising that the right should not generally apply to true and accurate information. Whilst a number of commentators, referring to the concepts of dignity and self-determination, argued that individuals in the position of Mr. Costeja, who wish to forget their embarrassing financial history, must be protected and therefore granted a broad RtbF, such wide RtbF should, however, be rejected for the reasons discussed below.

True and accurate information should be protected by default. Information which is inaccurate, outdated, false or illegal should be rectified or deleted at source as there is no reason why it should be preserved but be merely hidden from the general public and a third, uninvolved party be punished for revealing its existence [27]. On the other

---

[19] See also Graux, Ausloos and Valcke [58].

hand, where information is correct and legally obtained and processed, the rights to receive and impart information will weigh heavily in favour of preserving such information, even if an individual may prefer to have it cast into oblivion.

There is no right to a false image. Freedom of information confers upon individuals both a right to access information and a right to remember. As such, individuals 'should not have an unqualified right to control the accessibility of information about them' [21] or be allowed to remove true and accurate information about their past. And whilst individuals do have a right to dignity and self-determination [65], it does not give them an unqualified right to create a false image of themselves and demand that only this falsified image is made public [41].

Individuals should take responsibility for their actions. Individuals should be required to take responsibility for their actions rather than permitted to force others to forget their past mistakes. As one commentator has rightly observed:

> There is also something to be said for the deterrence value. If an individual presents an obnoxious or unflattering statement about himself because he is aware it can be deleted with impunity, he might remain unenlightened that his actions occasionally have consequences. However, if forced to be made aware that his behavior is unacceptable through social shaming, it might encourage people to operate with greater decorum' [63].[20]

Moreover, it is important to appreciate that people are, nowadays, well aware of the privacy risks associated with the use of the Internet and are 'fully attuned to the pitfalls of disclosing personal information online' [67] and therefore take appropriate measures to protect their data and identity.[21] The image of defenceless individuals who have absolutely no control over the use of their personal data online, as often painted by RtbF proponents, is not entirely accurate. As such, individuals should take responsibility for their use of websites and social media, rather than be allowed being reckless and permitted to subsequently delete any unfavourable content.

Information online does disappear. Interestingly, Ambrose observes that, '[o]ne study from the field of content persistence, a body of research that has been almost wholly overlooked by legal scholars, found that 85% of content disappears in a year and that 59% disappears in a week' [71] and further noted that the average lifespan of a webpage was merely around 100 days [71]. Moreover, information and news have different and 'expiring' relevance dates meaning that certain information becomes, over time, of little or no public interest and the internet does, in fact, 'forget' about it [23]. Whilst the proponents of the RtbF often rely on the notion that information, once online, remains there forever, the truth is that shelf life of online data is surprisingly low. Therefore, information should be allowed to 'be forgotten' in a natural way, rather than by forceful suppression and denial of the public's right to access it.

---

[20] See also Rosen [66].

[21] For example, an overwhelming number of people in Japan use pseudonyms on social network sites [68]. See also Madden [69] and note the option of using services providing expiration dates for data as discussed by Mayer-Schönberger [70].

4.4   A Limited RtbF

For the reasons discussed above, true, accurate and legal personal data should, by default, be preserved and any attempts of its de-listing resisted. This does not, however, mean that individuals should never be allowed to exercise a RtbF in respect of such information. As argued below, three situations should be recognised in which autonomy, dignity and privacy rights of individuals whose personal data is being processed will prevail and thereby legitimately limit the competing interests of website publishers, search engines and the general public. It is in these limited situations that a 'right to de-list' should be allowed to exist.

Victims of crimes. Whereas true and accurate criminal records, no matter how dated or embarrassing to the ex-convict, should never be de-listed unless expressly authorised by legislation (see Section 3.2.2), a different approach should apply where the information in question does not identify the perpetrator but the victim of the crime.

The arguments of public interest or the need to hold individuals to account for their own actions will not apply in such situations and there will be, therefore, no valid reason as to why the information should continue to be linked to the victims and the victims be repeatedly reminded of the painful memories and traumas of their past. Instead, victims should be permitted to dissociate themselves from the crimes and move on with their lives by demanding that any search results referring to these past crimes obtained through searches for their names be effectively de-listed.

Cyberbullying. Whilst the Protection from Harassment Act 1997 may protect individuals from harassing behaviour online (see Section 3.2.1), it will, arguably, fail to provide proper redress in all cases considering the potential sheer number and anonymity of bullies or 'trolls' [72] involved. Similarly, the fact that information expires and often loses the public's interest over time (as noted in Section 3.3.4), may not assist individuals whose personal information has gone viral in a matter of minutes and who are unable to wait for the information to be naturally forgotten and they are, as a result, required to switch schools/workplaces or even seek counselling [73]. Whereas the RtbF should not apply in *Google Spain* situations where the information in question is simply embarrassing, there may be serious cases of online cyberbullying where the scale and consequences of such acts would give the individuals concerned a legitimate claim for making a de-listing request.

Special categories of data. Whilst true and accurate data should not, normally, be deleted or de-listed, certain data will be so sensitive and personal by its very nature that making it readily available or easy to find and be attributable to a given individual should be prevented. Website providers, social media platforms and search engines have already recognised the existence of such special categories of data and have, consequently, provided a set of tools allowing individuals to control their use and processing. For example, Google has permitted victims of non-consensual pornography ('revenge porn') to ask for the removal of such content from search results based on their names [74][22] and suggested that private contact and identification data (such as,

---

[22] See also Microsoft's report on revenge porn removal requests on Bing [75].

for example, ID numbers, PINs, passwords or credit card details) or information that puts individuals at risk of identity theft could benefit from a de-listing process.[23] A 'right to de-list' could be expressly recognised to exist in relation to such categories of personal data.

Given that, on one hand, the public interest in the personal data being processed will be limited in the situations discussed above whilst, on the other hand, the individuals whose data is being processed will have a legitimate interest in dissociating themselves from such personal data or limiting access to it, the related de-listing requests will not raise the same freedom of expression concerns as other requests for de-listing of true and legally obtained information. As such, individuals should be entitled to make de-listing requests in these situations and search engines should, consequently, be permitted to remove relevant search results without the need to consult with or inform any other parties or involve courts and other public bodies.

5 Conclusion

'You are who Google says you are' [76].[24] As 'one's digital history may impact the opportunities offered, the reputation one maintains, and the self one embodies' [57], there is a clear value in giving individuals adequate tools to control their data, particularly where it is incorrect or may negatively affect their lives. The EU has tried to address this concern by equipping data subjects with the so-called RtbF which was formulated to allow individuals to regain control over their personal data being processed online. Regrettably, as it was argued in this article, the EU has failed to adequately define the scope and nature of the new right and to strike a fair balance between the rights of the various parties involved. As a result, the EU, its member states and numerous private parties must now make sense out of a misleadingly named right which lacks a clear definition, is subject to sets of ambiguous and, at times, conflicting criteria and, despite the fact that it clashes with fundamental human rights, is implemented by commercial bodies without democratic accountability or oversight.

The current situation is highly problematic. Indiscriminate de-listing of personal data can have grave consequences for fundamental human rights of various parties other than the data subject as data subjects and their personal data do not exist in a vacuum. Moreover, conflicting definitions of the RtbF and the lack of clear criteria for its application mean that the outcome of a de-listing request will often be difficult to predict. As a result, search engines, web publishers and even data subjects will face a real legal uncertainty as they struggle to ascertain when data will be permitted to be processed and when it will be required to be de-listed.

Fortunately, as argued in this article, there are a number of ways which could effectively address these problems. This could be achieved by, first and foremost, recognising that most situations which the RtbF was declared to cover are already

---

[23] See criteria 4.2.1.3 and 4.2.1.6 of the report prepared by The Advisory Council to Google [26].
[24] This appears to be an apt conclusion considering that Google accounts for 93% of online and mobile search traffic worldwide [77].

adequately addressed by existing member state laws. Requiring individuals to primarily rely on these rights would not only limit the scope of the seemingly limitless RtbF but also hand the decision-making and fundamental rights-balancing powers back to national courts where they belong [11]. Further clarity will be achieved by re-naming CJEU's RtbF as a 'right to de-list' and recognising that the GDPR's Art. 17 RtbF refers merely to a right to erasure. The final step would be achieved by defining the boundaries of the re-named 'right to de-list' by expressly recognising that it would only apply in specific circumstances: to protect victims of crimes and cyberbullying as well as to permit data subjects to de-list specific and strictly defined categories of data.

If the EU truly wants to be 'the Standard Setter for Modern Data Protection Rules in the Digital Age' [20], serve as an inspiring [78],[25] rather than discouraging [80, 81], example for other jurisdictions, and be in a position to respond to the fierce opposition the RtbF faces in the United States [82], it must address the controversies and legal uncertainty associated with the right, resolve the current lack of clarity and ensure that such problems are avoided in the future.

Appendix

1. Directive 95/46/EC

Article 12 - Right of Access

Member States shall guarantee every data subject the right to obtain from the controller:

(a) [...];
(b) as appropriate the rectification, erasure or blocking of data the processing of which does not comply with the provisions of this Directive, in particular because of the incomplete or inaccurate nature of the data;
(c) notification to third parties to whom the data have been disclosed of any rectification, erasure or blocking carried out in compliance with (b), unless this proves impossible or involves a disproportionate effort.

Article 14 - The Data Subject's Right to Object

Member States shall grant the data subject the right:

(a) at least in the cases referred to in Article 7(e) and (f), to object at any time on compelling legitimate grounds relating to his particular situation to the processing of data relating to him, save where otherwise provided by national legislation. Where there is a justified objection, the processing instigated by the controller may no longer involve those data; [...].

---

[25] See also the recent decision of the Brazilian courts not to recognise a RtbF, as discussed by Sganzerla [79].

2. Google Spain v AEPD and Mario Costeja González

94. Therefore, if it is found, following a request by the data subject pursuant to Article 12(b) of Directive 95/46, that the inclusion in the list of results displayed following a search made on the basis of his name of the links to web pages published lawfully by third parties and containing true information relating to him personally is, at this point in time, incompatible with Article 6(1)(c) to (e) of the directive because that information appears, having regard to all the circumstances of the case, to be inadequate, irrelevant or no longer relevant, or excessive in relation to the purposes of the processing at issue carried out by the operator of the search engine, the information and links concerned in the list of results must be erased.

3. Regulation (EU) 2016/679

Recitals

(65) A data subject should have the right to have personal data concerning him or her rectified and a 'right to be forgotten' [...]. That right is relevant in particular where the data subject has given his or her consent as a child and is not fully aware of the risks involved by the processing, and later wants to remove such personal data, especially on the internet. The data subject should be able to exercise that right notwithstanding the fact that he or she is no longer a child. [...]

Article 17 - Right to Erasure ('right to be forgotten')

1. The data subject shall have the right to obtain from the controller the erasure of personal data concerning him or her without undue delay and the controller shall have the obligation to erase personal data without undue delay where one of the following grounds applies:

(a) the personal data are no longer necessary in relation to the purposes for which they were collected or otherwise processed;

(b) the data subject withdraws consent on which the processing is based according to point (a) of Article 6(1), or point (a) of Article 9(2), and where there is no other legal ground for the processing;

(c) the data subject objects to the processing pursuant to Article 21(1) and there are no overriding legitimate grounds for the processing, or the data subject objects to the processing pursuant to Article 21(2);

(d) the personal data have been unlawfully processed;

(e) the personal data have to be erased for compliance with a legal obligation in Union or Member State law to which the controller is subject;

(f) the personal data have been collected in relation to the offer of information society services referred to in Article 8(1).

2. Where the controller has made the personal data public and is obliged pursuant to paragraph 1 to erase the personal data, the controller, taking account of available technology and the cost of implementation, shall take reasonable steps, including technical measures, to inform controllers which are processing the personal data that the data subject has requested the erasure by such controllers of any links to, or copy or replication of, those personal data. [...]

Article 19 - Notification Obligation Regarding Rectification or Erasure of Personal Data or Restriction of Processing

The controller shall communicate any rectification or erasure of personal data or restriction of processing carried out in accordance with Article 16, Article 17(1) and Article 18 to each recipient to whom the personal data have been disclosed, unless this proves impossible or involves disproportionate effort. The controller shall inform the data subject about those recipients if the data subject requests it.

References

1. Internet Live Stats. http://www.internetlivestats.com. Accessed 28 Nov 2016
2. Case C-131/12 Google Spain SL and Google Inc v Agencia Española de Protección de Datos (AEPD) and Mario Costeja González. EMLR 27 (2014)
3. Brock, G.: The Right To Be Forgotten: Careless, Muddled And Risky (European Journalism Observatory, 13 October 2016) (2016). http://en.ejo.ch/media-politics/the-right-to-be-forgotten-careless-muddled-and-risky. Accessed 15 Nov 2016
4. Siry, L.: Forget me, forget me not: reconciling two different paradigms of the right to be forgotten. Ky LJ 3(103), 311 (2015)
5. Directive 95/46/EC of the European Parliament and of the Council of 24 October 1995 on the protection of individuals with regard to the processing of personal data and on the free movement of such data. OJ L281/31 (1995)
6. de Azevedo Cunha, M.V., Itagiba, G.: Between privacy, freedom of information and freedom of expression: is there a right to be forgotten in Brazil? CLSR 32(4), 634 (2016)
7. House of Lords: European Union Committee, 2nd Report of 2015, 'EU Data Protection law: a 'right to be forgotten'?', HL Paper 40 (2015)
8. Posner, E.: We All Have the Right to Be Forgotten (Slate, 14 May 2014) (2014). http://www.slate.com/articles/news_and_politics/view_from_chicago/2014/05/the_european_right_to_be_forgotten_is_just_what_the_internet_needs.html. Accessed 14 Nov 2016
9. Bradley, P.: Data, data everywhere. LIM 14(4), 249 (2014)
10. Regulation (EU) 2016/679 of the European Parliament and of the Council of 27 April 2016 on the protection of natural persons with regard to the processing of personal data and on the free movement of such data, and repealing Directive 95/46/EC (General Data Protection Regulation). OJ L 199/1 (2016)
11. van Alsenoy, B., Kuczerawy, A., Ausloos, J.: Search engines after Google Spain: internet@liberty or privacy@peril? KU Leuven Interdisciplinary Centre for Law & ICT. https://ssrn.com/abstract=2321494. Accessed 8 Oct 2016
12. Guadamuz, A.: Who Wants to be Forgotten? (Society for Computers & Law, 14 October 2014) (2014). http://www.scl.org/site.aspx?i=ed38893. Accessed 24 Oct 2016

13. Peguera, M.: In the aftermath of Google Spain: how the "right to be forgotten" is being shaped in Spain by courts and the Data Protection Authority. IJLIT **23**, 325 (2015)
14. Kulk, S., Borgesius, F.Z.: Google Spain v. González: did the court forget about freedom of expression? EJRR **5**(3), 289 (2014)
15. Case C-73/07 Tietosuojavaltuutettu v Satakunnan Markkinapörssi Oy and Satamedia Oy. ECR I-9831 (2008)
16. Case C-101/01 Lindqvist v Aklagarkammaren i Jonkoping. ECR I-12971 (2003)
17. Case No 24061/04 Aleksey Ovchinnikov v Russia (2011)
18. Case No 35841/02 Österreichischer Rundfunk v Austria (2006)
19. Case No 39954/08 Axel Springer AG v Germany (2012)
20. Reding, V.: The EU Data Protection Reform 2012: Making Europe the Standard Setter for Modern Data Protection Rules in the Digital Age' (European Commission, 22 January 2012) (2012). http://europa.eu/rapid/press-release_SPEECH-12-26_en.htm. Accessed 12 Oct 2016
21. Article 19: Policy Brief – The "Right to be Forgotten": Remembering Freedom of Expression. https://www.article19.org/resources.php/resource/38318/en/policy-brief:-the-right-to-be-forgotten. Accessed 5 Oct 2016
22. Sartor, G.: The right to be forgotten: balancing interests in the flux of time. IJLIT **24**, 72 (2016)
23. Korenhof, P., Ausloos, J., Szekely, I., Ambrose, M., Sartor, G., Leenes, R.: Timing the right to be forgotten: a study into "Time" as a factor in deciding about retention or erasure of data. In: Gutwirth, S., Leenes, R., de Hert, P. (eds.) Reforming European Data Protection Law. LGTS, vol. 20, pp. 171–201. Springer, Dordrecht (2015). doi:10.1007/978-94-017-9385-8_7
24. McNealy, J.: The emerging conflict between newsworthiness and the right to be forgotten. N Ky L Rev. **39**, 119 (2012)
25. Article 29: Data Protection Working Party, 'Guidelines on the implementation of the Court of Justice of the European Union judgement on "Google Spain and INC v. Agencia Española de Protección de Datos (AEPD) and Mario Costeja González" C-131/12'. WP225, 26 November 2014
26. The Advisory Council to Google on the Right to be Forgotten, 6 February 2015. https://www.google.com/advisorycouncil. Accessed 12 Oct 2016
27. Fraser, D.: You'd better forget the right to be forgotten in Canada (Canadian Privacy Law Blog, 28 April 2016) (2016). http://blog.privacylawyer.ca/2016/04/youd-better-forget-right-to-be.html. Accessed 25 Oct 2016
28. Lee, D.: Google reinstates 'forgotten' links after pressure (BBC News, 4 July 2014) (2014). http://www.bbc.co.uk/news/technology-28157607. Accessed 4 Oct 2016
29. Gratton, E.: Challenges with the Implementation of a Right to be Forgotten in Canada (Eloïse Gratton, 28 April 2016) (2016). http://www.eloisegratton.com/blog/2016/04/28/challenges-with-the-implementation-of-a-right-to-be-forgotten-in-canada/. Accessed 25 Oct 2016
30. Trillmich, P., Hickman, T.: UK ICO recommends personal liability of directors for breaches of data protection law (Lexology, 27 October 2016) (2016). http://www.lexology.com/library/detail.aspx?g=45767c9b-1759-456b-b77c-8e4100302fa3. Accessed 9 Nov 2016
31. Shoor, E.: Narrowing the right to be forgotten: why the European Union needs to amend the proposed data protection regulation. Brook J. Int. L. **39**(1), 487 (2014)
32. Lee, E.: Judge Google: Why the EU Should Embrace Google's Role in the Right to Be Forgotten (The Huffington Post, 5 July 2015) (2015). http://www.huffingtonpost.com/edward-lee/judge-google-why-the-eu-s_b_7232688.html. Accessed 24 Oct 2016
33. Kuner, C.: The Court of Justice of the EU Judgement on Data Protection and Internet Search Engines, LSE Law, Society and Economy Working Papers 3/2015. https://www.lse.ac.uk/collections/law/wps/WPS2015-03_Kuner.pdf. Accessed 12 Oct 2016

34. Google: Transparency Report: European privacy requests for search removals' (Google, 26 December 2016) (2016). https://www.google.com/transparencyreport/removals/europe privacy/?hl=en>. Accessed 26 Dec 2016
35. Kerr, J.: What is a search engine? The simple question the court of justice of the European Union forgot to ask and what it means for the future of the right to be forgotten. Chi J. Int. L. **17**(1), 217 (2016)
36. Kaye v Robertson. FSR 62 (1991)
37. OBG Ltd. v Allan. UKHL 21 (2007)
38. Peck v UK. ECHR 44 (2003)
39. CTB v News Group Newspapers Ltd. EWHC 1326 (2011)
40. Murray v Big Pictures (UK) Ltd. EWCA Civ 446 (2008)
41. Campbell v MGN Limited. UKHL 22 (2004)
42. Applause Store Productions Ltd. v Raphael. EWHC 1781 (2008)
43. Prince Albert v Strange. 47 ER 1302 (1849)
44. Lachaux v Independent Print Ltd. EWHC 620 and the Defamation Act 2013 (2015)
45. Edmund Irvine v Talksport Ltd. 2 All ER 414 (2002)
46. Ratcliffe v Evans. 2 QB 524 (1892)
47. Pagallo, U., Durante, M.: Legal memories and the right to be forgotten. In: Floridi, L. (ed.) Protection of Information and the Right to Privacy - A New Equilibrium?. LGTS, vol. 17, pp. 17–30. Springer, Cham (2014). doi:10.1007/978-3-319-05720-0_2
48. Whitehead, T.: Venables protected by rare identity ban (The Telegraph, 4 March 2010) (2010). http://www.telegraph.co.uk/news/uknews/law-and-order/7361451/Venables-protected-by-rare-identity-ban.html. Accessed 3 Dec 2016
49. Information Commissioner's Office: Information Commissioner's Office, 'Bankruptcy'. https://ico.org.uk/for-the-public/bankruptcy/. Accessed 12 Oct 2016
50. Conway, L.: Discharge from bankruptcy (House of Commons Library, 8 October 2015) (2015). http://researchbriefings.parliament.uk/ResearchBriefing/Summary/SN03043. Accessed 12 Oct 2016
51. Klug, F., Starmer, K., Weir, S.: The Three Pillars of Liberty: Political Rights and Freedoms in the United Kingdom. Routledge, London (1996)
52. Public Order Act 1986
53. Obscene Publications Act 1959
54. Obscene Publications Act 1964
55. Protection of Children Act 1978
56. Terrorism Act 2006
57. Ambrose, M., Ausloos, J.: The right to be forgotten across the pond. J. Inf. Policy **3**, 1 (2012)
58. Graux, H., Ausloos, J., Valcke, P.: The Right to be Forgotten in the Internet Era (ICRI Working Paper, 12 November 2012) (2012). https://ssrn.com/abstract=2174896. Accessed 27 Oct 2016
59. Mosley v News Group Newspapers Ltd. EWHC 1777 (2008)
60. Facebook: How do I hide or delete posts I've shared from my Page? https://www.facebook.com/help/252986458110193. Accessed 12 Nov 2016
61. Korea Communications Commission: KCC Takes Measures to Guarantee "Right to be Forgotten". http://eng.kcc.go.kr/download.do?fileSeq=43299. Accessed 14 Oct 2016
62. California Penal Code. §647 (2014)
63. Bolton, R.L.: The right to be forgotten: forced amnesia in a technological age. J. Marshall J. Inf. Technol. Priv. L. **31**, 133 (2015)
64. Proposal for a Regulation of the European Parliament and of the Council on the protection of individuals with regard to the processing of personal data and on the free movement of such data (General Data Protection Regulation) COM. 11 final (2012)

65. Charter of Fundamental Rights of the European Union. Art. 1
66. Rosen, J.: The right to be forgotten. Stan. L. Rev. Online **64**, 88 (2012)
67. Sellars, S.: Online privacy: do we have it and do we want it? A review of the risks and UK case law. EIPR **33**(1), 9 (2011)
68. Tabuchi, H.: Facebook Wins Relatively Few Friends in Japan (The New York Times, 9 January 2011) (2011). http://www.nytimes.com/2011/01/10/technology/10facebook.html. Accessed 8 Dec 2016
69. Madden, M.: Privacy management on social media sites (Pew Research Centre, 24 February 2012) (2012). http://www.pewinternet.org/2012/02/24/privacy-management-on-social-media-sites. Accessed 30 Nov 2016
70. Mayer-Schönberger, V.: Delete: The Virtue of Forgetting in the Digital Age. Princeton University Press (2009). or Weber, R.: The right to be forgotten – more than an Pandora's Box? JIPITEC. **2**, 120 (2011). http://www.jipitec.eu/issues/jipitec-2-2-2011/3084. Accessed 12 Oct 2016
71. Ambrose, M.: It's about time: privacy, information life cycles, and the right to be forgotten. Stan. Technol. L. Rev. **16**(3), 101 (2013)
72. BBC News: Internet trolls targeted with new legal guidelines (BBC News, 10 October 2016) (2016). http://www.bbc.co.uk/news/uk-37601431. Accessed 14 Oct 2016
73. Garsd, J.: Internet Memes and "The Right To Be Forgotten" (NPR, 3 March 2015) (2015). http://www.npr.org/sections/alltechconsidered/2015/03/03/390463119/internet-memes-and-the-right-to-be-forgotten. Accessed 24 Oct 2016
74. Google: Remove "revenge porn" from Google. https://support.google.com/websearch/answer/6302812. Accessed 4 Dec 2016
75. Microsoft: Content Removal Requests Report. https://www.microsoft.com/about/csr/transparencyhub/crrr/. Accessed 10 Dec 2016
76. Angelo, M.: You Are What Google Says You Are (Wired, 2 November 2009) (2009). https://www.wired.com/2009/02/you-are-what-go. Accessed 12 Nov 2016
77. eMarketer: How Much Search Traffic Actually Comes from Googling? (eMarketer, 13 January 2015) (2015). https://www.emarketer.com/Article/How-Much-Search-Traffic-Actually-Comes-Googling/1011814. Accessed 30 Nov 2016
78. Yan, M.N.: Protecting the right to be forgotten: is mainland China ready? Eur. Data Prot. L. Rev. **1**, 190 (2015)
79. Sganzerla, T.: Brazil Superior Court Rules in Google's Favor, Against "Right to Be Forgotten" (advox, 21 November 2016) (2016). https://advox.globalvoices.org/2016/11/22/brazil-superior-court-rules-in-googles-favor-against-right-to-be-forgotten/. Accessed 12 Dec 2016
80. Toobin, J.: The Solace of Oblivion - in Europe, the right to be forgotten trumps the Internet (The New Yorker, 29 September 2014) (2014). http://www.newyorker.com/magazine/2014/09/29/solace-oblivion. Accessed 12 Oct 2016
81. Cunningham, M.: Free Expression, Privacy and Diminishing Sovereignty in the Information Age: The Internationalization of Censorship. Arkansas Law Review (2015). https://ssrn.com/abstract=2706730. Accessed 14 Oct 2016
82. Werro, F.: The right to inform v the right to be forgotten: a transatlantic clash. In: Ciacchi, A. C., et al. (eds.) Liability in the Third Millennium. FRG (2009)

A Refinement Approach for the Reuse of Privacy Risk Analysis Results

Sourya Joyee De[✉] and Daniel Le Métayer

Inria, Université de Lyon, Lyon, France
{sourya-joyee.de,daniel.le-metayer}@inria.fr

Abstract. The objective of this paper is to improve the cost effectiveness of privacy impact assessments through (1) a more systematic approach, (2) a better integration with privacy by design and (3) enhanced reusability. We present a three-tier process including a generic privacy risk analysis depending on the specifications of the system and two refinements based on the architecture and the deployment context respectively. We illustrate our approach with the design of a biometric access control system.

1 Introduction

With the adoption of the EU General Data Protection Regulation (GDPR) [18], conducting a data protection impact assessment will become mandatory for certain categories of personal data processing. A large body of literature has been devoted to data protection impact assessment and privacy impact assessment (*PIA*) [8–10,19,22,31,32]. However, most of these papers focus on legal and organizational aspects and do not provide many details on the technical aspects of the impact assessment (*Privacy Risk Analysis or PRA*, here) [12,14], which may be challenging and time consuming in practice. The objective of this paper is to fill this gap and to propose a methodology which can be applied to conduct a PRA in a systematic way, to use its results in the architecture selection process (following the *privacy by design* approach [4]) and to re-use its generic part for different products or deployment contexts. The aim of this work is therefore to improve the cost effectiveness of PIA through (1) a more systematic (and therefore repeatable) approach; (2) a better integration with privacy by design; and (3) enhanced reusability. Considering that some data controllers or technology providers may have to conduct many PIAs for similar lines of products (or implementation variants), reusability can be a major factor in saving costs. Reflecting this need, Recital 92 of the GDPR [18] finds it *"reasonable and economic"* to carry out a single PIA for *"a common action or processing environment across an industry sector or segment or for a widely used horizontal activity"* and the recently published WP 29 guidelines [1] also encourage the development of sector-specific PIA frameworks.

The proposed analysis proceeds in three broad phases:

1. A generic privacy risk analysis phase which depends only on the specifications of the system and yields *generic harm trees*.

© Springer International Publishing AG 2017
E. Schweighofer et al. (Eds.): APF 2017, LNCS 10518, pp. 52–83, 2017.
DOI: 10.1007/978-3-319-67280-9_4

2. An architecture-based privacy risk analysis which takes into account the definitions of the possible architectures of the system and refines the generic harm trees into *architecture-specific harm trees*.
3. A context-based privacy risk analysis which takes into account the context of deployment of the system (e.g., a casino, an office cafeteria, a school) and further refines the architecture-specific harm trees into *context-specific harm trees*. Context-specific harm trees can be used to take decisions about the most suitable architectures.

To illustrate our approach, we consider the design of a biometric access control system. Such systems are now used commonly in many contexts such as border security controls, work premises, casinos, airports, chemical plants, hospitals, schools, etc. [5,6]. However, the collection, storage and processing of biometric data raise complex privacy issues [2,23,27,29,35,40,41]. To deal with them, a wide array of dedicated techniques (such as secure sketches or fuzzy vaults) as well as adaptations of general privacy preserving techniques (such as homomorphic encryption or secure multi-party computation) have been proposed [3]. However, each technique is a building block solving specific privacy problems and suitable in specific contexts. In addition, a range of architectural options are generally possible to integrate these building blocks into a system. Therefore it would be beneficial to use the results of a privacy risk analysis to provide guidance to system designers and help them select a solution and justify it with respect to privacy risks.

In this paper, we choose the deployment of biometric access control systems in casinos as an illustration of the deployment context. The verification of the identities of casino customers is required by certain laws (to prevent access by minors or individuals on blacklists), which can justify the implementation of a biometric access control system to speed up the verification process [6].

We start with the definition of the terminology and some notions that are central to the paper in Sect. 2. In Sect. 3, we provide an overview of our three-phase approach before presenting each phase in Sects. 4, 5 and 6 respectively. We illustrate each phase with the biometric access control system introduced in Sect. 4. We discuss related works in Sect. 7 and conclude with avenues for further research in Sect. 8.

2   Preliminaries

In order to avoid any ambiguity about the terminology, we first introduce the key concepts used in the paper. The three main inputs of our PRA process are the *specification of the system*, the *architectures* and the *context*, which can be chatacterized as follows.

Definition 1. *The **specification of the system** is a high-level view of its functionalities and its interactions with its users (irrespective of any implementation).*

For example, the specification of a biometric access control system expresses that its goal is to grant access to authorized persons to a particular zone (e.g., office, casino, airport) based on their biometric identifiers. Biometric identifiers are collected during enrolment and stored as reference templates. During the access control phase, fresh biometric data is collected from the user, converted into a fresh template and compared with the stored template(s) using a pre-defined threshold. If the templates match, access control rules are used to grant or deny access. The specification does not contain any detail about the decomposition of the system into specific components, where each type of data is stored, where and how computations take place or who has control over the storage and processing units.

Definition 2. *An* **architecture** *includes the technical description of the components of the system (server, terminal, etc.), with their roles (storage, computation, etc.), the entities (system owners, users, etc.) controlling them and the data flows among them.*

A specification can generally be implemented by more than one architectures involving different components, performing different sets of functions, interacting in different ways and controlled by different entities.

Definition 3. *The* **context** *is defined as the environment (social, legal, economic, etc.) in which the system is deployed.*

For example, a biometric access control system may be implemented in a casino, an office cafeteria, an airport, to control access by employees, customers, travellers, etc. The context provides useful information about the possible misuses of the personal data and their likelihood.

Definition 4. *A* **risk source** *is any entity (individual or organization) that may process (legally or illegally) data belonging to a data subject and whose actions may directly or indirectly, intentionally or unintentionally lead to privacy harms.*

Examples of potential risk sources include cybercriminals, rogue system administrators and data controllers.

Definition 5. *A* **feared event** *is an event of the system that may lead to privacy harms.*

Examples of feared events include unauthorized access to personal data, use of personal data for unauthorized purposes and disclosure of personal data to unauthorized actors.

Definition 6. *A* **privacy harm** *is a negative impact of the use of the system on a data subject, or a group of data subjects (or society as a whole) as a result of a privacy breach.*

A wide variety of privacy harms can result from a feared event, including physical, mental, financial or reputation harms.

Definition 7. *A **harm tree** is a node-labeled tree describing the relationship among a privacy harm (root), feared events, risk sources and exploitations of personal data (leaves).*

The root node of a harm tree denotes a privacy harm. Leaf nodes represent the exploitation of data by the most likely risk source (for the root harm). Intermediate nodes represent the feared events caused by the risk sources. They can be seen as intermediate steps of potential privacy attacks. Children nodes are connected by an AND node if all of them are necessary to cause the parent node and by an OR node if any of them is sufficient. A harm tree can be associated with either an individual risk source or a group of risk sources, colluding or not, depending on the interactions needed to exploit the data. For conciseness, we do not discuss collusions in this paper but they can be dealt by the methodology.

The first objective of a risk analysis is to identify the privacy harms for a system in a given context and to assess the associated risks, generally measured in terms of likelihood and severity. Several factors can influence privacy risks. The first one is the *exploitability* of personal data in the system, characterized by the set of resources (e.g., technical resources, access rights, background knowledge) needed by a risk source to exploit it. The dual notion is the *capacity* of a risk source, defined as the resources (e.g., technical resources, access rights, background knowledge) available to this risk source. Another main factor affecting the likelihood that a risk source may carry out an attack is its *motivation*, resulting from the balance between its incentives[1] and disincentives to cause a feared event or a harm. The exploitability of a data item depends only on the architecture, while the motivation of a risk source depends only on the context. The capacity of a risk source depends on both: access rights depend on the architecture, while background information and technical resources depend on the context.

We assume that the control over a component allows a risk source to get access to all its data (even though it is fully secure). Risk sources that do not have the control over a component can get access to its data only by attacking it, *persistently* or *transiently*. By transient exploitation of a component, we mean an exploitation for a short period of time or infrequent exploitations; by persistent exploitation we mean an exploitation of a component for a long period of time (e.g., for several days or months). Persistent exploitation is therefore more demanding than transient exploitation. To summarize, we consider four decreasing levels of power of a risk source over a component: (1) control over the component; (2) ability to perform persistent exploitation; (3) ability to perform transient exploitation and (4) inability to perform any exploitation.

---

[1] Incentives should be taken in a general sense here, including lack of awareness in the case of unintentional breach.

3   General Approach

In this section, we provide an overview of our three-phase approach, leaving the details of each phase to the next sections. Figure 1 summarizes the inputs and outputs of each phase. In the remainder of the paper, the term "generic" refers to the types of privacy harms, risk sources and harm trees which depend only on the system specification[2].

Our approach is inspired by previous works on PRA [12–14, 16, 17, 36] while introducing three analysis levels to enhance reusability:

Phase 1 (*Generic PRA*) takes as inputs the specification and the generic components of the system and yields generic privacy harm trees. This phase has to be carried out only once for a given category of products, regardless of their architectures or deployment context. Its main steps are [12]:

- Definition of personal data involved;
- Definition of generic risk sources;
- Definition of generic feared events;
- Definition of generic privacy harms;
- Construction of generic harm trees.

Phase 2 (*Architecture-specific PRA*) takes as inputs the architectures to be analyzed and yields *architecture specific harm trees*. The main steps of Phase 2 (for each architecture) are:

- Definition of the exploitability values of personal data;
- Definition of relevant risk sources and their access rights;
- Refinement of generic harm trees to obtain harm trees specific to each architecture; the two refinement operations are the instantiation of generic components and the pruning of irrelevant subtrees.

Phase 3 (*Context-specific PRA*) takes as input the results of Phase 2 and the context of the deployment and yields a *context specific harm tree* for each architecture. It consists of:

- Definition of the background information available to the risk sources in the considered context (e.g., does the casino owner have enough information to identify a customer from his biometric data?).
- Definition of the technical resources available to the risk sources in this context (e.g., does an internal risk source have enough technical resources to get access to the access logs?)
- Definition of the motivation of each risk source for each feared event and harm (e.g., what are the incentives and disincentives for the employer to use biometric and access control data of his employees in order to track them?).

---

[2] And are independent of the architecture and the context.

- Refinement of architecture-specific harm trees based on the results of the previous steps. The refinement operation in this phase is the pruning of irrelevant subtrees to remove unlikely or irrelevant scenarios (e.g., one may consider that, in a casino, the owner is unlikely to perform further surveillance of its customers).
- Computation of the likelihood of each relevant harm using context specific harm trees, the exploitability of personal data and the capacity and motivation of the risk sources.

We do not discuss the decision making step here, based on the result of the risk analysis, which typically involves opinions about acceptable risk levels and may take consider other factors such as costs and usability. The detailed description of the three phases and their illustration on a biometric access control system are presented in Sects. 4, 5 and 6 respectively.

The benefits of this incremental approach are two-fold:

1. **Reusability of intermediate results:** The results of Phase 1 (generic harm trees) can be reused for another implementation (or architecture) of the same type of system and the results of Phase 2 (architecture-specific harm trees) can be reused for the deployment of a product or system in a different context. This approach aligns with the WP 29 guidelines [1] which encourage the development of sector-specific PIAs and Recital 92 of the GDPR [18] that proposes the use of a single PIA to assess multiple operations that are similar in the risks they present.
2. **Selection of appropriate architecture in a privacy by design approach:** Because the results of Phase 1 do not depend on a specific architecture, they can be refined in different ways to consider different architectural options. Appropriate design decisions can be taken based on the results of the analysis of each option.

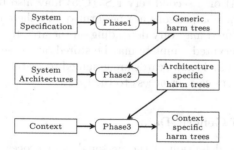

Fig. 1. Three phases of the selection process

4   Phase 1: Generic Privacy Risk Analysis

In this section, we present the first phase and illustrate it with our case study, the design of a biometric access control system. The following subsections describe successively the inputs of Phase 1 and the five steps introduced in Sect. 3.

4.1   Inputs: System Specification and System Components

The first step of a biometric access control system is the enrolment, involving the collection and storage of a biometric reference template br_i and identity ID_i for each user i of the system. As biometric data are sensitive, each reference template br_i is encrypted (into ebr_i) with a key (k_{br}) before being stored in a database ebr. Considering that some values are always stored with the identity of the user, we use the notation $\overline{x_i}$ (resp. $\overline{x}$) to denote the pair (x_i, ID_i) (resp. $\mathsf{list}(x_i, ID_i)$) for conciseness. The main authentication and access control steps are:

1. the input of fresh biometric raw data rd_i from the user i;
2. the conversion of rd_i into a fresh biometric template bs_i;
3. the comparison of bs_i with the enrolled template[3] br_i using a threshold thr;
4. if the templates match, the access control rules ac, are used to compute the decision dec_i (access grant or denial).

The system also manages an access trace (or access log) $\overline{at}$ consisting of the results of access control check dec_i and the associated time stamp ts_i along with the user's identity ID_i. Since access traces reveal information about users, they are usually stored as $\overline{eat}$, i.e., encrypted with a key k_{at}.

The components of a biometric access control system usually include a terminal T (C.1) to collect raw biometric data and a server S (C.2) to store information about users. In some cases, specific components such as a secure module M (C.3), a smart card C (C.4) or a second server S' (C.5) may also be used. The components on which the comparisons are performed and the encrypted biometric templates ebr_i are stored may vary depending on the architecture of the system. For example, the encrypted template may be stored on the server or on a smart card. Secure modules and smart cards are assumed to be tamper proof: only the actors controlling them can get access to their data.

4.2   Definition of Generic Data

The next step is the definition of the personal data processed by the system, which can be derived from its specification. Table 1 presents this list for the biometric access control system considered here. In a given architecture, each of these data is stored in one or more components, permanently or transiently. For example, the enrolled template ebr_i may be stored permanently in a database,

---

[3] The user's identity ID_i is used to fetch his enrolled template br_i.

and also transiently on the component performing the comparison with a fresh template. We assume that some data such as br_i and ebr_i are always associated with ID_i during enrolment (hence the use of $\overline{br}_i$ and $\overline{ebr}_i$ following our notation convention). So when a risk source has access to $\overline{br}_i$, it has also access to ID_i. For other data such as rd_i and bs_i, the identity ID_i may or may not be collected directly from the user during the access control phase. Therefore, we do not assume that they are always associated with ID_i. For example, in some scenarios, the user may be required to present a smart card containing his identity ID_i which is never transmitted to any of the components controlled by the owner (so that there is no trace of ID_i in these components although they may host rd_i and bs_i).

Table 1. Generic data

Code	Data
ID_i	Identity of user i
br_i	Biometric reference template of user i
ebr_i	Encrypted biometric reference template of user i
ebr	Encrypted database of biometric templates for all users
rd_i	Raw biometric data for user i
bs_i	Fresh biometric template derived from rd_i
dec_i	Decision (result of an access control check for user i)
ts_i	Time stamp associated with an access control of user i
$\overline{at}$	Access log of all users containing dec_i, ID_i and ts_i for all i
ac	Access control rules
k_{br}	Key used to encrypt and decrypt $\overline{ebr}$
k_{at}	Key used to encrypt and decrypt $\overline{at}$
$\overline{eat}$	Encrypted $\overline{at}$
thr	Threshold for comparing bs_i and $\overline{br}_i$

4.3 Definition of Generic Risk Sources

We assume that each component may be controlled either by the system owner (data controller in the GDPR) or by a security operator acting as a sub-contractor of the owner. The precise set of components controlled by each actor depends on the architecture. For example, in some architectures, the security operator may control only the component performing the comparison. In other architectures, it may also control the component storing the reference templates. In addition to the system owner (A.1) and the security operator (A.2) who are internal risk sources, cybercriminals (A.3) and states (A.4) may act as external risk sources. In some cases, the system owner or the security operator may have business links with third parties (A.5) such as insurance providers or marketing companies, which may also become risk sources. In a real PRA, other risk sources such as employees of the owner and the operator should also be considered, but we do not discuss them here for space considerations.

4.4 Definition of Generic Feared Events

Privacy harms result from the combination of one or more feared events. Generally speaking, we distinguish three types of feared events: the access to personal data, the use of personal data, and the disclosure of personal data. We consider two main types of personal data here, biometric data and access control results, which leads to the six generic feared events described in Table 2.

Table 2. Generic feared events for biometric access control systems

Code	Feared events
FE.1	Use of biometric data or data inferred from them for unauthorized purposes
FE.2	Use of result of biometric access control results and data inferred from them for unauthorized purposes
FE.3	Disclosure of biometric data to unauthorized actors
FE.4	Disclosure of results of biometric access controls to unauthorized actors
FE.5	Unauthorized access to biometric data
FE.6	Unauthorized access to results of biometric access controls

4.5 Definition of Generic Privacy Harms

The possibility for a risk source to get access to access control results dec_i and access logs $\overline{at}$ makes the users of the system vulnerable to surveillance (H.1). Surveillance may also result from the misuse of biometric templates. It may be carried out by the system owner itself or the state (with different motivations). For example, an employer may try to find out how frequently a particular employee takes breaks based on the number of times he visits the cafeteria. Harms occur when surveillance takes place beyond the intended purpose of the access control system. Identity theft (H.2) is another important concern for biometric access control systems. It can be caused by wrongful access to biometric reference templates br_i, fresh biometric templates bs_i or even raw biometric data rd_i along with the user identity ID_i. Other harms are also possible (e.g., inference of sensitive attributes such as health data or genetic information, weight or body mass index [11,35,41]), but we do not discuss them here because of space limitations.

4.6 Construction of Generic Harm Trees

Generic harm trees can be constructed for each of the harms discussed in Sect. 4.5 using the system components, risk sources and feared events identified in the previous subsections. In this section, we discuss only the generic harm tree for identity theft (H.2) (Fig. 2). The interested reader can find the generic harm tree for surveillance (H.1) in [15]. Generic harm trees can be refined to specific components and risk sources when the details of the architectures and the context are available (Sects. 5 and 6). We use the notation $C.i$, $C.k$, etc. to denote generic components (which will be instantiated in the next phases) in the harm trees.

Figure 2 shows that the harm identity theft (H.2) can result from the use of biometric data for unauthorized purposes (FE.1). FE.1 itself can be caused by a cybercriminal (A.3) via unauthorized access to biometric data (FE.5) or by third parties (A.5) receiving biometric data (FE.3) from either the security operator (A.2) or the owner (A.1). FE.3 and FE.5 may be caused by the exploitation of different types of data in different components of the system. These exploitations of personal data are pictured by the leaves in the harm trees. Commas in the leaves are used as concise notations for disjunctions (e.g., rd_i, bs_i means rd_i OR bs_i).

Although theoretically possible, some combinations of risk sources and harms do not make sense in practice, irrespective of the details of the architecture or the context. For example, the system owner, the operator and the state are unlikely to perform identity theft. These combinations are left out of the generic harm trees. Therefore, Fig. 2 does not have a branch where FE.1 is carried out by A.1 or A.2 or A.4.

ID_i may be obtained by a risk source either from a system component or as background information. These possibilities are differentiated by an OR subtree with two children in the harm trees. The abbreviation 'Bck' denotes background information. We assume that all other data can be obtained only from a system component (they are unlikely to be known as a background information by a risk source).

The generic harm tree only considers the most likely risk sources (with or without collusion) that may lead to a harm. When a harm is possible both via a single risk source or a collusion of risk sources, only the single risk source is represented (since it is less demanding and therefore more likely).

5   Phase 2: Architecture-Specific Privacy Risk Analysis

Phase 2 takes as input the architecture(s) under consideration and specific system components (if any). Its goal is to refine the generic harm trees resulting from Phase 1 to obtain harm trees specific to each architecture. In this paper, we illustrate our approach with three architectures:

1. Arch.1, a simple architecture with an encrypted database,
2. Arch.2, an architecture with an encrypted database and a hardware security module and
3. Arch.3, an architecture relying on the match-on-card technology.

Due to space considerations, we describe only the treatment of Arch.2 in the main body of the paper. Phase 2 for Arch.1 and Arch.3 is described in Appendix A.

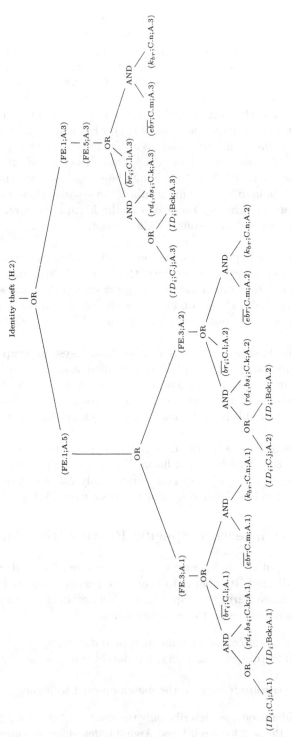

Fig. 2. Generic harm tree for identity theft (H.2) (Phase 1)

Figure 7 (Appendix A) shows the graphical representations of the biometric access control components used here. In the following subsections, the user and the enrolment site are not considered within the scope of the system. The issuer I is only involved in the enrolment phase. It is in charge of collecting and encrypting the enrolled biometric reference templates br_i along with user identities ID_i into $\overline{ebr_i}$ and storing them in the form of the database $\overline{ebr}$ in the server S. It has no role during the access control process and is included here for clarity only.

5.1 Description of Arch.2

In this architecture (Fig. 3), a hardware security module M is used to compare the fresh template with the enrolled template, so that the clear template is never used in the terminal T. The module M is assumed to be managed by a security operator (A.2). The server S stores the database of encrypted reference templates $\overline{ebr}$ and the access control rules ac. A second server S' stores $\overline{ebr}$ (updated periodically from S to take new enrolments into account), ac (updated periodically from S) and $\overline{eat}$ (updated periodically by T).

When a user presents his identity ID_i and a fresh biometric rd_i to the terminal T, T computes bs_i, fetches ebr_i from S' and sends them to the module M. M decrypts $\overline{ebr_i}$ using the key k_{br}, compares br_i with bs_i (taking into account the threshold thr) and uses ac to compute dec_i which is returned to T and used to grant or deny access. The access log $\overline{at}$ is encrypted into $\overline{eat}$ by M and sent to T which stores it into S'.

The separate server S' controlled by the security operator (A.2) prevents the owner (A.1) from knowing the identity ID_i of a user requesting access. Moreover, the owner does not have access to clear biometric templates or results of access control checks. Therefore, the owner cannot carry out any surveillance or disclose biometric data to other risk sources. The owner's role is to devise access control rules, enroll users and inform the security operator A.2 about ac and $\overline{ebr}$ updates from time to time. The owner maintains a copy of $\overline{eat}$ for future reference (e.g., in case of a dispute with the user).

The keys k_{at} and k_{br}, the threshold thr and access control rules ac are stored in M. The decision dec_i is erased just after its use. Similarly, rd_i, bs_i, $\overline{ebr_i}$, $\overline{br_i}$, $\overline{eat}$, ts_i, $\overline{at}$, ID_i, and ts_i are deleted from the components (i.e., T and M) which use or generate them as soon as their use is over.

The system components in this architecture are the terminal T (C.1), the servers S (C.2) and S' (C.5) and the hardware security module M (C.3).

5.2 Risk Sources for Arch.2

All risk sources have to be considered for Arch.2: the owner (A.1), the security operator (A.2), cybercriminals (A.3), the state (A.4) and third parties (A.5). We assume that the owner (A.1) controls only the server S while the security operator (A.2) controls the hardware security module M, the terminal T and the server S'. M is assumed to be secure and therefore cannot be (or is very unlikely to be) attacked.

5.3   Personal Data and Their Exploitability Values for Arch.2

Table 3 presents the personal data stored in each component with their exploitability values. Persistent exploitation is required to exploit the data stored on T because T stores these data only on a temporary basis. In contrast, transient exploitation is sufficient to exploit the data stored on S and S' which are used for long term storage. Since M is a secure component, the only possibility for a risk source to be able to exploit its data is to have control on it. Therefore, considering that the keys k_{br} and k_{at} are stored only on M, A.1, A.3 and A.4 cannot get access to them.

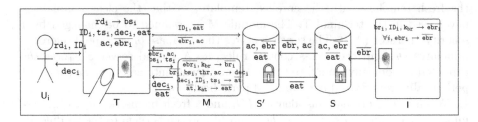

Fig. 3. Architecture Arch.2: hardware security module (HSM) (Color figure online)

In Fig. 3 (also in Figs. 8 and 10 in Appendix A), all data elements in red colour inside a certain component (for example, ac in the server S) are stored

Table 3. Personal data in Arch.2 and their exploitability values

System component	Data	Exploitability
T	dec_i	Persistent exploit of T
T	ID_i	Persistent exploit of T
M	$\overline{at}$	Control of M
M	dec_i	Control of M
M	ID_i	Control of M
M	k_{br}	Control of M
M	$\overline{ebr_i}$	Control of M
M	$\overline{br_i}$	Control of M
S'	$\overline{ebr}$	Transient exploit of S'
S	$\overline{ebr}$	Transient exploit of S
T	rd_i, bs_i	Persistent exploit of T
M	rd_i, bs_i	Control of M
S'	$\overline{eat}$	Transient exploit of S'
M	k_{at}	Control of M

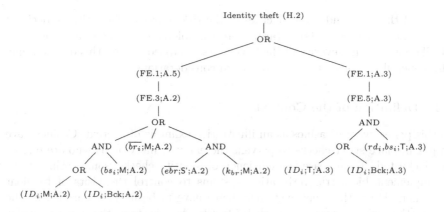

Fig. 4. Identity theft (H.2) harm tree for architecture Arch.2

persistently in the corresponding component whereas those in blue colour inside a component (for example, rd_i in the terminal T) are stored transiently in that component. We note that a data element that is stored persistently in one component can be stored transiently in another.

5.4 Refinement of Generic Harm Trees for Arch.2

Figure 14 in Appendix B shows how the generic harm tree for identity theft (H.2) (presented in Fig. 2) can be pruned to derive the corresponding harm tree for Arch.2 (presented in Fig. 4). In Arch.2, the owner of the system (A.1) has access only to S. Moreover, M is assumed to be a secure component. Therefore, no data element on any component other than S is accessible to A.1. So, A.1 can only access $\overline{ebr}$ (assuming that A.1 is unlikely to attack T for disclosing data to third parties (A.5)). However, to be able to exploit $\overline{ebr}$, the owner A.1 also needs to have access to k_{br} which is out of his reach since it is stored only in M. So, the branches in Fig. 14 where A.1 needs access to $\overline{br}_i$ and k_{br} are pruned (marked with red cross). Similarly, a cybercriminal (A.3) cannot access the secure component M containing $\overline{br}_i$ and k_{br}. So the corresponding branches are pruned. Both rd_i and bs_i are accessible to the security operator A.2 as it controls both M and T. In the harm trees, for simplicity, we only show A.2's access to bs_i in M. The definition of the architecture helps to instantiate the generic components C_i, C_j, C_k, C_l, C_m and C_n (as shown in Fig. 4).

6 Phase 3: Context-Specific Privacy Risk Analysis

As described in Sect. 3, the objective of Phase 3 is to take into account all context specific factors. The harm trees specific to each architecture produced in Phase 2 (Sect. 5) are further pruned based on the deployment context. The likelihoods of the harms can then be computed based on these pruned trees, the exploitability values of the data and the capacities of the risk sources. The ultimate decision as to which architecture(s) is (are) more suitable can be taken based on these likelihoods and the severity of the harms. As discussed before, this decision may also generally involve other non-technical considerations.

6.1 Definition of the Context

In this paper, we use casinos as an illustrative example of context. Casinos have to put in place strict checks to prevent the entry of individuals who are minors or blacklisted. To increase the efficiency of identity checks, some casinos want to implement biometric verification systems to control the visits of frequent customers. Users (frequent customers here) have to be initially enrolled by the owner (the casino here) to verify their identity. At this stage, the owner may also provide other relevant information (such as the location of the casino[4]) that may later be useful to determine the capabilities and motivations of the risk sources. In the following subsections, we discuss the main contextual factors for our case study.

6.2 Definition of the Background Information Available to Risk Sources

We assume that in this context, none of the risk sources is likely to possess the identity of the users as background information[5]. By availability of ID_i, we mean the availability of any information that can reveal ID_i.

6.3 Definition of the Technical Resources Available to the Risk Sources

The system owner (A.1) and the security operator (A.2) are assumed to have technical resources for the transient exploitation of all components over which they do not have control. Third parties (A.5) also have technical resources for this transient exploitation. The state (A.4) and cybercriminals (A.3) are assumed to have the technical resources required for the persistent exploitation of any component.

---

[4] For example, different locations correspond to different applicable laws (the motivation of a risk source may vary depending on the existence of data protection regulations and how strongly they are enforced), the strength (e.g., technical resources) or motivation of the local state to interfere [33], etc.

[5] This assumption should be valid at least for large scale attacks. However, one could argue that casinos may possess background information about certain frequent customers. Similarly, the state would be considered as having potentially a lot of background information but it is a more relevant risk source for surveillance than for identity theft. In any case, the assumptions made in this paper are for illustrative purposes only: different assumptions about background information could be made within the same framework.

The access rights of each risk source have already been specified in Phase 2. For a given architecture, the capabilities of each risk source can be derived by comparing the exploitability of the data and their technical resources and access rights. A risk source having control over a component has the highest capability (with respect to the data stored on this component) because it can exploit it irrespective of exploitability values. A risk source having technical resources for persistent exploitation also has high capability for data for which the exploitability value is persistent or transient and low otherwise. A risk source having technical resources for transient exploitation only has high capability for data with exploitability value equal to transient and low otherwise.

6.4   Definition of the Motivation of the Risk Sources

The motivations of the risk sources for the casino context are presented in Table 4. They depend on the feared events and sometimes also on specific harms. For example, the motivation of cybercriminals (A.3) to exploit biometric data for unauthorized purpose (FE.1) is high when the objective is identity theft (H.2) and medium for surveillance (H.1), since identity theft is a more lucrative scenario for cybercriminals, compared to surveillance. In contrast, the motivation of states (A.4) is high for surveillance to keep an eye on the citizens. The motivation for the casino owner to disclose data (FE.3, FE.4) or for unauthorized access to data (FE.5, FE.6) is only medium as such actions may have several incentives (such as monetary benefits from selling data) and many disincentives (such as bad reputation). Similarly, third parties (A.5) and security operators (A.2) may have several incentives and disincentives influencing their motivations.

Not all combinations of harms, feared events and risk sources are meaningful. For example, states are very unlikely to carry out identity theft against its own

Table 4. Relevant risk sources and their motivations in the casino context

Risk Sources	Harms	Feared events	Motivation
Owner (A.1)	H.1	FE.3, FE.4, FE.5, FE.6	Medium
	H.2	FE.3, FE.5	Medium
	H.1	FE.1, FE.2	×
	H.2	FE.1	×
Security operator (A.2)	H.1	FE.1, FE.2	×
	H.2	FE.1	Low
	H.1	FE.3, FE.4, FE.5, FE.6	Medium
	H.2	FE.3, FE.5	Medium
Cybercriminal (A.3)	H.1	FE.1, FE.2, FE.3, FE.4, FE.5, FE.6	Medium
	H.2	FE.1, FE.3, FE.5	High
State (A.4)	H.1	FE.1, FE.2, FE.3, FE.4, FE.5, FE.6	High
	H.2	FE.1, FE.3, FE.5	×
Third party (A.5)	H.1	FE.1, FE.2, FE.3, FE.4, FE.5, FE.6	Medium
	H.2	FE.1, FE.3, FE.5	Medium

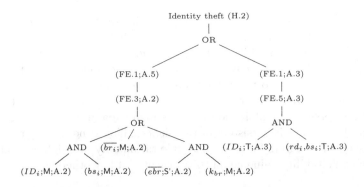

Fig. 5. Identity theft (H.2) final harm tree for architecture Arch.2

citizens. All unlikely combinations are marked with "×" under motivation in Table 4.

6.5 Final Pruning of Harm Trees

The specific harm trees produced in Phase 2 can be further pruned depending on the contextual information (as described in Sects. 6.2, 6.3 and 6.4). For example, for the harm tree for Arch.2 in Fig. 4, we observe that ID_i appears as background information in some of the branches. As discussed in Sect. 6.2, it is unlikely that any of the risk sources will possess ID_i as background information. Hence, the corresponding branches can be pruned. The pruned tree is shown Fig. 5. Similarly, the harm trees for Arch.1 and Arch.3 can be pruned. For Arch.1, the pruned harm tree is shown in Fig. 13 (Appendix B). For Arch.3, the pruning leads to an empty tree. The pruning is shown in Fig. 16 in Appendix B.

Generally speaking, the context is of prime importance to distinguish relevant and irrelevant combinations of harms and risk sources. For example, casino owners are unlikely to track their customers beyond the purpose of the access control system. In contrast, an employer may be tempted to track his employees (e.g., to know how many breaks they take) beyond the purpose of the biometric access control system (e.g., to restrict the access of a cafeteria only to employees).

6.6 Computation of Likelihoods Based on Harm Trees

The computation of the likelihood of the harms based on the final harm trees can be carried out in two steps:

1. The first step is the assessment of the likelihood of the leaves of the harm trees (likelihood of exploitation of personal data) from the *motivation* and the *capability* of the relevant *risk sources*. This assessment is based on the motivations of the risk sources listed in Table 4 and the combination rules presented in Table 5.

2. The second step is the computation of the likelihood of each feared event and harm according to the following rules (applied bottom-up), where P_i is the likelihood of the ith child node:

R1. AND node with independent child nodes: $\prod_i P_i$.

R2. AND node with dependent child nodes[6]: $Min(P_i)$, i.e., minimum of the likelihoods of the child nodes.

R3. OR node with independent child nodes: $1 - \prod_i (1 - P_i)$.

R4. OR node with dependent child nodes[7]: $Min(1, \sum_i P_i)$.

For the computations of the second step, the symbolic likelihood values of Table 5 must be translated into numerical values. This transformation must be done by the privacy expert in collaboration with the owner and should be documented. In this paper, we use as an illustration the following correspondance for the likelihood values (p):

1. *Negligible (N)*: $p < 0.01\%$;
2. *Limited (L)*: $0.01\% \le p < 0.1\%$;
3. *Intermediate (I)*: $0.1\% \le p < 1\%$;
4. *Significant (S)*: $1\% \le p < 10\%$;
5. *Maximum (M)*: $p \ge 10\%$.

Figure 6 depicts the computation of the likelihood for H.2 for Arch.2.

The likelihoods of the harms for the three architectures can be computed similarly (see Table 6). Needless to say, the analysis could lead to different results for different scenarios or different assumptions.

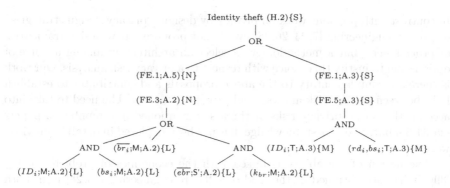

Fig. 6. Likelihood computation using the final pruned harm tree for identity theft (H.2) for Arch.2 (after Phase 3)

---

[6] In order to err on the safe side in terms of privacy protection, we consider dependent nodes such that one node may imply the other nodes.

[7] In order to err on the safe side in terms of privacy protection, we consider dependent nodes such that each node may exclude the other nodes.

6.7   Choice of Architecture

The results of the previous sections can be used by the owner (with the help of the privacy expert and, ideally, after consultation of the stakeholders in the context of a PIA) to decide upon an acceptability threshold for each harm. Based on Table 6, and this threshold, he can select one or more acceptable architectures or decide to enhance them with further privacy protection measures. Let us assume that the system designer decides that the acceptability threshold for each of harm is "Limited". Then, none of the architectures considered here is acceptable. If the owner accepts "Significant" risks of state surveillance, then Arch.3 is the only acceptable architecture. The owner may be ready to accept a higher level of risk (for his customers) related to surveillance by the state and want to use Arch.2, as he does not want to manage the process related to the distribution and management of smart cards. Then, he has to decide (in collaboration with a privacy expert) upon additional counter-measures to reduce the risks. The harm tree in Fig. 6 is a key source of information to make this decision. It shows that the target should be to better protect the terminal from cybercriminals.

If the storage of or an operation on a data element in a component seems to be a large contributor to the harm likelihood, one can think about replacing it by another component or reducing its role in the architecture. For example, the comparison between templates in the terminal (T) contributes more to the harm likelihood than doing it in the security module (M). So the harm tree helps to justify the roles of different components.

7   Related Works

In contrast with previous work on privacy by design, "privacy design strategies" or privacy engineering [7,24–26,38], we do not propose a new design framework or process here, but a methodology to select an architecture among a range of options and to justify this choice with respect to a privacy risk analysis. Our work is therefore complementary to the above proposals and contributes to establish links between privacy risk analysis and privacy by design. The need to take into account the actual privacy risks or threats is mentioned in a number of papers [25,34,38] but, to our best knowledge, has not been explored in detail in previous works.

The notion of reusability is linked with the economics of problem solving [39]. It has been studied in the field of software engineering [20,28] from both the economic and the technical viewpoints [30]. In this paper, we show how reusability can also be applied to privacy risk analysis. The framework presented in this paper builds on previous work on privacy risk analysis [12,13] precisely to make reusability possible at several stages. Our methodology supports vertical reuse [37], i.e., the reuse of the generic harm trees resulting from Phase 1 for all architectures and the architecture-specific harm trees resulting from Phase 2 for all contexts. To our best knowledge, previous works on PRA or PIA [14,17,21, 31,42] do not consider reusability.

Table 5. Measurement rule for likelihood of exploitation

Likelihood of exploitation	Risk source capability	Motivation
Negligible	Low	Low
Limited	High	
Negligible	Low	Medium
Significant	High	
Limited	Low	High
Maximum	High	

Table 6. Comparison of the likelihoods of harms

	Surveillance by the state (H.1, A.4)	Identity theft (H.2)
Encrypted Database (Arch.1)	Maximum	Maximum
HSM (Arch.2)	Maximum	Significant
Match-on-Card (Arch.3)	Significant	Negligible

Similar types of trees (sometimes called "threat trees" or "attack trees") have been used for PRA [12,13,16,17,36]. However, the focus of the work described here is not the risk analysis itself, but its adaptation and application to the architecture selection process. To this aim, we introduce generic harm trees and show how they can be successively refined.

8   Conclusion and Future Work

In this paper, we have presented a novel, incremental, approach to privacy risk analysis. We have also shown how the results of the analysis can be used by system designers to compare the privacy risks of different architectures and to choose the best option or find appropriate countermeasures.

We believe that establishing better links between privacy risk analysis and privacy by design is of prime importance in practice, especially in the context of the GDPR, which promotes both approaches. It is also important to improve the cost effectiveness of privacy risk analysis through the reuse and capitalization of results: in our framework, only the third phase has to be reconsidered in case of a change in the context; only the second and third phases for changes in the architectures; Phase 1 needs to be updated only when new types of privacy harms, feared events or risk sources emerge for a given system. This phase can be seen as a preliminary risk analysis valid for a whole line of products.

Another benefit of the three-phase process described here is a better clarity of the PRA process through a better separation of concerns.

One of the advantages of the order chosen here (considering first the specification, then the architectures and finally the context) is that the provider of a given solution (relying on a specific architecture) can build on the results of the second step to derive refined trees for different contexts (e.g. for different customers). In some situations however, it might be more efficient to consider the context before the architectures (e.g. to discard irrelevant harms). Space considerations prevent us from describing this option here but it is essentially a variant of the methodology described in this paper.

We have also not discussed certain features of the harm trees that can turn out to be useful in other contexts or for other systems or architectures. For example, harm trees can include information about the possibility of collusion among risk sources. The motivations of the risk sources have to be properly defined when collusions are considered.

Last but not least, further types of risks (such as unavailability or loss of integrity) and considerations (such as usability and cost) have to be taken into account in practice. Any privacy risk that can be analyzed using harm trees can be dealt with by our methodology. As far as usability and costs are concerned, they have to be integrated in the decision process (which is not described in this paper as it can involve a variety of non-technical considerations).

Acknowledgments. This work has been partially funded by the French ANR-12-INSE-0013 project BIOPRIV and Inria Project Lab CAPPRIS.

A   Description of Phase 2 for Arch.1 and Arch.3

A.1   Arch.1: Use of an Encrypted Database

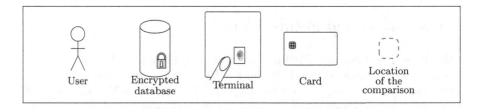

Fig. 7. Graphical representation of biometric access control systems

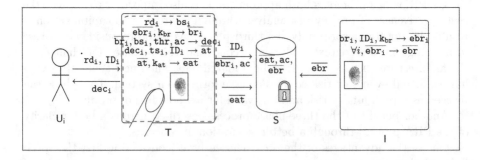

Fig. 8. Architecture Arch.1: Encrypted database (Color figure online)

Description of Arch.1. In the simple biometric access control architecture pictured in Fig. 8, the server S stores the database of encrypted reference templates $\overline{ebr}$ and the access control rules ac. When the user presents his identity ID_i and fresh biometric rd_i to the terminal T, T fetches the encrypted reference template $\overline{ebr_i}$ from S, decrypts it using the key k_{br} and compares br_i with bs_i produced from rd_i by T (taking into account thr). The access control decision dec_i is used to allow or deny access. The access logs $\overline{at}$ of different users are encrypted into $\overline{eat}$ and sent back by the terminal T at regular intervals to be stored in the server S. The access log $\overline{at}$ is updated after each access control.

The keys[8] k_{at} and k_{br}, the threshold thr and access control rules ac are persistently stored in the terminal T[9]. In contrast, $\overline{at}$ is stored in T only for short time intervals. dec_i, rd_i, bs_i, $\overline{br_i}$, ts_i, $\overline{at}$, $\overline{eat}$, $\overline{ebr_i}$, ID_i are deleted from the terminal T as soon as their use is over[10].

The components in this architecture are therefore: the terminal T (C.1) and the server S (C.2).

Risk Sources for Arch.1. Since the architecture does not include any security components, we assume that no security operator is involved. The risk sources are therefore: the owner (A.1), cybercriminals (A.3), the state (A.4) and third parties (A.5). The owner (A.1) controls both the server S and the terminal T.

Personal Data for Arch.1 and Their Exploitability. At this stage, the privacy analyst presents each data element stored in each system component and its exploitability (see Table 7). As explained in Sect. 2, by "transient exploitation" of a component we mean exploitation for a short period of time or infrequent exploitation, (e.g., once in several months), whereas "persistent exploitation" means the exploitation of a component for a long period of time (e.g., for several days or months). For example, dec_i provides the result of one access control for user i, whereas $\overline{at}$ provides the access log of all users for all previous days. So to know the access log of all users over t days, the risk source must either access all dec_i for all users for each of the t days (persistent exploitation) or access $\overline{at}$ at the end of the t days (transient exploitation).

Refinement of Generic Harm Trees for Arch.1. In this phase, we consider the harm identity theft (H.2). Figure 9 shows the harm tree corresponding to this harm. Figure 12 in Appendix B shows how the generic harm tree (Fig. 2) for identity theft is pruned to obtain the architecture specific harm tree in Fig. 9. From Sect. A.1, we know that the risk sources for Arch.1 do not include A.2.

---

[8] Keys are assumed to be protected by techniques which are not discussed here (e.g. obfuscation).

[9] Data elements that are stored persistently in a component are marked in red in Figs. 3, 8 and 10.

[10] Data elements that are stored transiently in a component are marked in blue in Figs. 3, 8 and 10.

Table 7. Personal data in Arch.1 and their exploitability values

System component	Data	Exploitability
T	dec_i	Persistent exploit of T
T	ID_i	T
T	$\overline{at}$	Transient exploit of T
S	$\overline{eat}$	Transient exploit of S
T	k_{at}	Transient exploit of T
T	k_{br}	Transient exploit of T
T	$\overline{ebr_i}$	Persistent exploit of T
T	$\overline{br_i}$	Persistent exploit of T
S	$\overline{ebr}$	Transient exploit of S
T	rd_i, bs_i	Persistent exploit of T

Therefore, all branches of the generic harm tree for identity theft (H.2) that contain A.2 are pruned (pruned branches are marked by a red cross in Fig. 12). The definition of the architecture also makes it possible to instantiate the generic components C_i, C_j, C_k, C_l, C_m and C_n.

A.2   Arch.3: Match-on-Card Technology

Description of Arch.3. Arch.2 is more protective than Arch.1 as the former uses a secure component M to perform the comparison between the fresh template and the reference template. In addition, it involves a security operator (A.2) for a better separation of responsibilities. However, in Arch.2, the fresh reference template bs_i is still available in T along with ID_i. Moreover, the clear template $\overline{br_i}$ can still be accessed by the security operator (A.2) who controls M. In fact, A.2 has access to a lot of personal data. One way to overcome these

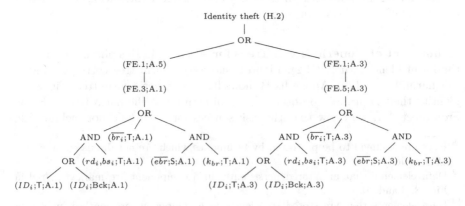

Fig. 9. Identity theft (H.2) harm tree for architecture Arch.1

difficulties is to use the match-on-card technology. In Arch.3, pictured in Fig. 10, each user possesses a smart card C that stores his identity ID_i along with his enrolled template br_i (i.e., it stores $\overline{br_i}$), the threshold thr and access control rules ac and performs the matching operation without disclosing ID_i or br_i to the terminal T. The owner does not store any database of reference templates.

The user inserts the card into the terminal T and submits the fresh biometric raw data rd_i. T derives a fresh template bs_i from rd_i and transfers it to C. C compares bs_i with br_i using the threshold thr and transfers the result of the access control dec_i to T. T informs the user about dec_i and sends it to the physical access control mechanism. The card C does not transfer any information apart from dec_i (not even the user identity ID_i) to T. C is assumed to be completely secure (e.g., it is tamper-resistant and personalized by a certified issuer during the enrolment phase). Both rd_i and bs_i as well as dec_i are deleted from T and C as soon as their uses are over. No access log $\overline{at}$ is recorded.

The system components in this architecture are: the terminal T (C.1) and the smart card C (C.4).

Risk Sources for Arch.3. We assume that there is no security operator (A.2) in this architecture, since the security relies only on the smart cards possessed by the users. Therefore, the risk sources to be considered include: the owner (A.1), cybercriminals (A.3), the state (A.4) and third parties (A.5). The owner (A.1) controls the terminal T.

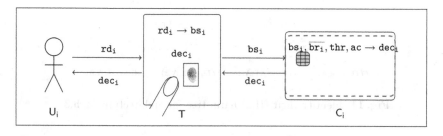

Fig. 10. Architecture Arch.3: Match-On-Card technology (Color figure online)

Table 8. Personal data in Arch.3 and their exploitability values

System component	Data	Exploitability
T	dec_i	Persistent exploit of T
T	rd_i, bs_i	Persistent exploit of T

Personal Data and Their Exploitability for Arch.3. Table 8 presents each data item stored in each system component and the corresponding exploitability values for Arch.3. A risk source must have enough technical resources to exploit T persistently to get access to dec_i, rd_i or bs_i. However, in contrast with Arch.1 and Arch.2, ID_i is not stored in any component in Arch.3. Thus, in order to exploit dec_i or rd_i, bs_i, risk sources must have ID_i as background information. Since C is considered to be secure and belongs to the user, it does not appear in Table 8.

Refinement of Generic Harm Trees for Arch.3. Figure 15 in Appendix B shows how the generic harm tree for identity theft (H.2) (presented in Fig. 2) can be pruned to derive the corresponding harm tree for Arch.3 (presented in Fig. 11). In Arch.3, ID_i, $\overline{br_i}$, $\overline{ebr_i}$ and k_{br} are not present at any moment in any of the components that the risk sources may access (i.e., terminal T). So all branches in the generic tree corresponding to these data elements are pruned. Also, the risk source A.2 is not a part of Arch.3. So all branches concerning A.2 are pruned too. The definition of the architecture also makes it possible to instantiate the generic components C_i, C_j, C_k, C_l, C_m and C_n.

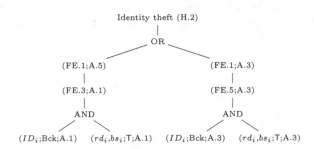

Fig. 11. Identity theft (H.2) harm tree for architecture Arch.3

B Pruning of Harm Trees and Likelihood Computation for Identity Theft (H.2)

In this appendix, we present the harm trees for identity theft, showing in detail how branches of the generic tree are pruned based on different conditions (related to the architecture and the context) discussed in the paper.

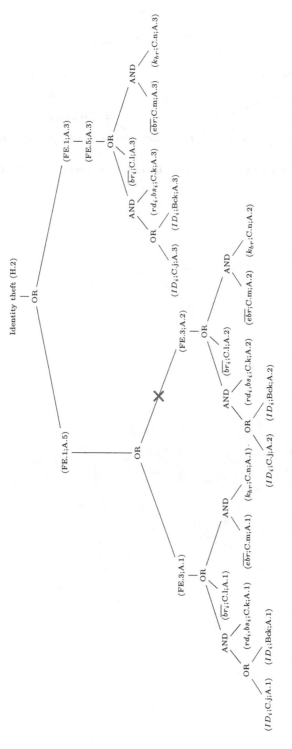

Fig. 12. Pruning of the generic harm tree for identity theft (H.2) to derive the harm tree for Arch.1 (Phase 2)

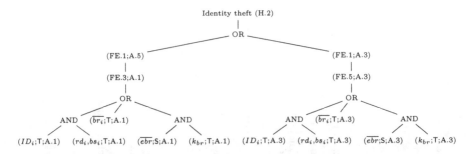

Fig. 13. Identity theft (H.2) final harm tree for architecture Arch.1

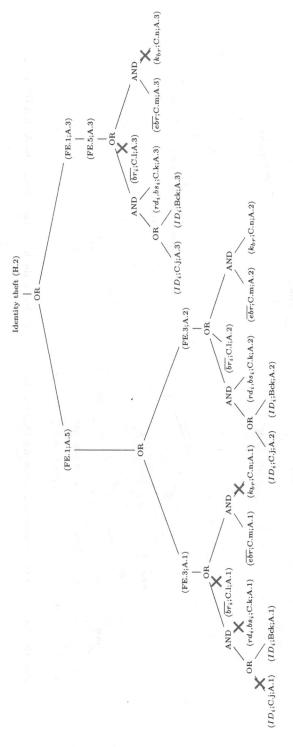

Fig. 14. Pruning of the generic harm tree for identity theft (H.2) to derive the harm tree for Arch.2 (Phase 2) (Color figure online)

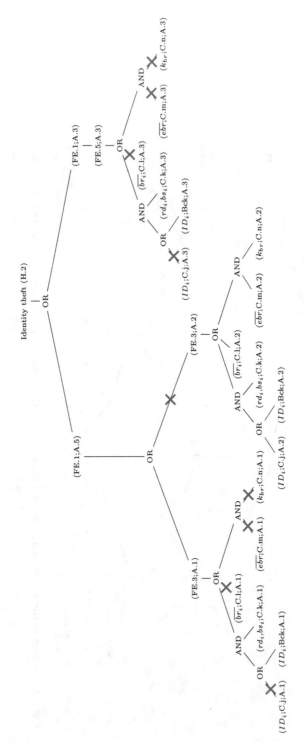

Fig. 15. Pruning of the generic harm tree for identity theft (H.2) to derive the harm tree specific to Arch.3 (Phase 2)

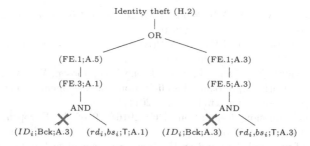

Fig. 16. Final pruning of the harm tree for identity theft (H.2) for architecture Arch.3 (Phase 3)

References

1. Article 29 Data Protection Working Party: Guidelines on Data Protection Impact Assessment (DPIA) and determining whether processing is "likely to result in a high risk" for the purposes of Regulation 2016/679 (2017)
2. BBC Technology: Millions of Fingerprints Stolen in US Government Hack (2015)
3. Bringer, J., Chabanne, H., Métayer, D., Lescuyer, R.: Privacy by design in practice: reasoning about privacy properties of biometric system architectures. In: Bjørner, N., de Boer, F. (eds.) FM 2015. LNCS, vol. 9109, pp. 90–107. Springer, Cham (2015). doi:10.1007/978-3-319-19249-9_7
4. Cavoukian, A.: Privacy by Design: The 7 Foundational Principles Implementation and Mapping of Fair Information Practices. Office of the Information and Privacy Commissioner, Ontario, Canada Standards (2010)
5. Cavoukian, A., Chibba, M., Stoianov, A.: Advances in biometric encryption: taking privacy by design from academic research to deployment. Rev. Policy Res. **29**(1), 37–61 (2012)
6. Cavoukian, A., Stoianov, A.: Privacy by Design Solutions for Biometric One-to-Many Identification Systems (2014)
7. Colesky, M., Hoepman, J., Hillen, C.: A critical analysis of privacy design strategies. In: 2016 IEEE Security and Privacy Workshops, SP Workshops 2016, San Jose, CA, USA, 22–26 May 2016, pp. 33–40 (2016)
8. Commission Nationale de l'Informatique et des Libertes (CNIL): Methodology for Privacy Risk Management - How to Implement the Data Protection Act (2012)
9. Commission Nationale de l'Informatique et des Libertes (CNIL): Privacy Impact Assessment (PIA) Methodology (How to Carry Out a PIA) (2015)
10. Commission Nationale de l'Informatique et des Libertes (CNIL): Privacy Impact Assessment (PIA) Tools (templates and knowledge bases) (2015)
11. Dantcheva, A., Elia, P., Ross, A.: What Else Does Your Biometric Data Reveal? A Survey on Soft Biometrics (2015)
12. De, S.J., Métayer, D.: PRIAM: a privacy risk analysis methodology. In: Livraga, G., Torra, V., Aldini, A., Martinelli, F., Suri, N. (eds.) DPM/QASA -2016. LNCS, vol. 9963, pp. 221–229. Springer, Cham (2016). doi:10.1007/978-3-319-47072-6_15
13. De, S.J., Le Métayer, D.: Privacy harm analysis: a case study on smart grids. In: International Workshop on Privacy Engineering (IWPE). IEEE (2016)
14. De, S.J., Le Métayer, D.: Privacy risk analysis. In: Synthesis Series. Morgan & Claypool Publishers (2016)

15. De, S.J., Le Métayer, D.: A Risk-based Approach to Privacy by Design (Extended Version). No. RR-9001, December 2016
16. De, S.J., Le Métayer, D.: PRIAM: A Privacy Risk Analysis Methodology. INRIA Research Report (RR-8876), July 2016
17. Deng, M., Wuyts, K., Scandariato, R., Preneel, B., Joosen, W.: A privacy threat analysis framework: supporting the elicitation and fulfilment of privacy requirements. Requirements Eng. **16**(1), 3–32 (2011)
18. European Commission: Regulation (EU) 2016/679 of the European Parliament and of the Council of 27 on the protection of natural persons with regard to the processing of personal data and on the free movement of such data, and repealing Directive 95/46/EC (General Data Protection Regulation), April 2016
19. Expert Group. 2 of Smart Grid Task Force: Data Protection Impact Assessment Template for Smart Grid and Smart Metering Systems (2014)
20. Frakes, W.B., Kang, K.: Software reuse research: status and future. IEEE Trans. Softw. Eng. **31**(7), 529–536 (2005)
21. Friginal, J., Guiochet, J., Killijian, M.O.: A privacy risk assessment methodology for location-based systems. http://homepages.laas.fr/guiochet/telecharge/MOBIQUITOUS2013.pdf. Accessed 13 July 2016
22. Garcia, M., Lefkovitz, N., Lightman, S.: Privacy Risk Management for Federal Information Systems (NISTIR 8062 (Draft)). National Institute of Standards and Technology (2015)
23. Gartland, C.: Biometrics Are a Grave Threat to Privacy (2016). The New York Times
24. Gürses, S., Troncoso, C., Diaz, C.: Engineering privacy by design. Comput. Priv. Data Prot. **14**(3) (2011)
25. Gürses, S., Troncoso, C., Diaz, C.: Engineering Privacy by Design Reloaded. Amsterdam Privacy Conference (2015)
26. Hoepman, J.-H.: Privacy design strategies. In: Cuppens-Boulahia, N., Cuppens, F., Jajodia, S., Abou El Kalam, A., Sans, T. (eds.) SEC 2014. IFIP AICT, vol. 428, pp. 446–459. Springer, Heidelberg (2014). doi:10.1007/978-3-642-55415-5_38
27. Kobie, N.: Surveillance State: Fingerprinting Pupils Raises Safety and Privacy Concerns (2016). The Guardian
28. Mcilroy, M.: Mass produced software components (1969)
29. Miglani, S., Kumar, M.: India's Billion-member Biometric Database Raises Privacy Fears (2016). Reuters
30. Mili, A., Chmiel, S.F., Gottumukkala, R., Zhang, L.: An integrated cost model for software reuse. In: Proceedings of the 2000 International Conference on Software Engineering, pp. 157–166. IEEE (2000)
31. Oetzel, M.C., Spiekermann, S.: A systematic methodology for privacy impact assessments: a design science approach. Eur. J. Inform. Syst. **23**(2), 126–150 (2014)
32. Oetzel, M.C., Spiekermann, S., Grüning, I., Kelter, H., Mull, S.: Privacy Impact Assessment Guideline for RFID Applications (2011)
33. Oppenheim, C.: Big Brother Spying is Reaching Scary Levels (2013). http://edition.cnn.com/2013/12/10/opinion/oppenheim-privacy-reform/
34. Pearson, S., Benameur, A.: A decision support system for design for privacy. In: Fischer-Hübner, S., Duquenoy, P., Hansen, M., Leenes, R., Zhang, G. (eds.) Privacy and Identity 2010. IFIP AICT, vol. 352, pp. 283–296. Springer, Heidelberg (2011). doi:10.1007/978-3-642-20769-3_23
35. Prabhakar, S., Pankanti, S., Jain, A.K.: Biometric recognition: security and privacy concerns. IEEE Secur. Priv. **1**(2), 33–42 (2003)

36. del Prado, N., Cortez, M., Friginal, J.: Geo-location inference attacks: from modelling to privacy risk assessment. In: Tenth European Dependable Computing Conference (EDCC), pp. 222–225. IEEE (2014)
37. Prieto-Díaz, R.: Status report: software reusability. IEEE Softw. **10**(3), 61–66 (1993)
38. Spiekermann, S., Cranor, L.F.: Engineering privacy. IEEE Trans. Softw. Eng. **35**(1), 67–82 (2009)
39. Standish, T.A.: An essay on software reuse. IEEE Trans. Softw. Eng. **10**(5), 494–497 (1984)
40. Tillman, G.: Opinion: Stolen Fingers: The Case Against Biometric Identity Theft Protection (2009). Computer World
41. Woodward, J.D.: Biometrics: privacy's foe or privacy's friend? Proc. IEEE **85**(9), 1480–1492 (1997)
42. Wright, D., De Hert, P.: Privacy Impact Assessment. Springer, Netherlands (2012)

Neutralisation and Anonymization

A Gamified Approach to Explore Techniques
of Neutralization of Threat Actors
in Cybercrime

Andreas Rieb[(✉)], Tamara Gurschler, and Ulrike Lechner

Universität der Bundeswehr München,
Werner-Heisenberg-Weg 39, 85577 Neubiberg, Germany
{Andreas.Rieb,Tamara.Gurschler,
Ulrike.Lechner}@unibw.de

Abstract. In the serious game "Operation Digital Chameleon" red and blue teams develop attack and defense strategies as part of an IT security Awareness training. This paper presents the game design and selected results from a structured evaluation of techniques of neutralization applied by cybercrime threat actors. Various motives and five neutralization techniques are identified in fifteen instances of "Operation Digital Chameleon". We argue that "Operation Digital Chameleon" is not only an instrument to raise IT security awareness but also a sensible method to explore techniques of neutralization in cybercrime.

Keywords: Theory of neutralization · Threat actors · Cybercrime

1 Introduction

Cybercrime is becoming more commonplace, more dangerous, and more sophisticated. Public as well as private sector and especially critical infrastructures face cyber intrusions from different kinds of threat actors. On the one hand, there are threat actors with a high level of skills as Nation States [1] or Hacktivists [2] and on the other hand, there are cyber criminals and script kiddies with more modest skills that rely on established tools and techniques. Researchers and public institutions alike argue that the sector undergoes professionalization with, e.g., underground forums, business models and well established organizational routines (see e.g. [3–5]). To develop adequate IT security measures, an understanding of threat actors and why they break into IT systems is useful. Current approaches in threat intelligence focus more on the "how" do threat actors attack systems and not on the "why". Neutralization captures herein the rationalization of deviant behavior that helps to overcome the barrier to engage in criminal behavior.

According to the German Bundeskriminalamt (BKA), cybercrime should be seen through the lens of socio-technical explanations. This perspective fosters the understanding of offenders regarding their motivation, their justification, their behavior and their environment. Moreover, the offender-oriented analysis of cybercrime can help to develop strategies for intervention and prevention as demonstrated e.g. in the seminal paper on why employees fail to comply with IT security policies [6].

© Springer International Publishing AG 2017
E. Schweighofer et al. (Eds.): APF 2017, LNCS 10518, pp. 87–103, 2017.
DOI: 10.1007/978-3-319-67280-9_5

We follow criminology in the socio-technical analysis and use neutralization theory as the theoretical underpinning of our analysis. We propose a gamification approach: "Operation Digital Chameleon". In the game, team red (the attacker team) takes a role, team blue (the defender team) knows the role of team red. Team red is expected to act in accordance to the characteristics of the role in terms of resources, technical skills and motives. We observed in the games that it is a lot of fun to adapt the attackers' position (team red) and to think of what eventually team blue will do. We observed also, how difficult it is to anticipate team red's possible courses of action and how difficult it is to develop adequate IT security measures to prepare for an upcoming threat when team blue cannot anticipate team red's motivation. These observations motivate the analysis of techniques of neutralization in the paper at hand.

We argue that "Operation Digital Chameleon" is not only a good IT security awareness training following previous analysis on reasonable complexity and realism of attack and defense and on innovativeness [7]. We argue that our game is a good way to explore criminal intentions in cyberspace - as an alternative to the typical methods of interviews, surveys or after action reviews. The paper presents the State of the Art, the method and design of the game "Operation Digital Chameleon", results of 15 games, 27 offenders, and an analysis of these games.

2   State of the Art

From a criminological point of view, cybercrime comprises all crimes against Internet, networks, IT systems, or data. To name just a few: data manipulation, computer sabotage, or cyber blackmail with ransomware. Furthermore, cybercrime covers all crimes that has been done employing information technology [8]. According to BKA, offender-oriented analysis of cybercrime can help to develop strategies for intervention and prevention [6].

2.1   Deterrence, Theory of Neutralization, and Techniques of Neutralization

In criminology and penology, deterrence is a theory about preventing or controlling actions or behavior through fear of punishment or retribution [9]. Deterrence is also studied in the domain of cybercrime. With respect to offenders' behavior, Young et al. interviewed hackers at the DefCon conference in Las Vegas: Hackers engage in a criminal behavior because they rate the risk of punishment very low [10]. Young et al. conclude that the severity of penalties does not have a significant effect of deterrence if the probability of getting punished is considered low. Siponen and Vance provide an overview of deterrents in cybersecurity and the effectiveness of deterrents [11].

Deterrence Theory assumes rationality and this assumption of rationality draws criticism. The theory of neutralization as proposed by Sykes and Matza suggests that people psychologically enable themselves to commit crimes or rule-breaking or any other anti-social behavior by techniques of neutralization [12]. These techniques provide the (potential) criminal a temporary release from conventional restraints. Techniques of neutralization rationalize deviant behavior. Neutralization theory claims that both law-abiding citizens and those who commit crimes or rule-breaking actions believe in the norms and values of the community in general (Siponen and Vance [11] following Sykes and Matza 1957 [12]). Techniques of neutralization offer a way for persons to render existing norms inoperative by justifying behavior that violates those norms. Sykes and Matza identify five techniques of neutralization in their seminal work [12]:

- **Denial of responsibility.** The offender will propose that he/she was victim of circumstance or was forced into the action in question which was beyond his/her control.
- **Denial of injury.** The offender justifies the action by minimizing harm/damage.
- **Denial of the victim.** The offender believes that the victim deserves whatever action the offender committed.
- **Condemnation of the condemners.** The offenders maintain that those who condemn his/her offense are doing so purely out of spite, or are shifting the blame off of themselves unfairly.
- **Appeal to higher loyalties.** The offender suggests that the offense was for the greater good, and justifies the aberrant behavior as being part of a higher order ideal or value equal to or greater than his/her own self-interest.

2.2 Techniques of Neutralization in Cybercrime

The five techniques of neutralization have many applications in cybercrime. To give a few examples: An example for *denial of responsibility* in cybercrime is "a lack of transparency of a policy" was used by employees to neutralize a failure to comply with a policy to encrypt confidential emails in an analysis by Puhakainen [13]. Parker cites the neutralization of cybercriminals, that their action did not cause any harm to humans as an example for the technique of neutralization *denial of injury* [14]. In cybercrime, a popular *Denial of the Victim* is "if people do not want me to get access to their computer or computer systems, they should have better computer security" [15]. Offenders engaged in cybercrime claim that the law was unjust – an example for *Condemn the Condemners* [14]. In digital piracy the statement "I see nothing wrong in giving people copies of pirated media to foster friendships." is a typical neutralization in category *appeal to higher loyalties* [15].

In scholarly discussion of cybercrime more techniques of neutralization were identified. Exemplarily the *Defense of Necessity* was developed by Minor [16], and *the Metaphor of Ledgers* by Klockars [17]. Coleman proposed three further techniques of neutralization: *the denial of the necessity of the law, the claim of entitlement* and *the claim that everybody else is doing it* [18]. Spafford published further techniques of neutralization when analyzing given reasons to justify computer intrusions [19]. Moore and McMullan [20] as well as Haupt [21, 22] put their focus on digital piracy and were able to identify further techniques of neutralization. According to Spafford, the so-called *security argument* is the most common technique of neutralization offered within the computer community.

- **Security argument.** The offender believes that breaking into systems is a service that exposes security flaws. After publication the public or the victim (e.g. the administrator of the hacked organization) is able to fix the vulnerability to raise the level of IT security [19].

This technique of neutralization is in accordance with the seminal work of Siponen and Vance [11] on employee's justifications for their failure to comply with information systems security policies. For this, they interviewed 395 employees by a questionnaire containing hypothetical scenarios. Their empirical results highlight neutralization as an important factor to take into account with regard to developing and implementing organizational security policies and practices. Research in the domain of cybercrime related to the theory of neutralization is presented in Tables 1 and 2.

2.3   Techniques of Neutralization in Cybersecurity and Cybercrime

Tables 1 and 2 present a non-exhaustive overview of scholarly literature on techniques of neutralization in cybercrime. In our search we used the search engines Google, Google Scholar and Mendeley Literature Search. Keywords were *techniques of neutralization, neutralization theory, justifications, cybercrime, hacking, Internet*. Note that we also used combinations and variations as well as German versions of the search terms. We used the method of snowballing to identify more related articles. From our analysis we excluded search results that are non-related to IT security for critical infrastructures as, e.g., Porn or Adult-Child sex websites (see e.g. [23]). We identified 12 relevant articles to be presented in the paper at hand.

Further studies in the topic cybercrime have been done by Spafford [19]. Higgings et al. [24] analyzed digital piracy and the research field of Hutchings [25] was online victimization.

Table 1. State of the Art: 9 neutralization techniques in digital piracy identified by Haupt [22]

Techniques of neutralization applied by Haupt [22]
Glossy naming
Dehumanization
Ascription of guilt
Downplay of the consequences
Condemnation of the condemners
Moral justification
Shift of responsibility
Minimized comparison
Diffusion of the responsibility

The tables illustrate that the techniques of neutralization studied in cybercrime are relatively stable with a few studies that develop individual sets of techniques of neutralization, e.g. for the threat actor group of employees by Siponen and Vance [11] or by Li and Cheng [26]. The studies on music or digital piracy came up with a different collection of techniques of neutralization (e.g. [27]).

Table 2. State of the art techniques of neutralization in cybercrime

#	Author(s)	Field of research	Method	Techniques of neutralization														
				Denial of responsibility	Denial of injury	Denial of the victim	Condemnation of the condemners	Appeal to higher loyalties	Claim of entitlement	Defense of necessity	Metaphor of the ledger	Denial of necessity of the law	Claim that everybody else is doing it	Claim of Normalcy	Digital rights management software defiance	Claim of the future patronage	Denial of negative Intent	Claim of relative acceptability
1	Morris [15]	Cybercrime	785 Students; Survey	X	X	X	X	X		X	X							
2	Walkley [28]	Cybercrime	No empirical testing	X	X	X	X	X										
3	Turgeman-Goldschmidt [29]	Cybercrime	54 Israeli hackers; Interviews	X	X	X	X	X										
4	Haupt [22]	Digital Piracy	15 Copyists of music; Interviews	to preserve the clarity, these techniques are presented in Table 1														
5	Holt/Copes [30]	Digital Piracy	Content analysis of message boards catering to digital piracy, Interviews with digital pirates	X	X	X	X	X										
6	Moore/McMullan [20]	Digital Piracy	Students; Qualitative interviews	X	X	X	X	X	X	X	X	X	X					
7	Smallridge/Roberts [27]	Digital Piracy	304 Students; Survey	X	X	X	X	X	X	X	X	X		X	X	X		
8	Li/Cheng [26]	Employees	428 Employees; Survey	X	X	X	X	X			X							X
9	Siponen/Vance [11]	Employees	395 Employees; Survey with hypothetical scenarios	X	X	X	X	X		X	X							
10	Nicho/Kamoun [31]	Malicious Insiders	3 Case studies	X	X	X	X	X		X	X							
11	Goode/Cruise [32]	Software Cracking	28 People; Survey	X	X	X	X	X										
12	Hinduja [33]	Software Piracy	507 Students; Survey	X	X	X	X	X			X			X			X	X

2.4   Motivation and Subculture

The theoretical concepts to capture deviant behavior are manifold. Several authors study motivations to engage in cybercrime: Money, power, self-expression, or curiosity are typical motives in cybercrime [34]. Hald and Pederson classify offenders regarding their motivations (revenge, money, curiosity, and notoriety), capabilities, triggers, methods, and trends to support defenders in doing their threat assessment [3]. Holt and Kilger [35] with reference to [36] identify entertainment, ego, status, entrance to a social group, money, and cause as typical motivations for cybercrime. For a more detailed list, see [25] or [37].

Bässmann [6] refers to Taylor [38] who points out that motivations in cybercrime have to be strictly differentiated between offenders' justification. This strict separation is in accordance to externalism, coined by Falk as an opposite to internalism, where motivation and justification are close together [39]. Motivation, justification as well as neutralizations are indeed close as an analysis of an cybersecurity incident in the Darknet [40] illustrates: An offender associated with Anonymous knocked down a fifth of the websites on the Darknet offline in protest against child pornography (justification). He motivated his attack: The victim hosted more than 50% child pornography despite his claim to have a zero tolerance policy to child pornography (motivation) [40]. Neutralization techniques as *denial of the victim* or *appeal to higher loyalties* can be applied to this case.

While neutralization refers to a temporary rendering of norms, subculture refers to a more persistent deviation of norms and rules: A subculture is an ethnic, regional, economic, or social group exhibiting characteristic patterns of behavior sufficient to distinguish it from others within an embracing culture or society a criminal subculture [6].

3   Method

The overall research follows a design oriented research approach as described by Hevner et al. [41]. We use an iterative approach in the design and evaluation of "Operation Digital Chameleon" and the paper at hand describes the state of the design after pretest and 15 games done in 2015 until 2017 (Table 3).

Table 3. Games of "Operation Digital Chameleon"

#	Date	Duration training	Duration game	Number of participants	Number of red teams	Threat actors (teams red)
1	10/2015	3d	6 h	11	1	Hacktivists
2	01/2016	5d	9 h	9	1	Hacktivists
3	03/2016	2d	6 h	10	1	Hacktivists
4	03/2016	2d	10.5 h	19	3	Cyber criminals, employees, nation states

(continued)

Table 3. (*continued*)

#	Date	Duration training	Duration game	Number of participants	Number of red teams	Threat actors (teams red)
5	05/2017	2d	10 h	18	2	Cyber criminals, hacktivists
6	05/2017	2d	10 h	20	3	Cyber criminals, employees, hacktivists
7	07/2016	2d	10.5 h	17	3	Cyber criminals, employees, hacktivists
8	09/2016	2d	11.7 h	21	2	Cyber criminals, employees
9	10/2016	2d	5.8 h	11	1	Hacktivists
10	11/2016	2d	11.8 h	14	2	Hacktivists, script kiddies
11	11/2016	2d	12.3 h	15	2	Employees, nation states
12	12/2016	2d	7.9 h	15	2	Cyber criminals, hacktivists
13	01/2017	1d	4 h	11	1	Nation states
14	02/2017	1d	3 h	9	1	Hacktivists
15	03/2017	3d	12.1 h	14	2	Cyber criminals, employees

For data generation and data collection, the first author who acted as game master on the basis of ten years + experience in IT security consulting and awareness training took notes during the game, collected the gaming material, and summarized observations in a structured way. The empirical basis of this analysis (done in February/March 2017) comprises 15 games with IT experts/IT security experts of critical infrastructures within Europe in two game variations: "Operation Digital Chameleon" and "Operation Digital Owl".

Regarding the target group, we assume that the experts of our 15 games are familiar with different threats and threat actors due to their daily work as a risk manager, member of a CERT, IT security administrator, chief information security officer, investigators in Cybercrime, and others.

4   The Game Design of "Operation Digital Chameleon"

"Operation Digital Chameleon" is designed as a table-top game and adopts the method of wargaming to the cyberdomain. The game is created for IT security professionals with experience and expertise on an operational, conceptual, or strategic level.

4.1   The Game Board and Game Activities

The game board (cf. Fig. 1) depicts a generic IT infrastructure of a critical infrastructure – without any IT security instruments.

Fig. 1. The board of "Operation Digital Chameleon"

This IT infrastructure comprises (mobile) clients, various servers, a database, and with reference to critical infrastructures an industrial network with a human machine interface, an industrial system with control systems, and an industrial Ethernet switch. Note that these elements are typical for production plants, harbors, energy systems, water power plants, and others [42].

Industrial systems and their subcomponents are designed for long lifetimes and there are many systems in operation that run Windows NT and Windows XP [43]. For this reason, the game board does also include older systems for which patches are no longer available.

"Operation Digital Chameleon" games are managed by a game master. The game master ensures that teams comply with the rules of the game, assesses the solutions, determines the winner and manages the reflection of the game. Additionally, the white team can include observers.

The red team's job is to develop an attack against the critical infrastructure protected by the blue team. Team red chooses one of five threat actors as a role. The roles are described in detail in Sect. 4.2. Red teams are instructed to declare a goal related to their role. In addition to that, they are instructed to justify their attack before designing their attack chain and before deciding on a goal. The justifications are part of the model of the attack chain. I.e. red teams have to think about motivation and technique of neutralization of the threat actor that they enact.

The development of attack chains and defense strategies is followed by a presentation and the decision about which team(s) win(s). Red teams present goal, technique of neutralization and attack chain. Results of teams red and blue are assessed in a group discussion led by the game master regarding plausibility of the concepts with the chosen threat actor and feasibility.

The gaming phase is followed by a debriefing. The debriefing aims to solicit emotions, proposals on improvements of the gaming experience, and a self-assessment of IT security awareness levels. A discussion of the threat actor including their attacks and Team Blue's defense strategies is part of the debriefing.

For more details regarding the model of the game, see [7].

4.2   Threat Actors

A red team's job is to develop an attack against the critical infrastructure protected by the blue team. Team red chooses one out of five threat actors as role. These threat actors are (in alphabetical order):

- **Cyber criminals.** Cyber criminals are primary driven by money. Within their well-organized team, they do have specialized skills and use a plethora of methods [3]. According to ENISA's Threat Landscape Report of 2016, cyber criminals use ransomware, botnets, web application attacks and other attack vectors [5].
- **Employees.** Employees as insiders' usual work alone in their attack and they have physical as well as privileged digital access to the IT infrastructure of their employer. Negative work-related events can trigger intensions like financial ones or revenge [3]. According to ENISA's Threat Landscape Report Employees/Insiders are a threat regarding data breaches, physical manipulation and others [5].
- **Hacktivists.** Hacktivists are ideologically motivated and their attacks are driven by fame and glory, revenge, or mere fun. Hacktivist groups normally have a core of high talented members and a bunch of members with a lower level of skills [3]. According to ENISA's Threat Landscape Report, denial of service or web-based attacks are common attack vectors for Hacktivists [5].
- **Nation states.** Nation state attackers typically have access to more funds, better equipment and more thorough intelligence than any other group of attackers. In general, this threat actor is triggered by geo-political conflicts [3]. According to ENISA's Threat Landscape Report, cyber espionage, information leakage and others are typical for Nation State attackers [5].
- **Script kiddies.** Script kiddies are motivated by curiosity and notoriety and do not need special triggers to execute an attack. Script kiddies work alone and their capability skills are defined as very low [3]. For Holt and Kilgers, script kiddies can be a big threat to organizations as script kiddies' tools can be compromised by more talented threat actors, which use script kiddies as men in the middle [35].

These roles come with a description of a profile with motivation, intention and capabilities. Note that the five chosen different threat actors are taken from the threat actor classification of Hald and Pedersen [3]. These five threat actors coincide with ENISA's Threat Landscape Report 2016 [5] and Robinson's identified actors who threaten critical infrastructures [44].

5   Results

This section reflects the games and their results with a focus on techniques of neutralization. In the after-action review of the 15 games, the game master's notes as well as the notes of the 27 red teams have been reviewed and reflected. All justifications and neutralizations were categorized to the techniques of neutralization presented in Subsect. 2.2. Category "Other" subsumes the cases in which no justification or no clear neutralization was given. An example for "Other" is "personal financial gain" ("persönliche finanzielle Bereicherung") as this is a motive but not a neutralization. Table 4 lists the chosen threat actors as well as the techniques they used.

Table 4. Techniques of neutralization used in "Operation Digital Chameleon"

Technique of neutralization	Cyber criminals	Employees	Hacktivists	Nation states	Script kiddies
Denial of responsibility	0	1	0	0	1
Denial of injury	1	1	0	0	0
Denial of the victim	1	3	2	0	0
Condemnation of the condemners	0	0	0	0	0
Appeal to higher loyalties	2	0	3	2	0
Security argument	0	1	4	0	0
Other	3	0	1	1	0

Note that the role of Hacktivists is the most popular one. An approach to explain this is the high media exposure of this threat actor. Note also that the technique of neutralization *Condemnation of the Condemners* was not used by the 27 red teams.

The authors categorized the team's justifications to the techniques of neutralization by themselves. If there were more techniques possible due to longer justifications, the most plausible one according to the attackers' goal and attacking scenario was chosen. The first author conducted a first classification of the statements to techniques of neutralization. The second author reviewed the classification and conflicts in first and second authors' classification were resolved in discussion until a mutual agreement could be reached.

The subsequent five subsections present the analysis of the results regarding the five threat actors in cybercrime with a brief and selective discussion of the played roles and the used techniques of neutralization, in the literature and in real cases.

5.1   Techniques of Neutralization of Cyber Criminals

In the context of cyber criminals, we discovered *appeal to higher loyalties*, *defense of the victim* and *denial of injury* as techniques for neutralization (cf. Table 4). In game No. 8 in more detail the threat actor cyber criminals used *Denial of Injury* as neutralization technique. Game No. 8 (named "Operation Digital Owl" ("Operation Digitale Eule")) was played on a game board with the infrastructure of a university. The cyber criminals targeted results of cutting-edge research projects to sell them on the black market. The neutralization was that universities in Germany are publicly funded and so they are paid from tax money and do not need the revenues from selling research results anyway. On this way of interpretation, the attack does not put a risk on jobs or employees and can be executed without bad conscience. Understanding this motive is useful. The blue team did not anticipate this neutralization and the neutralization was essential in identifying the particular target in the university. We observed this neutralization was sort of an eye-opener for the professors participating in this particular game. They tend to circumvent IT security measures and to deviate from the IT security policies of the university and neutralize this with a "who is commercially interested in my research results, anyway?". We argue here, that understanding such a neutralization contributes both to effectiveness and efficiency of cybersecurity measures.

5.2 Techniques of Neutralization of Employees

In the course of "Operation Digital Chameleon" different techniques of neutralization have been identified (see Table 4). In sum five teams played the employee-role. Three of them decided to use the *Denial of the Victim* technique to overcome the natural inhibition threshold and to start so the modeling of an attack chain.

One of the red teams in game No. 7 acted with the intention of data disclosure. Therefore, this red team applied the attack vectors command injection, spear phishing with attachment, zero-day exploit, hardware keylogger and sniffing using hardware. The self-motivation of the attackers was clearly evident to categorize by Chiesea: Anger and frustration [37]. The company has been constantly in arrears with the payment of the salaries. This fact has been leaded to an easy justification of the deviant behavior of the threat actor: "The payment of the salaries is always not carried out, so they want it this way" ("Ständig zahlen die die Löhne nicht, die haben's ja so gewollt").

One out of many real employee attacks happened in February 2014 [45]. After the employment of a system administrator was terminated the employee had still access to servers via VPN. The dissatisfied ex system administrator, Brian Johnson, has taken this opportunity and caused over a million dollars in damage. He installed his own software and monkeyed around with the industrial control systems. The FBI raided Johnson's home, there they found a VPN connection into the company's servers on his private laptop. The offender was sentenced to 34 months in prison and to repay the damage. This example gives insight into how employees neutralize the behavior with the technique *Denial of the Victim* in the real world.

These detailed attacks, with motivation and justification of an employee, shows on one hand how easy it could be for a company to get frustrated employees. On the other hand, they reveal which different internal and external risks a company has to face to guarantee a high IT security level and secure services.

Note that the range of motivations and neutralizations of employees is manifold and Siponen and Vance provide here a seminal analysis of techniques of neutralization of employees [11]. Technically, a mishap or weak security policies may be the reason why employees violate IT security policies or cause IT security incidents, e.g. by being successfully targeted in Social Engineering. For instance: An employee in the human resource department is the victim of a spear-phishing attack, receives and opens a malicious mail attachment which is called "CV John Doe". This could be the beginning of an extensive system infection. Note that we identified here only neutralizations of employees that actively damage or abuse their business IT system. For the role of employees, the findings are in line with literature and real cases. In game, these neutralizations were an eye-opener and the institution reacted (game No. 8). Understanding neutralization through contextualization proved to be useful.

5.3   Techniques of Neutralization of Hacktivists

The role of Hacktivists is the most popular role in "Operation Digital Chameleon" – ten times this threat actor has been chosen to fight against a blue team and won for 3 times. The behavior of the threat actor was explained with the techniques *appeal to higher loyalties, denial of the victim* and *the security argument* (cf. Table 4).

Four times *the Security Argument*, breaking into systems as a service to depict vulnerabilities, was utilized. For instance, in game No. 10 the role's motivation, categorized by Chiesea, could have been *attract media attention on the hope of becoming famous* [37]. Therefore, the players wanted to disclose weaknesses in the IT system and set transparency in this field. To reach their targets different attack vectors were in operation: Spear-phishing with attachment, spear-phishing with link and USB sticks.

In game No. 9 - similar to game No. 10 - the aim of the team was the disclosure of vulnerabilities and the technique of neutralization was again *the Security Argument*. In this specific game, the IT infrastructure was of a national institution. The justification for the deviant behavior was formed by the argument "Show the public that the system is not safe. If the state can't protect its own system, how can it protect the population?" ("Der Öffentlichkeit zeigen, dass das System nicht sicher ist. Wenn der Staat schon nicht sein eigenes System schützen kann, wie kann er die Bevölkerung schützen?").

The Security Argument is popular among Hacktivists. In reality, the range of techniques of neutralization is wider. E.g. consider "Operation Payback" of 2010 [46]. 13 insiders of Anonymous performed a coordinated series of cyber-attacks against the websites of the Recording Industry Association of America, the Motion Picture Association of America and the United States Copyright Office. One of the offenders justified his behavior in court with the following words: "I never harmed society; I contributed to society". Under these circumstances, we speak about *Appeal to higher Loyalties* and *Denial of the Victim* techniques because he argues he had done the whole exploit just for society and that society was not harmed.

A second occurrence happened in February of 2016. A subdivision of the Anonymous hacker collective has leaked details for 52 officers and employees of the Cin-cinnati Police Department [47]. The deeds were motivated by the unnecessary death of Paul Gaston. The man was shot numerous times by police officers because he reached for a pellet gun while officers were trying to arrest him. With reference to a video statement, published by an Anon at YouTube (which is also embedded in [47]), the motivation, the justification or rather the neutralization techniques can be categorized as *Denial of the Victim* and *Appeal to higher Loyalties* [48].

5.4   Techniques of Neutralization of Nation States

Historically the threat actor Nation States is the youngest. Typically, the members of this group have more thorough intelligence, better equipment and access to high financial means. Through the classification, the threat actor has the power of a state and so nearly every possibility. In "Operation Digital Chameleon" the role has been played for three times (cf. Table 4).

In game No. 11 the aim of the Nation States was to espionage the victim's IT system for a benefit in knowledge. On this basis, they wanted to generate political influence and financial advantage. This motivation can be classified by Chiesea in the categories *political reasons* and *money* [37]. As a justification the offenders applied the technique of neutralization *Appeal to higher Loyalties*: "get knowledge and insight to exert influence in world politics. In addition, there is an economic advantage" ("Wissen und Einsicht gewinnen, um so Einfluss in der Weltpolitik ausüben zu können. Hinzu kommt ein wirtschaftlicher Vorteil"). This neutralization was part of the attack strategy developed by team red. Economic advantage is a popular justification to neutralize other actions. See the arguments of the US President Donald Trump on jobs to neutralize actions that potentially harm the environment.

The attacker in game No. 13 was played from IT and IT law students. They declared themselves as ISIS and targeted the defacement of a state-owned website. Thereby they hoped to gain more political influence and saw the opportunity to destabilize the government. ISIS acts with religious motives - a case of *Appeal to higher Loyalties*.

5.5 Techniques of Neutralization of Script Kiddies

The threat actor script kiddies marks up by different characteristics. Script Kiddies have little understanding of the mechanics of the attack and do not have a functional appreciation for the ways that an exploit impacts system processes [35]. In comparison to the other four threat actors in "Operation Digital Chameleon" this role can be seen as the weakest and has nearly no opportunity to win the game. Due to the fact that the red teams can select which actor they capture the threat actor script kiddy has been played just once.

In the 10th game the Script Kiddies' aim was to disclose data. Therefore, the threat actor applied phishing with attachment and WLAN-crack as attack vectors. The attack in sum can be classified as no danger for the business and was justified by "need for recognition" ("Geltungsbedürfnis"). In the mapping of the different techniques this justification can be found in the section *denial of responsibility*. When attempting to detect a valid motivation by Chiesea et al., the authors assign the motive to the category *attract media attention on the hope of becoming famous* [37].

A real case scenario happened in 2010. The student Armin Razmdjou, a 16 years old teenager, had found security gaps on the websites of in sum 17 banks [49]. The gaps are so-called cross-site scripting problems. Razmdjou had done this deeds in the motivation of curiosity, this category can be also found in the classification by Chiesa [37]. The article, which describes the occurrence, contains no justification thus the mapping for a classification of a technique of neutralization cannot be done.

The literature on script kiddies and their motivations is not as well developed as the one on Hacktivists. However, understanding their ways to act from a socio-technical perspectives would allow to develop socio-technical IT security measures. This is motivated by the assumptions that script kiddies are willingly or unwillingly engaged by more professional actors – that use e.g. script kiddies' software to mask or piggyback their attacks [35].

6 Discussion and Conclusion

6.1 Limitations

This paper should be interpreted in light of its limitations. The study has its sole focus on non-criminals. Because of the participants' daily work as investigators in cybercrime, IT security administrators, and members of CERTs. We assume that they are familiar with the attackers' methods and behavior. Notwithstanding the game participants lack of criminal careers in cybercrime, the results illustrate the relevance of understanding neutralization and motivation of hackers and the potential of this approach to add to the understanding of the socio-technical aspects in cybercrime, in a field that lacks empirical basis.

A second limitation is the generalizability of our results – as more games with different participants would potentially yield different results. Also, we do not consider other threat actors like cyber fighters or cyber terrorists (see [5]) yet.

6.2 Implications for Practice and Research

In this article we offer information about techniques of neutralization according to different threat actors, applied by 27 red teams in the first 15 instances of "Operation Digital Chameleon".

Such a understanding of techniques of neutralization is useful for cybersecurity in practice: According to Bersoff, unethical behavior decreases when offenders' abilities to construct neutralizations are impeded [50]. Cornish and Clarke terms this removal of excuses, which is one in five principals in prevention of crime. Note that these principals are also adapted by the BKA [51]. Other authors derive IT security measures from techniques of neutralization: Ethical trainings [15], campaigns and company seminars [11] or public relations work [21] can inhibit these techniques of neutralization.

Currently most studies analyze techniques of neutralization in cybercrime in general and there are only a few studies that study techniques of neutralization for specific threat actors. We argue that the combination of threat actor and neutralization brings benefit to the development of IT security measures. Herein we close a gap in literature and a gap in methods in cybersecurity also through our gamified approach.

Our analysis does not go that far to develop security measures. We illustrate that it is potentially useful to collect and study techniques of neutralization and that "Operation Digital Chameleon" is a useful tool for data collection: First, the 15 games that we analyzed in this publication provide a significant number of techniques of neutralization. Second, the techniques that we identified are in line with techniques of neutralization in literature and with real incidents, i.e. they are realistic. Third, we demonstrate that both understanding of cyberthreat actor roles and techniques of neutralization contributes to the effectiveness of IT security strategy.

In addition to that, our results highlight a number of opportunities for future research. First, a large-scale analysis can shed light on threat actors, where little is known about socio-technical aspects at this point. Second, future studies should take threat actors into account that we did not consider – e.g. cyber fighters or cyber terrorists. Especially, if the techniques of neutralization vary because of the target (e.g. service providers, single persons, churches) such as the motives and the used attack vectors do (see e.g. [2]). Or if e.g. hacktivists use different techniques of neutralization depending on their educational level, age, or other socio-demographic data. We argue that a development of IT security can be more effective if they are not generalized but are targeted according to neutralization and threat actor as e.g., offering ethical trainings regarding cybercrime in early school years and in study.

Acknowledgments. We would like to acknowledge the funding from BMBF for project "Vernetzte IT-Sicherheit Kritischer Infrastrukturen" (FKZ: 16KIS0213). We thank all participants for making "Operation Digital Chameleon" a success.

References

1. Gaycken, S.: Cyberwar: Das Internet als Kriegsschauplatz. Open Source Press (2010)
2. Füllgraf, W.: Hacktivisten: Abschlussbericht zum Projektteil der Hellfeldbeforschung, Wiesbaden (2015)
3. Hald, S., Pedersen, J.: An updated taxonomy for characterizing hackers according to their threat properties. In: 2012 14th International Conference on Advanced Communication Technology (ICACT), pp. 81–86 (2012)
4. TrendMicro: U-Markt - Peering into the German Cybercriminal Underground (2015)
5. ENISA: ENISA Threat Landscape Report 2016: 15 Top Cyber-Threats And Trends (2017)
6. Bässmann, J.: Täter im Bereich Cybercrime, Wiesbaden (2015)
7. Rieb, A., Lechner, U.: Operation digital chameleon – towards an open cybersecurity method. In: Proceedings of the 12th International Symposium on Open Collaboration (OpenSym 2016), Berlin, pp. 1–10 (2016)
8. Bundeskriminalamt: Bundeslagebild Cybercrime 2015 (2016)
9. Logan, C.H., Blumstein, A., Cohen, J., Nagin, D.: Deterrence and Incapacitation: Estimating the Effects of Criminal Sanctions on Crime Rates (1980)
10. Young, R., Zhang, L., Prybutok, V.R.: Hacking into the minds of hackers. Inf. Syst. Manag. **24**, 281–287 (2007)
11. Siponen, M., Vance, A.: Neutralization: new insights into the problem of employee information systems security policy violations. MIS Q. **34**, 487–502 (2010)
12. Sykes, G.M., Matza, D.: Techniques of neutralization: a theory of delinquency (1957)
13. Puhakainen, P.: A Design Theory for Information Security Awareness. Oulu University Press, Oulu (2006)
14. Parker, D.B.: Fighting Computer Crime: A New Framework for Protecting Information. Wiley, New York (1998)
15. Morris, R.: Computer hacking and the techniques of neutralization: an empirical assessment. In: Corporate Hacking and Technology-Driven Crime: Social Dynamics and Implications, pp. 1–17. Information Science Reference, Hershey (2011)
16. Minor, W.W.: Techniques of neutralization: a reconceptualization and empirical examination. J. Res. Crime Delinq. **18**, 295–318 (1981)

17. Klockars, C.B.: The Professional Fence. Free Press, New York (1974)
18. Coleman, J.W.: The Criminal Elite: The Sociology of White Collar Crime. St. Martin's Press, New York (1994)
19. Spafford, E.H.: Are computer hacker break-ins ethical? J. Syst. Softw. **17**, 41–47 (1992)
20. Moore, R., McMullan, E.C.: Neutralizations and rationalizations of digital piracy: a qualitative analysis of university students. Int. J. Cyber Criminol. **3**, 441–451 (2009)
21. Haupt, S.: Internet-Piraten ohne Gewissensbisse - warum Aufklärung und Strafaktionen nicht wirken (2007)
22. Haupt, S.: Musikkopisten und ihre Rechtfertigungen. VDM Verlag Dr. Müller, Saarbrücken (2007)
23. D'Ovidio, R., Mitman, T., El-Burki, I.J., Shumar, W.: Adult-child sex advocacy websites as social learning environments: a content analysis. Int. J. Cyber Criminol. **3**, 421–440 (2009)
24. Higgins, G.E., Wolfe, S.E., Marcum, C.D.: Music piracy and neutralization: a preliminary trajectory analysis from short-term longitudinal data. Int. J. Cyber Criminol. **2**, 324–336 (2008)
25. Hutchings, A.: A qualitative analysis of online offending and victimisation. In: Global Criminology: Crime and Victimization in the Globalized Era, pp. 93–114. Taylor and Francis (2013)
26. Li, W., Cheng, L.: Effects of neutralization techniques and rational choice theory on internet abuse in the workplace. In: PACIS 2013 Proceedings (2013)
27. Smallridge, J.L., Roberts, J.R.: Crime specific neutralizations: an empirical examination of four types of digital piracy. Int. J. Cyber Criminol. **7**, 125–140 (2013)
28. Walkley, S.: Regulating cyberspace: an approach to studying criminal behaviour on the internet (2005). http://hdl.handle.net/1885/9994
29. Turgeman-Goldschmidt, O.: The rhetoric of hackers' neutralisations. In: Schmalleger, F., Pittaro, M. (eds.) Crimes of the Internet, pp. 317–335. Pearson Education, Upper Saddle River (2009)
30. Holt, T.J., Copes, H.: Transferring subcultural knowledge on-line: practices and beliefs of persistent digital pirates. Deviant Behav. **31**, 625–654 (2010)
31. Nicho, M., Kamoun, F.: Multiple case study approach to identify aggravating variables of insider threats in information systems. Commun. Assoc. Inf. Syst. **35**, 333–356 (2014)
32. Goode, S., Cruise, S.: What motivates software crackers? J. Bus. Ethics **65**, 173–201 (2006)
33. Hinduja, S.: Neutralization theory and online software piracy: an empirical analysis. Ethics Inf. Technol. **9**, 187–204 (2007)
34. Australian Institute of Criminology: Hacking motives (2005)
35. Holt, T.J., Kilger, M.: Know Your Enemy: The Social Dynamics of Hacking. Honeynet Proj. 17 (2012)
36. Kilger, M., Arkin, O., Stutzman, J.: Profiling. In: Know Your Enemy: Learning about Security Threats, pp. 505–556. Addison Wesley Professional (2004)
37. Chiesa, R., Ducci, S., Ciappi, S.: Profiling Hackers: The Science of Criminal Profiling as Applied to the World of Hacking. CRC Press, Boca Raton, London, New York (2009)
38. Taylor, P.: Hackers: Crime and the Digital Sublime, New York (1999)
39. Falk, W.D.: "Ought" and motivation. In: Proceedings of the Aristotelian Society, pp. 111–138 (1947)
40. McGoogan, C.: Anonymous hacker knocks 20pc of dark web offline in campaign against child pornography. http://www.telegraph.co.uk/technology/2017/02/06/anonymous-knocks-20pc-dark-web-offline-campaign-against-child/?WT.mc_id=tmg_share_fb
41. Hevner, A.R., March, S.T., Park, J., Ram, S.: Design science in information systems research. MIS Q. **28**, 75–105 (2004)

42. Kamath, M.: Hackers can remotely take over nuclear power plants by exploiting vulnerability in IES. http://www.techworm.net/2015/08/security-flaws-in-industrial-ethernet-switches.html
43. Neitzel, L., Huba, B.: Top ten differences between ICS and IT cybersecurity (2014). https://www.isa.org/standards-and-publications/isa-publications/intech-magazine/2014/may-jun/features/cover-story-top-ten-differences-between-ics-and-it-cybersecurity/
44. Robinson, M.: The SCADA threat landscape. In: 1st International Symposium on ICS SCADA Cyber Security Research 2013 (ICS-CSR 2013), pp. 30–41 (2013)
45. Thomson, I.: Paper factory fired its sysadmin. He returned via VPN and caused $1m in damage. Now jailed. https://www.theregister.co.uk/2017/02/18/it_admin_/
46. Unknown: Payback 13: Last of Anonymous anti-copyright hacktivists sentenced in Virginia. https://www.rt.com/usa/234191-anonymous-payback-collins-blake/
47. Cimpanu, C.: Anonymous Leaks Data of 52 Cincinnati Police Officers. http://news.softpedia.com/news/anonymous-leaks-data-of-52-cincinnati-police-officers-500801.shtml
48. Verdict, A.: Message to Cincinnati Police Department. YouTube (2016)
49. Schmidt, J.: 16-jähriger demonstriert Sicherheitslücken bei 17 Banken. https://www.heise.de/security/meldung/16-jaehriger-demonstriert-Sicherheitsluecken-bei-17-Banken-1104841.html
50. Bersoff, D.M.: Why good people sometimes do bad things: motivated reasoning and unethical behavior. Pers. Soc. Psychol. Bull. **25**, 28–39 (1999)
51. Bässmann, J.: Situative Kriminalprävention; Chancen eines Kooperationsansatzes im Bereich Cybercrime (2014). http://www.praeventionstag.de/dokumentation/download.cms?id=1832&datei=20140508_19DPT_13-05-2014__Vortrag_Bae_sit_F2761-1832.pdf

Privacy by Design Data Exchange Between CSIRTs

Erich Schweighofer[1(✉)], Vinzenz Heussler[1], and Peter Kieseberg[2]

[1] Centre for Computers and Law, University of Vienna, 1010 Vienna, Austria
{erich.schweighofer,
vinzenz.klaus.heussler}@univie.ac.at
[2] SBA Research, 1040 Vienna, Austria
pkieseberg@sba-research.org

Abstract. Computer Security Incident Response Teams ('CSIRTs') may exchange personal data about incidents. A privacy by design solution can ensure the compliance with data protection law and the protection of trade secrets. An information platform of CSIRTs is proposed, where incidents are reported in encoded form. Without knowledge of other personal data, only the quantity, region and industry of the attacks can be read out. Additional data–primarily from own security incidents–can be used to calculate a similarity to other incidents.

Keywords: NIS directive · GDPR · CSIRTs · Information platform · Privacy by design

1 Introduction

Data, information and knowledge are the raw material of the age of knowledge and networks, and are commonly referred to as the 'oil of the 21st century'. In contrast to land and industrial goods, information, however, is reproducible. The personal and economic value of information is influenced by every reproduction, and thus by every information exchange. There are therefore legal limits for the exchange of information in the virtual as well as in the analogue world. What can be passed on or published is only found after examination of the relevant legislation.

Sharing information in the context of cyber security allows governments to gain an overview of national risk situation on potential threat scenarios. Comprehensive data is key for governments to develop and adjust strategies, policies, legislation and the allocation of resources [1]. In regard to incidents impairing the network and information security, it is necessary to collect and exchange information in the course of the incident-handling procedures, which may lead to data protection issues. The Computer Security Incident Response Teams (CSIRTs) play a key role in the collection of relevant information and their exchange. Similarly to a fire-brigade they issue (early) warning and participate in incident-handling. Hereinafter, a technical solution is proposed in the form of an information platform for CSIRTs where security incidents are reported in encoded form, taking into account the privacy by design principle.

© Springer International Publishing AG 2017
E. Schweighofer et al. (Eds.): APF 2017, LNCS 10518, pp. 104–119, 2017.
DOI: 10.1007/978-3-319-67280-9_6

2 Framework of Data Exchange: NIS Directive

First, the sector-specific European Union (EU) legal framework in the field of the security of network and information systems (NIS) shall be addressed. The EU considered a comprehensive approach at Union level necessary to respond effectively to the challenges of security of NIS. Against this background, the Directive 2016/1148 concerning measures for a high common level of security of network and information systems across the Union (NIS Directive) was adopted. The NIS Directive is to be transposed by the Member States into national law by 9 May 2018 (Article 25 (1)).

The NIS Directive lays down measures to achieve a high common level of security of NIS within the Union so as to improve the functioning of the internal market (Article 1 (1)). In essence, this high level of security of NIS is to be achieved by strengthening cooperation between Member States (strategic coordination and operational cooperation) as well as introducing mandatory safety measures, adequate IT risk management and the reporting of significant incidents.

Chapter 2 of the NIS Directive establishes national frameworks on the security of NIS. As part of these national frameworks, Article 8 provides for authorities and requires Member States to designate one or more national competent authorities on the security of NIS ('competent authority') whose task is to monitor the application of the Directive at national level. Moreover, Member States must designate a national single point of contact on the security of NIS which will exercise a liaison function to ensure cross-border cooperation of Member State authorities as well as with the Cooperation Group (see Article 11) and the CSIRTs network (see Article 12).

According to Article 9, the national framework on the security of NIS also includes CSIRTs, which is basically a different term for the well-known Computer Emergency Response Teams (CERTs) (see recital 34). Each Member State must designate one or more CSIRTs. A CSIRT can also be established within a competent authority. CSIRTs are responsible for risk and incident handling in accordance with a well-defined process (Article 9 (1)).

The requirements of CSIRTs are laid down in particular in Annex I (1). According to Annex 1, the requirements of CSIRTs have to be adequately and clearly defined and supported by national policy and/or regulation. E.g. CSIRTs must ensure a high level of availability of their communications services by avoiding single points of failure, and must have several means for being contacted and for contacting others at all times. Furthermore, the communication channels must be clearly specified and well known to the constituency and cooperative partners (Annex I (1) (a)). Moreover, CSIRTs have to rely on an infrastructure of which the continuity is ensured due to reasons of business continuity (Annex I (1) (c) (iii)).

Annex I (2) (a) specifies the tasks of CSIRTs. These tasks include at least monitoring incidents at a national level, providing early warning, alerts, announcements and dissemination of information to relevant stakeholders about risks and incidents, responding to incidents as well as providing dynamic risk and incident analysis and situational awareness.

Aiming to facilitate cooperation, CSIRTs have to promote the adoption and use of common or standardized practices for incident and risk-handling procedures and incident, risk and information classification schemes (Annex I (2) (c)).

It should also be noted that Member States must ensure that their CSIRTs have access to an appropriate, secure, and resilient communication and information infrastructure at national level (Article 9 (3)).

3   Data Protection Law

In order to effectively address threats to the security of NIS, e.g. through cyber attacks, information must be collected and exchanged. The purpose of collecting information is to support the prevention and the reaction in dealing with cyber threats. For instance, when an organization is aware of the fact that attacks originate from a particular IP address or that certain attack methods are used or certain targets are aimed at, this information could contribute to the prevention or minimization of damage to other organizations [2].

Data protection law is probably the most referenced potential hurdle to data sharing. A report on threat data exchange among CERTs by ENISA shows that interviewees have doubts about whether a particular set of information can be shared at all, with whom, on what conditions etc., the grounds being that data protection and privacy law are perceived to be fragmented. Also different interpretations of the law by different bodies are problematic in this regards [3].

Hereinafter, it is demonstrated how data protection may be a hurdle to data sharing at the example of IP addresses. Log data, spam filters, blocking lists, and other forms of data collection might contain IP addresses. According to an important recent decision in 2016 [4] the European Court of Justice (ECJ) ruled that IP addresses can qualify as personal data. The court had to decide "whether Article 2(a) of Directive 95/46 must be interpreted as meaning that a dynamic IP address registered by an online media services provider when a person accesses a website that provider makes accessible to the public constitutes, with regard to that service provider, personal data within the meaning of that provision" [5]. The ECJ concluded that the dynamic IP address constitutes personal data in relation to a provider "where the latter has the legal means which enable it to identify the data subject with additional data which the internet service provider has about that person" [6]. Consequently, the questions whether data constitutes personal data depends on the specific data holder and the answer can differ depending on the data holder. Moreover, in order to determine if data qualifies as personal data, not only the data holder's information enabling the identification of the data subject must be considered but also information that the data holder can obtain with the assistance of third parties. Summing up, IP addresses can constitute personal data which must be determined on a case to case basis.

Generally, the NIS Directive recognizes the need for processing personal data. Particularly in recital 72 the Directive states that "sharing of information on risks and incidents within the Cooperation Group and the CSIRTs network and the compliance with the requirements to notify incidents to the national competent authorities or the CSIRTs might require processing of personal data [...]." Article 2 stipulates that the processing of personal data pursuant to the Directive shall be carried out in accordance with Directive 95/46/EC and that the processing of personal data by Union institutions and bodies shall be carried out in accordance with Regulation (EC) No 45/2001. Moreover, the Directive states in recital 75 that it "respects the fundamental rights, and observes the principles, recognised by the Charter of Fundamental Rights of the European Union, in particular the right to respect for private life and communications, the protection of personal data [...]" and that the "Directive should be implemented in accordance with those rights and principles". The NIS Directive itself, however, does not lay down specific rules and provision on data protection.

Since a CSIRT is very likely to process personal data, which it receives, for example, from an operator of an essential services in compliance with the notification obligation in the case of an incident pursuant to the NIS Directive, the CSIRT needs a legal basis for the processing these data.

In the EU, the primary legal basis for processing data can be found in the Directive 95/46/EC [7] and in the national laws implementing this Directive. In Austria, for example, the primary legal basis is the Data Protection Act 2000 [8]. However, the General Data Protection Regulation (GDPR) [9] will be applicable from 25 May 2018 and is going to replace the Directive 95/46/EC and the national implementation acts. Unlike the Directive 95/46/EC, the GDPR is directly applicable and does not require transposition into national law.

It is important to note, though, that according to Article 2 (2) (b) the GDPR does not apply to the processing of personal data by the Member States when carrying out activities which fall within the scope of Chapter 2 of Title V of the Treaty on European Union (TEU), thereby excluding matters concerning the national security from the scope of application. Moreover, the processing of personal data by competent authorities for the purposes of the prevention, investigation, detection or prosecution of criminal offences or the execution of criminal penalties, including the safeguarding against and the prevention of threats to public security, are excluded according to Article 2 (2) (d) of the GDPR. In such cases, the Directive 2016/680/EU [10] and its national implementing measures are to be applied. Since the NIS Directive stipulates in Article 9 (1) that a CSIRT may be established within a competent authority, these exemptions may be relevant. However, CSIRTs are often operated by private entities for which the GDPR is applicable.

According to recital 49 of the GDPR, the "processing of personal data to the extent strictly necessary and proportionate for the purposes of ensuring network and information security, i.e. the ability of a network or an information system to resist, at a given level of confidence, accidental events or unlawful or malicious actions that compromise the availability, authenticity, integrity and confidentiality of stored or transmitted personal data, and the security of the related services offered by, or accessible via, those networks and systems, by public authorities, by computer emergency response teams (CERTs), computer security incident response teams (CSIRTs), by providers of electronic communications networks and services and by providers of security technologies and services, constitutes a legitimate interest of the data controller concerned." Hence, a CSIRT has a legitimate interest in processing personal data to the extent strictly necessary and proportionate for the purposes of ensuring NIS.

Apart from notification duties, there is, however, also an interest in voluntary exchange of information. Notification duties have the disadvantage that they are only applicable after a breach has occurred. A broader, pro-active exchange of information is important in order to achieve resilience too. Voluntary information exchange is based on the intention to improve the understanding of companies and authorities on cyber threats independently of a specific event. The purpose of such voluntary exchange of information lies in mutual assistance and the exchange of experience in the handling of incidents and of appropriate prevention and defense measures. There is an interest in voluntarily exchanging information in the case of abnormalities which do not necessarily have to be the result of an attack or a technical disruption. A number of legal questions arise though, such as: Are personal data exchanged? What is the purpose of the exchange? Who are the recipients? What data security measures are used when exchanging? Article 20 of the NIS Directive provides for a voluntary notification stating that "entities which have not been identified as operators of essential services and are not digital service providers may notify, on a voluntary basis, incidents having a significant impact on the continuity of the services which they provide." This provision, however, does not include the exchange of information in the case of abnormalities which do not necessarily have to be the result of an incident. Apart from the voluntary and obligatory notification according to the NIS Directive, no legitimate interest can be derived from recital 49 of the GDPR, neither for CSIRTs exchanging information among each other nor for providers of critical infrastructures who wish to share certain information with CSIRTs. It should also be remarked that there might be the interest of providers of critical infrastructures to share certain information horizontally among each other.

In order to enable such an exchange of information, technical solutions can be considered, which correspond to the principles relating to processing of personal data stipulated in Article 5 GDPR. For example, only those data should be exchanged which are adequate, relevant and limited to what is necessary in relation to the purposes for which they are processed ("data minimisation"). The processing of personal data should also be carried out in such a manner that the personal data can no longer be attributed to a specific data subject without the use of additional information ("pseudonymisation").

These measures can be considered as privacy by design solutions. The GDPR regulates "data protection by design" – a variation of the term privacy by design – in Article 25 (1) according to which "[...] the controller shall, both at the time of the determination of the means for processing and at the time of the processing itself, implement appropriate technical and organisational measures, such as pseudonymisation, which are designed to implement data-protection principles, such as data minimisation, in an effective manner and to integrate the necessary safeguards into the processing in order to meet the requirements of this Regulation and protect the rights of data subjects." In the Directive 95/46/EC, data protection by design was, if at all, only indirectly addressed, e.g. in Article 17 (Security of processing) where appropriate safeguards are demanded. However, this provision was mainly directed to security instead of privacy guarantees. The Article 29 Data Protection Working Party proposed to innovate the legal framework by introducing additional principle of privacy by design in order to counterbalance the risks for individuals' privacy and data protection due to technological developments [11]. With the GDPR, the concept of privacy by design has finally found its way into legislation as one of the key principles in the revised data protection legal framework which must be considered a major step forward in designing and implementing more data protection and privacy friendly technologies. Nevertheless, the concrete implementation of privacy by design remains unclear at the present moment as there is a gap between the legal framework and the available technological implementation measures [12]. One example, though, of how privacy by design can work in practice is the Ma^{3}tch technology as it achieves data anonymisation and enhances data minimisation as well as data security, which are the fundamental elements of privacy by design [13]. In particular data anonymisation brings the advantage that the anonymized data fall outside the scope of the GDPR. Anonymous data is information which does not relate to an identified or identifiable natural person or to personal data rendered anonymous in such a manner that the data subject is not or no longer identifiable (see recital 26 of the GDPR).

Before going into further detail about the Ma^{3}tch technology, it's worth mentioning that sharing certain information might not only concern data protection law but also law protecting business confidentiality such as trade secret law. Recital 41 of the NIS Directive states that where "information is considered to be confidential in accordance with Union and national rules on business confidentiality, such confidentiality should be ensured when carrying out the activities and fulfilling the objectives set by this Directive." Information about vulnerabilities, e.g. in the IT infrastructure of a company, may be protected under trade secret law. The relevant national laws in the Member States governing trade secrets are about to be harmonized by the Directive 2016/943 [14] which was adopted on 8 June 2016 [15]. The Directive aims to harmonize the national laws against the unlawful acquisition, disclosure and use of trade secrets. According to Article 2 (1), in order to be considered a 'trade secret' information must meet the following requirements: (a) it is secret in the sense that it is not, as a body or in the precise configuration and assembly of its components, generally known among or readily accessible to persons within the circles that normally deal with the kind of information in question; (b) it has commercial value because it is secret; (c) it has been subject to reasonable steps under the circumstances, by the person lawfully in control of the information, to keep it secret. The qualification of certain information as trade secret will largely depend on the nature of the information and various circumstances. In practice, a case-by-case evaluation will have to be carried out. However, it can't be ruled out that certain information in relation to incidents qualifies as trade secret. Here too, technical solutions can be considered to exchange such sensitive information while keeping it secret and not endangering the commercial value thereof.

Finally, it should not go unmentioned that intellectual property law must also be considered when sharing information. Intellectual property grants rights holders exclusive rights such as the exclusive power to disseminate and duplication their works. The legal implications of sharing information protected under IP law cannot be dealt with at this point.

4   Encrypted Codes as a Privacy by Design Solution

The required information infrastructure of CSIRTs represents a challenge for Member States, a typical balancing problem between information needs and privacy. A proportional solution must take into account all available technical solutions of privacy by design.

A possible solution may be seen in the data exchange of Financial Intelligence Units (FIUs). A decentralised network of the European FIUs, "FIU.net", started in 2000 and has been operational since 2002 [16]. The system was integrated into EUROPOL in 2016 [17]. Member States use this method for transposing the 4th Anti-Money Laundering Directive [18], requiring extensive data exchange on money laundering and terrorism financing.

Udo Kroon, one of the developers of FIU.net, described the technology as «cloud inside out». It consists of a decentralised architecture, in which information physically stays at the respective authority. From the point of view of data protection, this architecture has the advantage that storage, processing and analysis of the data take place locally. Local storage and processing of data at the premises of the information owner can contribute to higher data security too. Authorities can use the applicable legal and administrative rules to process their data ("flexibility by design") [19]. The 4th Anti-Money Laundering Directive indicates a strong preference for FIU.net as an appropriate solution (see recital 56 and Article 51, 53 and 56). This is in principle to be welcomed, as the exchange of data between the EU-FIUs is to be based on a data protection friendly basis.

All "obliged entities" (refer to Article 2 (1) 4th Anti-Money Laundering Directive), including the most important professional groups involved in handling money or valuables, have to report unusual or suspicious transactions to the FIU in their Member State. These reports are analyzed by the FIUs and forwarded to law enforcement authorities in the event of a criminal offense. In particular, with respect to credit and financial institutions, the use of software to meet their due diligence requirements (for example identification, reconciliation of data from customers or beneficial owners with monitoring lists and transaction monitoring) involves very large amounts of data for combating money laundering [20]. It has to be noted that highly personal data are involved and banks have to balance between customer relationship and compliance obligations. Data anonymization and data minimisation constitute a necessity.

The "Ma^{3}tch technology" was built on the FIU.net described above. The technology aims at improving the exchange of information among FIUs by excluding unnecessary requests, improving timeliness and enhancing privacy. Ma^{3}tch enables connected FIUs to 'match' their data with that of the other FIUs in order to check whether other FIUs have information on a particular individual in their databases. A match may lead to the conduction of joint analyses for detection of relations and networks and identification of trends, irregularities, classifications, correlations, discriminants or outliers between the distributed data sources. This is achieved through the creation of anonymous filters. These filters can be used to determine approximation matches between FIUs without the need for any FIU to share or expose personal data or even reference data. Ma^{3}tch filters capture the 'characteristics' of the original data, e.g. if the technology is applied to a list of four records containing personal details, the result is a filter like "Nm0a", which is neither an encryption nor just hashing. In facts, it is 'hashing' the hash [21]. The anonymisation of personal data is achieved through a combination of anonymisation algorithms, space efficient probabilistic data structures, and hashing, fuzzy logic and approximation technologies [22] (principle of data anonymisation). In case of an existing match, i.e. indentification of money laundering and terrorism financing, an ordinary exchange of necessary information with related parties is initiated. Instead of exchanging everything, this serves the principle of data minimisation. The system follows the logic of an existing "hit/no hit principle". Only after a hit is found in the database, the regular exchange of information/data between the relevant FIUs may begin. FIUs do not receive information about another FIU investigating a particular individual.

Although the exchange of information using the Ma^{3}tch technology is generally positive as it is in accordance with key principles of privacy by design, the potential drawbacks of this technology should not be disregarded. Ma^{3}tch can do much more than just exchange personal data in an anonymous form and secure channels. Ma^{3}tch can also generate knowledge and, among other things, recognize profiles and predict behavior patterns. The analysis of social networks is also being attempted by the developers of the Ma^{3}tch technology [19]. The implications thereof cannot be dealt with at this point. It should also be pointed out that no security check of this technology has yet been published.

5 Definition and Modelling of Incidents

The Ma^{3}tch technology was designed to balance the problem between the need for information and respect of privacy in financial matters. In the sector of IT security, however, different characteristics need to be considered. First, the legal framework is examined to figure out the characteristics that are key in incidents.

The NIS Directive provides for a notification duty for operators of essential services in Article 14 (3) and providers of digital services in Article 16 (3) when an incident has a significant impact on the availability of the service provided, whereby the notification must be carried out without undue delay to the competent authority or the CSIRT. According to the NIS Directive, 'incident' means "any event having an actual adverse effect on the security of network and information systems" (Article 4 (7)). The Directive lists parameters that have to be taken into account in particular in order to determine the significance of the impact of an incident. These parameters, thus, specify the broad term 'incident'. The parameters for operators of essential services comprise the number of users affected by the disruption of the essential service, the duration of the incident and the geographical spread with regard to the area affected by the incident (Article 14 (4)). In regard to digital service providers, the parameters listed are the number of users affected by the incident, in particular users relying on the service for the provision of their own services, the duration of the incident, the geographical spread with regard to the area affected by the incident, the extent of the disruption of the functioning of the service and the extent of the impact on economic and societal activities (Article 16 (4)). Accordingly, digital service providers must take two more parameters into account in comparison to operators of essential services. The European Commission must adopt implementing acts in order to specify further the parameters relevant for digital service providers by 9 August 2017. The parameters relevant for operators of essential may be specified further in the national laws implementing the Directive.

Pursuant to Article 1 (3) of the NIS Directive security and notification requirements provided for in the NIS Directive do not apply to undertakings which are subject to the requirements of Article 13a and 13b Directive 2002/21/EC (Framework Directive) [23]. Directive 2009/140/EC [24] (which amended the Framework Directive) introduced these Articles 13a and 13b containing among other things the obligation to notify the competent national regulatory authority in case a breach of security or loss of integrity results in a significant impact on the operation of networks or services. According to ENISA, the EU was highly diversified in terms of security measures, however, Article 13a brought a certain amount of uniformity in the approach taken regarding security of telecommunication services. Nevertheless, there are areas of further improvement. For instance, the scope of Article 13a should be clarified in order to provide clear information on the types of networks and services that should be covered. Reinforcing cross-border collaboration could contribute to a higher degree of resilience of European networks and services too [25]. The evaluation of Article 13a reveals the importance of a clear scope of information duties and the significance of (cross-border) collaboration to contribute to more resilient networks and services. This is input that should be taken into close consideration when implementing the NIS Directive.

In order to successfully share information, many factors are significant and prerequisite for effectiveness. For instance, it must be clear who should be contacted and provided with information depending on the particular context, there should be knowledge about the shared information and it is paramount that the same or comparable information classifications are utilized. From a legal point of view, particularly in relation to information sharing, the Directive 2013/40/EU [26] on attacks against information systems provides common definitions of cybercrimes.

Based on the legal assessment, we can derive several side parameters for the practical implementation of information exchange. From the technical perspective, there are several dimensions that are relevant for the operator of a CSIRT in the case of a security incident, of which some do possess components that can result in issues with respect to data protection regulations. In addition, they often also contain information which is harmless from the legal perspective regarding the protection of sensitive personal information, nevertheless deserving extremely high protection from the point of the operator of the respective infrastructure. This especially includes internal processes and workflows, but of course also the fact of being vulnerable due to the attack itself. In the process of our analysis, which have not been fully published until now, we identified the following relevant information particles:

- *Sender information:* Sender and sector of the critical infrastructure under attack, which includes contact information and other assets.
- *Attack information:* This includes the system level of the attack and the affected component(s), as well, whether this was a targeted attack or rather a general approach. Furthermore, critical infrastructures are required to identify other targets

that could be related to this kind of attack. If possible, the attacked infrastructure is also required to deliver as many details as possible on the attack and, in case this is not a new issue, links to the respective CVE [27] entry.

- **Attacker information:** If available, the critical infrastructure under attack will provide as much information as possible on the attacker. This can include IP addresses, internal and external user names. Especially in the case of DDoS attacks (and especially in case of amplification attacks), the list of IPs can grow drastically [28]. Especially when dealing with IP addresses it is also required to provide a specific timestamp for each address, as due to dynamic address allocation, the address alone is an insufficient and incomplete information particle. Especially in cases of phishing, and especially in cases of very specific and targeted spear phishing attacks, the email addresses used can be very helpful for further investigations.

- **Damage information:** In order to estimate the severity of the attack, the CSIRT not only requires details on the attacked component(s), but also on the resulting damage, as the CSIRT, while providing expert knowledge in the area of IT security, can typically not estimate damages specific to an industrial application. This damage estimation not only includes the actual damage caused by the attack, but also the potential damage that could have been caused under certain circumstances, including details on them. The damage should also be split into a pure economical part, which also contains damage done through the unavailability of service or liabilities to stakeholders, as well as into a technical damage report that focusses purely on the technological side. In order to support the CSIRT in gaining situational awareness, it is important to also provide information on other processes inside the company, and especially inside other companies and industries that rely on the attacked components or the services provided by them. This also includes any reduction in service due to mitigation measures or countermeasures applied.

- **Meta-information:** In order to fully use the potential of collecting information on issues and attacks through various stages of the incident, some meta-information is required. It must be made possible to encode the timeline of different notifications on the same incident, possible with revised information, i.e. changes on information that was originally reported differently. Furthermore, in case a bidirectional information exchange needs to be implemented, the messages containing questions to/from the CSIRTs and the respective answers need to be collected and annotated. Furthermore, with the advent of the NIS directive, it is important to distinguish between information sent to the CSIRTs on a voluntary basis, and those sent due to the notification duty. In addition, and in order to ease the subsequent sensitivity analysis, the infrastructures can also annotated, whether sensitive and/or personal information is stored within the information sent to the CSIRT.

- **Additional Information:** Especially attachments can be very useful in order to supply all the information needed to the CSIRTs. This may include code fragments, output from shell commands or pictures and documents, thus, a general form of attachment is required, since all these diverse information types cannot be encoded otherwise. It is important though to especially secure the use of attachments, as they could pose a potential threat to the information system by introducing malware into the CSIRT information process.

In order to speed up the communication between industries and CSIRTs, especially when considering large amounts of attacks of different severity level and the introduction of sensor information into the CSIRT information process, standardizing the communication method is of the utmost importance. This is especially useful in order to allow the (semi-) automated aggregation and alignment of information derived from different sources, e.g. in the course of a coordinated attack on several targets.

Thus we propose to use the STIX-standard [29, 30] for encoding the communication in order to provide interoperability. In addition, due to the widespread use of this standard, this also allows structured communication between the CSIRTs and other partners through unified interfaces.

While most information outlined before is strictly speaking not sensitive with respect to the GDPR, this is different for IP and email addresses. Especially in combination with a time interval it is often possible to assign a person to an address, which results in IP addresses being classified as personal information, even though in the case of dynamic IP addresses additional help from the provider hosting the address is required.

The principle used in the Ma^{3}tch approach can of course also be used for IP and email addresses, by just exchanging the „hashes of hashes". Also in this case it is possible to just exchange a reduced version, which will only be compared fully on match.

In addition, our system approach plans to provide aggregates, e.g. for further publication. The main problem with respect to aggregates are dynamic datasets with different ranges: Let X_0 and X_1 be two different versions of the same data set taken at times t_0 and t_1. Then it is often possible to identify data records by constructing the difference between the aggregates, i.e. based on the differences of the aggregates built from the two data sets it can be possible to retrieve detailed information on their symmetric difference.

6 Data Protection Friendly Coding of Identifiers

Based on the selected STIX-encoding, each identifier will be encoded alone in order to allow for better analysis and detection of similarities. Especially when dealing with composite identificators it is important to encode each particle separately, since otherwise the matching would become very difficult. Example: The composite identificator «name» typically consists of one or more components of the type «first name» and «last name» . Thus, in case of using a cryptographic hash functions H in order to protect this information, the application of H in order to construct H(«first name(s)»||«last name(s)») does not allow one to draw any conclusions on H(«last name(s)»||«first name(s)»), where "||" denotes string concatenation. This is due to the intrinsic requirements regarding cryptographic hash functions that must not allow calculating a hash value from other hash values, even in case the source information is similar. Otherwise, the hash function would not protect the encoded information.

The basic concept behind the approach is that not the data itself is exchanged, or stored into a shared data pool, but only encrypted versions, like it is done in the Ma^{3}tch approach. This "encryption" can either be done by using a secure cryptographic hash function like SHA-3 [31], or by using a shared public key with the corresponding private key being used for de-anonymization.

Another important aspect is the definition of ranges of validity for certain aspects: While information particles like names do change rather rarely over the lifetime of a person, the case is completely different for dynamically allocated IP addresses. These are only tied to a specific internet access point for a certain time and can be allocated to other persons outside of this timeframe. This could result in false accusations, thus, in order to mitigate this problem when using approaches like Ma^{3}tch, it is important to add a time interval. This time interval cannot be trivially encrypted though, as this would thwart comparison (or, even when utilizing homomorphic encryption, it would still take a lot of time). This problem exists for every data type, where ranges instead of fixed values need to be compared. Of course there exist several possibilities like functional encryption, or, for some range types, binning, where the value range is replaced by a representative value. Still, this might not be possible for all range typed values and is currently not intended in the standard design of Ma^{3}tch.

In the case two users produce the same hash value, they have encountered the same characteristic in the data set, i.e. the same value in the same identifier. Still, this approach can cause further problems: One of the (legitimate) users could try to enumerate all valid values of the preimage (e.g. by having access to a list of all inhabitants of a certain area in question) and produce all hashes in order to detect, whether one of the inhabitants has been saved in the lists of the other users while never having had an entry in his own list. It has to be kept in mind, that salting the hashes does not work against this kind of preimage attack, as in order for the original approach to work, the salt has to be known by all legitimate users, salting the hashes thus would only work against external (illegitimate) attackers. In general, there are two ways of dealing with this issue:

- *Organizational:* The partners could introduce methods for the detection of brute-force enumeration and comparison. This works well, in case the partners share all their hashes in a pool and the comparison takes places at a central instance (that also stores the hashes), but not on the partner premises, i.e. in order to find suitable hashes, the users do not download the hashes of all other partners to their servers and do the comparison there, but every user submits his hashes to a central pool, which then does the comparisons and informs the respective users. Submitting large amounts of data would be quite suspicious in such a setting, thus effectively thwarting brute-force enumeration. Still, the major drawback of this solution lies in the trust factor: The central entity is required to be trustworthy. While this trustworthiness can of course be split over several parties in order to mitigate this problem a bit, still, the trustworthiness of the central component(s) remains a problematic issue.
- *Technical:* In case of direct exchange of information without a central instance that controls the submitted values, the partners could still exchange their lists in a privacy preserving way: The value of each identifier is split at an exactly specified point and the hashes of the first part are exchanged. When a user finds a suitable match, then he directly enquires for more information by submitting the hash of the second part to the partner originally issuing the original hash value. The original partner then states whether the second part matches. One of the main problems with

this approach though is the fact, that this allows an enquiry for single specific records, but still thwarts the outlined brute-force enumeration. Furthermore, it puts the load of brute-force detection into the hands of each individual partner in the system, with one partner failing to follow this obligations posing a threat to the privacy of at least parts of sensitive information. Still, more advanced versions can be built on this approach by adding zero-knowledge protocols [32].

7 Sanitizing Data from External Sources

Information collection through CSIRTs has especially high potential, if the analysis workflows behind the pure collection strive to determine patterns (as it is e.g. done in [33]). This can be especially useful in order to detect large scale attacks, attacks launched against a specific type of industry, or just a large amount of low-level and low-impact attacks that, in combination, cause potentially large overall damage.

In order to allow for an automated reconciliation of information from different sources, but also from different information particles from the same source, the encoding in STIX format is one of the major prerequisites as it allows relatively simple matching and caters for the structural requirements as put forth by technologies like Ma^3tch. While the comparison of identifiers as outlined in chapter 6 is an important issue in the generation of additional knowledge, for the further analysis it is vitally important to apply some data cleansing steps before the submission of the information to the other partners in the CSIRT network. The major reason for this is the danger of clogging the data pool with wrong information, either due to simple errors from the side of the infrastructure, but also due to attackers deliberately trying to introduce wrong information into the system in order to damage the reputation of a CSIRT or to obscure other attacks.

Thus, before introducing the information into any data pool and exchanging it with other CSIRTs, all information gathered will be analyzed with respect to its quality: The information will be automatically checked for missing vital information in all fields that are mandatory, especially concerning the sender information. The sending of the information, as well as certain key facts will be checked back with the contact through a second communication channel. Furthermore, the intrinsic quality of the information provided will be checked: Especially, in cases the message contains information from a very early stage of the attack, the information will either be held back and not issued into the shared data pool, or marked as preliminary information. This also means that the exchange mechanisms utilized (e.g. Ma^3tch) needs some way of revoking information, as well as marking its preliminary status. Messages that contain different information particles on the same incident by the same industry will be aggregated and summarized into a single data record. The mechanisms applied may vary, still, especially considering very preliminary information it must be possible for the CSIRT to ask for feedback on (technical) questions.

In addition, the CSIRT can enrich the gathered information before submitting it to the shared data pool, especially when the same, or related, incidents have been reported from different victims. In this case, instead of pushing all aggregated information tickets to the pool, where several of them might miss important aspects due to the reporting infrastructure not being aware of the finer details, the CSIRT might reconcile these different information particles into a single message for the shared data pool. Since the role of a CSIRT allows to see a much broader part of the infrastructure spectrum and the arising attacks than each infrastructure on its own, this adds major value to the recognition of large scale attacks and attack patterns.

In addition to the pure aggregation and basic feedback, it is also possible to add an (semi-)automated sanitization process: For example, in case of CVE-links provided in the message, the CSIRT can check, whether they fit the components described in the message. In case of a mismatch, this can also be important information for the infrastructure under attack, as well as being an indicator for an erroneous or even forged message. Depending on the role of the CSIRT, it might even have more information stored on the internal systems of each critical infrastructure, thus enabling the CSIRT to provide additional checks concerning the validity of the introduced information. Especially in scenarios, where the CSIRT operates its own sensors on the backbone infrastructure, the information gathered by these can be used to sanitize and enrich the messages provided by the infrastructure operators. Furthermore, many CSIRTs do operate internal incident databases which can be used to enrich the information provided by the operators, e.g. with annotating known effects or countermeasures. Since all this depends on the actual role of the CSIRT in the national infrastructure, no general proposition can be put forward at this point, still it should be noted that the matching of information inside the shared data pool must not rely on the existence of such additional information channels, but solely on the minimum all CSIRTs can gather. Still, this information should be encoded using additional STIX-fields in order to allow for a clear and concise separation between the information entered into the system by the infrastructure operators and the data added by the CSIRT.

8 Conclusions

Sharing information in the context of cyber security allows governments to gain an overview of the national risk situation on potential threat scenarios. Comprehensive data is key for governments to develop and adjust strategies, policies, legislation and the allocation of resources. In regard to incidents impairing the network and information security, it is necessary to collect and exchange information in the course of the incident-handling procedures. CSIRTs may thereby have to exchange personal data concerning incidents. A privacy by design solution can ensure the compliance with data protection law and the protection of trade secrets. In this work, an information platform for the CSIRTs is proposed, where incidents are reported in encoded form. In this closed user community, CSIRTs can easily exchange anonymized or pseudonymized data, which is essential for the knowledge of the security situation and threat scenarios, but does not violate data protection law and the protection of trade secrets. The knowledge of the same personal data leads to a "hit" in the platform and ultimately means an intentional cooperation of the affected parties in the incident handling process. Furthermore, by using standardized methods for information exchange, the information gathering process of each CSIRT can be automated for large parts. This is especially important when considering the introduction of automatically harvested sensor information into the CSIRT knowledge bases. Altogether, the approach outlined in the work provides a significant contribution to practical cyber security by introducing means for CSIRTs to share vital information in a privacy preserving way that is adhering to the new legal prerequisites.

Acknowledgments. This work has received funding as part of the project Cyber Incident Situational Awareness (CISA) within the Austrian security research program KIRAS.

References

1. ENISA, Anna, S., Konstantinos, M.: Stocktaking, Analysis and Recommendations on the Protection of CIIs, p. 33 (2016)
2. Kuratorium Sicheres Österreich: KSÖ Rechts- und Technologiedialog – Whitepaper, 2nd ed., p. 20. Vienna (2016)
3. ENISA, Bourgue, R., Budd, J., Homola, J., Wladenko, M., Kulawik, D.: Detect, SHARE, Protect – Solutions for Improving Threat Data Exchange among CERTs, p. 8 (2013)
4. ECJ Judgement Case C-582/14 19 October 2016 (Breyer), ECLI:EU:C:2016:779
5. ECJ, C-582/14, no. 31
6. ECJ, C-582/14, no. 49
7. Directive 95/46/EC of the European Parliament and of the Council of 24 October 1995 on the protection of individuals with regard to the processing of personal data and on the free movement of such data, OJ L 281, pp. 31–50, 23 November 1995
8. Federal Act concerning the Protection of Personal Data (DSG 2000), Federal Law Gazette I No. 165/1999
9. Regulation (EU) 2016/679 of the European Parliament and of the Council of 27 April 2016 on the protection of natural persons with regard to the processing of personal data and on the free movement of such data, and repealing Directive 95/46/EC (General Data Protection Regulation), OJ L 119, pp. 1–88, 4 May 2016
10. Directive (EU) 2016/680 of the European Parliament and of the Council of 27 April 2016 on the protection of natural persons with regard to the processing of personal data by competent authorities for the purposes of the prevention, investigation, detection or prosecution of criminal offences or the execution of criminal penalties, and on the free movement of such data, and repealing Council Framework Decision 2008/977/JHA, OJ L 119, pp. 89–131, 4 May 2016
11. Article 29 Data Protection Working Party and Working Party on Police and Justice: The Future of Privacy – Joint contribution to the Consultation of the European Commission on the legal framework for the fundamental right to protection of personal data. 02356/09/EN, adopted on 01 December 2009
12. ENISA, Danezis, G., Domingo-Ferrer, J., Hansen, M., Hoepman, J., Le Métayer, D., Tirtea, R., Schiffner, S.: Privacy and Data Protection by Design – from policy to engineering, p. iii (2014)
13. Balboni, P., Macenaite, M.: Privacy by design and anonymisation techniques in action: case study of Ma3tch technology. Comput. Law Secur. Rev. **29**(4), 330–340 (2013)
14. Directive (EU) 2016/943 of the European Parliament and of the Council of 8 June 2016 on the protection of undisclosed know-how and business information (trade secrets) against their unlawful acquisition, use and disclosure. OJ L 157, pp. 1–18, 15 June 2016
15. Kalbfus, B.: Die EU-Geschäftsgeheimnis-Richtlinie. Welcher Umsetzungsbedarf besteht in Deutschland? GRUR 2016, pp. 1009–1018 (2016)

16. Wikipedia: Gebruiker:FIU.NET. https://nl.wikipedia.org/wiki/Gebruiker:FIU.NET
17. EUROPOL: EUROPOL joins forces with EU FIUs to fight terrorist financing and money laundering. https://www.europol.europa.eu/newsroom/news/europol-joins-forces-eu-fius-to-fight-terrorist-financing-and-money-laundering
18. Directive (EU) 2015/849 of the European Parliament and of the Council of 20 May 2015 on the prevention of the use of the financial system for the purposes of money laundering or terrorist financing, amending Regulation (EU) No 648/2012 of the European Parliament and of the Council, and repealing Directive 2005/60/EC of the European Parliament and of the Council and Commission Directive 2006/70/EC, OJ L 141, pp. 73–117, 5 June 2015
19. Kroon, U.: Ma^{3}tch: Privacy AND Knowledge. In: 2013 IEEE International Conference on Big Data
20. Schweighofer, E., Böszörmenyi, J.: A review of tools to comply with the proposed 4th EU Anti-Money Laundering Directive In: International Review of Law, Computers & Technology, vol. 29, Special Issue: BILETA 2014, pp. 63–77 (2015)
21. Balboni, P., Macenaite, M.: Privacy by design and anonymisation techniques in action: Case study of Ma3tch technology, pp. 332–333
22. Balboni, P., Macenaite, M.: Privacy by design and anonymisation techniques in action: Case study of Ma3tch technology, p. 334
23. Directive 2002/21/EC of the European Parliament and of the Council of 7 March 2002 on a common regulatory framework for electronic communications networks and services, OJ L 108, pp. 33–50, 24 April 2002
24. Directive 2009/140/EC of the European Parliament and of the Council of 25 November 2009 amending Directives 2002/21/EC on a common regulatory framework for electronic communications networks and services, 2002/19/EC on access to, and interconnection of, electronic communications networks and associated facilities, and 2002/20/EC on the authorisation of electronic communications networks and services, OJ L 337, pp. 37–69, 18 December 2009
25. ENISA, Tofan, D., Moulinos, K., Karsberg, C.: ENISA Impact Evaluation on the Implementation of Article 13a Incident Reporting Scheme within EU, p. 41 (2016)
26. Directive 2013/40/EU of the European Parliament and of the Council of 12 August 2013 on attacks against information systems and replacing Council Framework Decision 2005/222/JHA, OJ L 218, pp. 8–14, 14 August 2013
27. Mell, P., Grance, T.: Use of the common vulnerabilities and exposures (cve) vulnerability naming scheme (No. NIST-SP-800-51). National Inst of Standards and Technology Gaithersburg Md Computer Security Div. (2002)
28. Bhuyan, M.H., Bhattacharyya, D.K., Kalita, J.K.: An empirical evaluation of information metrics for low-rate and high-rate DDoS attack detection. Pattern Recogn. Lett. **51**, 1–7 (2015)
29. Structured Threat Information eXpression (STIX™). https://stixproject.github.io/
30. Barnum, S.: Standardizing cyber threat intelligence information with the Structured Threat Information eXpression (STIX™). MITRE Corporation, 11 (2012)
31. Bertoni, G., Daemen, J., Peeters, M., Van Assche, G.: Keccak specifications. Submission to NIST (Round 2) (2009)
32. Feige, U., Fiat, A., Shamir, A.: Zero-knowledge proofs of identity. J. Cryptology **1**(2), 77–94 (1988)
33. D'Amico, A., Whitley, K., Tesone, D., O'Brien, B., Roth, E.: Achieving cyber defense situational awareness: a cognitive task analysis of information assurance analysts. In: Proceedings of the human factors and ergonomics society annual meeting, vol. 49, No. 3, pp. 229–233. SAGE Publications, Sage CA (2005)

Mr X vs. Mr Y: The Emergence of Externalities in Differential Privacy

Maurizio Naldi[✉] and Giuseppe D'Acquisto

Department of Civil Engineering and Computer Science,
University of Rome Tor Vergata, Rome, Italy
maurizio.naldi@uniroma2.it, dacquisto@ing.uniroma2.it

Abstract. The application of differential privacy requires the addition of
Laplace noise, whose level must be measured out to achieve the desired level
of privacy. However, the protection of the data concerning a Mr. X, i.e., its
privacy level, also depends on the other data contained in the database: a
negative externality is recognized. In this paper we show that an attack on
Mr. X can be conducted by an oracle, by computing the likelihood ratio
under two scenarios, where the database population is made of either independent or correlated entries. We show that the target Mr. X can be spot-
ted, notwithstanding the addition of noise, when its position happens to be
eccentric with respect to the bulk of the database population.

Keywords: Differential privacy · Statistical databases · Negative
externalities

1 Introduction

A well-known conundrum in privacy protection is the wish to reconcile the protection of the individual's personal data with the release of information that
may be useful for the general public. A typical example is provided by the use
of statistical databases [17], where answers to queries about aggregate characteristics have to be provided while protecting the information concerning any
specific individual.

Among the measures that can be put into place to achieve both goals (see
[1] for an early but still useful survey and [3] for the privacy-by-design notion),
differential privacy has emerged as the most prominent [4,7], and even mar-
ketplaces based on differential privacy have been envisaged [12]. In differential
privacy the characteristics of the individual are masked by adding noise following a Laplace distribution. The statistical characteristics of the mechanisms are
explored in [18].

However, the differential privacy mechanism is not immune to attacks aimed
at uncovering the true individual data (see, e.g., the mechanism based on Bayes
estimation [13]). A related problem concerning the practical application of the
differential privacy mechanism is the choice of the right level of noise to add
(which is tightly related to the level of differential privacy achieved): too little

© Springer International Publishing AG 2017
E. Schweighofer et al. (Eds.): APF 2017, LNCS 10518, pp. 120–140, 2017.
DOI: 10.1007/978-3-319-67280-9_7

makes the mechanism ineffective; too much makes the released information useless. Mechanisms based on economics [10] or estimation theory [14], have been proposed for this purpose.

In this paper we investigate the relationship between the differential privacy level and the actual level of protection that can be achieved.

In particular, after describing the notion of differential privacy in Sect. 2, we obtain the following results:

- we see that an *any query* attack may be conducted by an oracle to recover the noisy record concerning the target (which we hereafter name Mr. X) once it knows all the true records (Sect. 3);
- for this kind of attack we investigate the effect of externalities, masking noise level, and correlation among database entries (for the case of a Gaussian copula) in both Sects. 3 and 4;
- we find a sufficient condition for differential privacy through the bounds on the likelihood ratio, conditioned on the actual values of the data to be protected and those injected to protect them (Sect. 4);
- we provide a closed form for the upper bound on the likelihood ratio when the database entries are independent and identically distributed (Sect. 4);
- we provide a MonteCarlo simulation evaluation of the average likelihood ratio for the cases of independent and correlated database entries (Sect. 4).

2 Differential Privacy

In this section we review the notion of differential privacy and highlight its limitations. We adopt the approach taken by Wasserman and Zhou in [18].

We consider a database D as a collection of n m-tuples (the records), which in turn are a random sample $\{\underline{X}_1, \underline{X}_2, \ldots, \underline{X}_n\}$ drawn from some population P. Each record $\underline{X}_i$, $i = 1, 2, \ldots, n$ is therefore a vector made of m components.

Here we do not pose any constraint on the nature of the $\underline{X}_i$'s: its elements could be strings of text, dates, Boolean or real values.

For the purpose of protecting the individuals' true data that are contained in D, we may build a sanitized database D^*, which may be publicly released in the place of D. The sanitized database is made of the collection $\{\underline{Z}_1, \underline{Z}_2, \ldots, \underline{Z}_k\}$ and has a size k that may be different from the size n of the original database: the sanitized database may omit some records or even add brand new ones, generated for the purpose of protecting the true data. It has been stated that, for some schemes, a large value of k can lead to low privacy and high accuracy, while the reverse may take place with small values of k [18].

The response to a query concerning D is therefore provided through a data release mechanism that outputs a function of the collection $\{\underline{Z}_1, \underline{Z}_2, \ldots, \underline{Z}_k\}$ that follows a probability distribution conditioned on the true values $\{\underline{X}_1, \underline{X}_2, \ldots, \underline{X}_n\}$.

As a simple example of the kind of transformation that leads from the true database to the sanitized one, we may consider the case where $k = n$ and $\underline{Z}_i = \underline{X}_i + \eta_i$, $i = 1, 2, \ldots, n$, with $\{\eta_1, \eta_2, \ldots, \eta_n\}$ being zero-mean independent observations drawn from a common probability distribution (which we hereafter refer to as the *noise*).

The choice of the probability distribution of the noise is critical. In [2] the uniform and the Gaussian distributions have been considered. Dwork has proven that for a mechanism that adds noise bounded by E there exists an adversary that can reconstruct the database to within $4E$ positions [5]. Probability distributions with a bounded domain should therefore be excluded from the set of possible choices.

Over the past years the concept of differential privacy has emerged, with a tight relationship with the choice of distribution for the noise. According to the general definition, a randomized function $\mathcal{K}$ gives ϵ-differential privacy if, for all neighbouring databases D_1 and D_2 (i.e., differing just for one record), and all $U \subseteq \text{Range}(\mathcal{K})$, we have $\mathbb{P}[\mathcal{K}(D_1) \in U] \leq e^\epsilon \mathbb{P}[\mathcal{K}(D_2) \in U]$ [4]. As the privacy level ϵ gets closer to 0, the privacy guaranteed to an individual grows, since its inclusion in the database does not change appreciably the response of the database. Dwork et al. have shown that adding Laplace-distributed noise (which represents the randomized mechanism $\mathcal{K}$) achieves ϵ-differential privacy if the parameter of the Laplace distribution obeys some condition [5]. Namely, if noise following a Laplace density function

$$f_\eta(x) = \frac{\lambda}{2} e^{-\lambda |x|} \tag{1}$$

is added, we obtain ϵ-differential privacy if $\lambda = \epsilon / \Delta f$, with Δf representing the maximum difference in the value of the response when exactly one input to the database is changed [5,6]. For a counting query we have $\Delta f = 1$ [5,16], since the addition of a record may modify the response by 1 at most. Since the variance of the Laplace distribution is $2/\lambda^2$, the standard deviation of the Laplace distribution can be expressed as $\sqrt{2}/\epsilon$. There is therefore a tight relationship between the amount of noise injected and the level of differential privacy: larger values of the standard deviation of noise lead to more differential privacy (i.e., lower values of ϵ).

In fact, the definition of differential privacy requires the added random noise to be such that for any two values η_1 and η_2 differing by 1 ($|\eta_1 - \eta_2| = 1$) we have $f_\eta(\eta_1) \leq e^\epsilon f_\eta(\eta_2)$. For dealing at the same time with the cases where $\eta_1 < \eta_2$ or $\eta_1 > \eta_2$, that inequality may be rewritten as

$$e^{-\epsilon} \leq \frac{f_\eta(\eta_1)}{f_\eta(\eta_2)} \leq e^\epsilon, \tag{2}$$

so that the noise is capable of hiding the difference between values that the query output may take on a pair of databases that differ in only one row. For example, let's consider the two cases where: (a) the true value is 10 and the added noise is 2; (b) the true value is 11 and the added noise is 1. In both cases we end up with an output equal to 12. If we ask ourselves what the probability is of getting that response when the true value is either 10 or 11, we must consider the probability densities of the random noise for the values 2 and 1 respectively. If we set $\epsilon = 0.01$, after recalling the relationship $z = x + \eta$ between the true value x and the sanitized value z, we have

$$e^{-0.01} \leq \frac{\mathbb{P}[\hat{z} = 12 | x = 10]}{\mathbb{P}[\hat{z} = 12 | cx = 11]} \leq e^{0.01}$$

$$0.99 \leq \frac{\mathbb{P}[\eta = 2]}{\mathbb{P}[\eta = 1]} \leq 1.01, \tag{3}$$

i.e. we cannot practically distinguish if the true value was 10 or 11. The choice of the Laplace distribution with $\lambda = \epsilon$ satisfies the inequality (2) and therefore provides differential privacy. In fact, for $\eta_1 > 0$ (but the same expression can be obtained for $\eta_1 < 0$) we have

$$\frac{f_\eta(\eta_1)}{f_\eta(\eta_1 + 1)} = \frac{\frac{\epsilon}{2} e^{-\epsilon|\eta_1|}}{\frac{\epsilon}{2} e^{-\epsilon|\eta_1 + 1|}} = e^\epsilon \tag{4}$$

It is to be noted that the level of privacy protection is higher the lower ϵ, since that guarantees that both bounds in the inequality (2) are very close to 1.

Notwithstanding the use of differential privacy, the protection of the personal data contained in a database is subject to several limitations. The importance of context in deciding whether anonymisation has actually been delivered, especially because of the additional knowledge or capability held by an attacker, has been pointed out in [8]. Privacy may be easily compromised even if we just allow for aggregate queries, i.e. queries spanning a set of individuals rather than a specific one. In particular we are concerned with the following two issues:

– semantically identical queries;
– innocent queries.

If noise is added to the outcome of a query, the first way to protect the privacy of the data subjects included in a database is avoiding repeatedly answering identical queries. Two queries are semantically identical if they ask exactly for the same question to the database (namely they sort out exactly the same records), though expressed in two formally different ways. For example, if we consider two attributes A and B, we could be interested in the number of people that possess both. The query can be formulated in at least two formally different but logically (and semantically) identical ways, e.g. as A AND B or, alternatively, $\bar{A}$ OR $\bar{B}$ (obtained by applying De Morgan's laws). Those two queries can be discovered to be identical by the database curator; consequently the second one should not be allowed after the first one has already been answered. If that were not the case, an attacker could repeat the same query over and over again, making the noise addition mechanism ineffective in masking the true query output (a simple averaging operation could be applied to smooth out the noise). This is particularly true for differential privacy, which relies on the addition of Laplace noise.

On the other hand, this cautiousness might be wasted by a clever combination of different innocent queries, though formulate in a different way, since noise could be averaged out. Innocent queries are legitimate by themselves, so that they can neither be identified as such nor blocked (and it may even be argued that this would constitute a form of censorship), but their aggregation may allow to uncover information that was intended to be private. For example the following three queries are all legitimate and refer to a potentially very large set of people in a population: "How many people have blue eyes?", "How many people earn between 50,000 and 55,000 euros?", and "How many people have blue eyes OR earn between 50,000 and 55,000 euros?". However, the attacker may combine the answers to those queries to compute how many people have blue eyes AND earn between 50,000 and 55,000 euros (e.g., by summing the answers to the first two queries and then subtracting the third one), which would not be an innocent query. In fact, the intersection of two large sets (those pertaining to the first two queries) may be quite small, even so small as to reveal a single person. The addition of noise to query answers has been considered so far the most effective way to circumvent this limitation.

Lately, it has been observed that the existence of correlation among the database entries may add to the problem, since it may reduce the masking effect of noise injection [11,15]. Those observations have been countered by the statement that differential privacy keeps its promise if you consider that is actually meant to help protect "my secret" (something I know and I don't want to disclose) rather than "a secret about me" (something I wish to protect that may however be known to others). But, quantifying the real promise of differential privacy (especially in presence of correlated data) is still a topic of research. The key indicator as to this effort is the parameter ϵ introduced in the definition of differential privacy, which symbolizes the actual disclosure level on the attributes of a record when noise is added to a query response.

However, there is not a general consensus on how that value should be set (and not even on the range of values it should take), though it is generally held that it should be a social choice, i.e., something that might be determined ex-ante by a "regulator" and generally accepted by people. A proposal to relate it to a statistically-sound decision criterion has been put forward in [14]. Actually, we will show that its value is tightly related to the database population distribution. More, it is a personal attribute. Each data subject has its own specific ϵ, depending on its dummy substitute Mr. Y (namely, on how eccentric Mr. X is in a dataset), and an overall "privacy expectation" (expected value of ϵ), strongly dependent on the distribution (shape and correlation structure) of the population to which it belongs.

3   A Case for the Emergence of Externalities

In Sect. 2 we have hinted that the differential privacy mechanism exhibits some limitations. In this section we show that the addition of (Laplace) noise may not be enough to prevent the attacker from inferring either Mr. X's data or even its presence in the database.

Our database may be subject to a variety of attackers. We consider the worst case of an attacker who knows as much about the sample as the database curator. Since the curator knows the whole database, we call this attacker an *oracle*. Any other attacker has a less complete knowledge than the oracle: whatever the oracle cannot do cannot be done by any other attacker *a fortiori*.

The database contains the data concerning Mr. X, which is the entity whose data we want to protect. The protection may consist in hiding either the values of Mr. X's attributes or its very same presence. The latter kind of protection is of course much stronger than the former.

A test to assess if the latter kind of protection is achieved may consist in allowing the oracle to put any query on two databases differing by just one single record (one of which contains the anonymized attributes of Mr. X) and see if the oracle is capable of correctly identifying the database containing Mr. X. We are not considering the repetition of the same query on the same database, since we have assumed that this attack is thwarted if we can identify semantically identical queries.

Let's consider the case of a set of localization data, which we can plot on the uv plane, where u and v represent the spatial coordinates of a subject. For the purpose of this example, we use a toy database, made of 4 points on the plane. We call this database $D1$ and show it in Fig. 1. The subject who is located at $(1, 1)$ is our Mr. X.

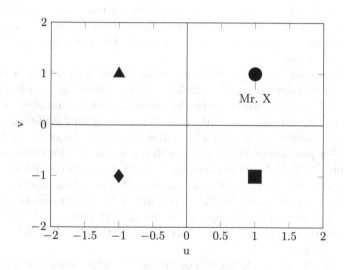

Fig. 1. True location database $D1$

Let's imagine the presence of an oracle, which, as previously stated, knows exactly the original location of all points of $D1$, including that of Mr. X.

According to the differential privacy scheme, the exact coordinates of each entity can be masked by adding Laplace noise. In Fig. 2 we report the location

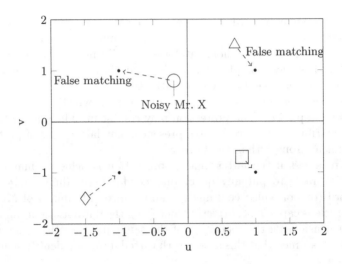

Fig. 2. Noisy location database $D1^*$ and matching assignments

of the entities after the addition of some noise. We call this noisy database $D1^*$ and keep the same set of symbols (though empty) as for $D1$ to represent the four subjects. Though the noisy locations are different from the true ones, they still retain some utility, e.g., since the addition of noise does not significantly alter the average distance of the points from the origin: in the case of Fig. 2 the true average distance is $\sqrt{2} \simeq 1.414$, while the noisy average distance is approximately 1.416.

The oracle could try to spot the presence of Mr. X by posing a number of queries to the two databases. The oracle could ask "How may people are located in Region R?". Alternatively, since the oracle knows the number of subjects contained in the database, it could ask "What is the probability of a generic subject to be located in Region R?". After querying, the oracle can actually spot the noisy position of Mr. X and match noisy and true locations, (e.g., by a simple minimum Euclidean distance algorithm that assigns the noisy location to the closest true point, which the oracle knows). However, this matching may not work. In our case, as shown in Fig. 2, two out of four assignments are correct, but there are two false matchings, since the subject represented by a triangle is matched with the true position of Mr. X, while the true Mr. X is assigned a different location.

Simply removing Mr. X would not protect it either, since the oracle would see two database differing by just one record (Mr. X) and would easily spot that containing Mr. X's data, i.e., that with the higher number or records.

If we now replace Mr. X by introducing a Mr. Y, drawn from the same general distribution of the database population, so as to hide the presence of Mr. X in the database, we get the database $D2^*$ and the oracle may arrive at the matchings reported in Fig. 3. For simplicity, we do not move the other points (actually, they would be located through the addition of newly generated noise, and their position would change). We see that the assignments do not change and the new Mr. Y is assigned the same wrong location as the previous noisy Mr. X. The two databases $D1^*$ and $D2^*$ are similarly puzzling to the oracle's eyes. The oracle cannot say which of the two databases contains Mr. X. Mr. X is therefore well protected, since its presence is hidden (which is a stronger protection than just hiding its exact location).

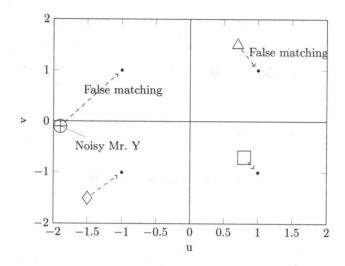

Fig. 3. Noisy location database $D2^*$ with Mr. X replaced by Mr. Y

Let's consider now an outlying Mr. X, whose true position is well removed from the other points. Let's call the resulting original database $D3$, which we can see in Fig. 4.

As in the previous case, the first protection measure is the addition of noise, so as to hide the true location of Mr. X. The resulting database $D3^*$ is shown in Fig. 5. Now we see that, nothwithstanding the addition of noise, by querying the database for the location of each entity and then performing, for instance, a minimum distance matching, the original location of Mr. X is anyway correctly recovered.

In this case, not even the replacement of Mr. X by Mr. Y helps. Introducing a dummy Mr. Y, which is generated according to the general distribution governing the position of the points in the database, produces, e.g., the noisy database $D4^*$ shown in Fig. 6. By putting a set of queries, the oracle is now able to compare the two databases $D3^*$ and $D4^*$, and guess which one contains Mr. X: in the matching assignment the point associated to the true location of Mr. X (which the oracle knows) in $D4^*$ (the triangle), is much farther away from the true location of Mr. X than the associated point (the circle) in $D3^*$. The oracle can therefore safely conclude that Mr. X must be in $D3^*$.

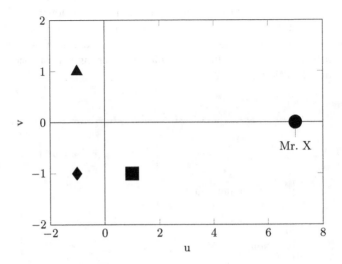

Fig. 4. True location database $D3$

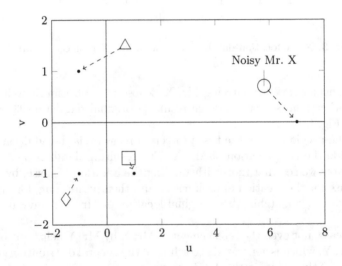

Fig. 5. Noisy location database $D3^*$ and matching assignments

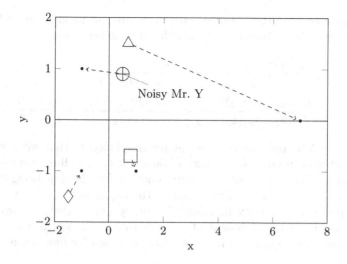

Fig. 6. Noisy location database $D4^*$ and matching assignments

4 The Likelihood Ratio

As recalled in Sect. 2, in the differential privacy approach we consider two databases differing just for one record. A random distortion is applied to those data so that any query on the two databases provides the same result, leaving the presence of that record masked. Actually, the result will never be exactly the same, but the extent to which the results differ is an indication of the (poor) level of privacy offered. Under a probabilistic framework, the difference in results can be measured through the likelihood ratio. In this section we wish to investigate the actual level of privacy achieved when the database is populated with data drawn from a certain distribution. In addition, we consider the impact of correlation.

Let's consider a vector $[x_1, x_2, \ldots, x_n]$ of true responses to a query, where $x_k = x$ for some $k \in \{1, 2, \ldots, n\}$ is a datum concerning me. Without loss of generality, let's suppose that we have $x_n = x$. The data are supplied in response to the query after addition of Laplace noise. The actual response to the query is then the vector $[z_1, z_2, \ldots, z_n]$, where $z_i = x_i + \eta_i$, with η_i, $i = 1, 2, \ldots, n$ being i.i.d. variables drawn from a Laplace distribution.

If the x value is replaced by a y value to mask the presence of x, the masking effect is accomplished if the likelihood ratio is quite close to 1, i.e. if the probability of getting the same response z is approximately equal when the true value is either x or y:

$$L = \frac{f_{x_1, x_2, \ldots, x_{n-1}, x}(\underline{z})}{f_{x_1, x_2, \ldots, x_{n-1}, y}(\underline{z})} \simeq 1 \tag{5}$$

In this case, it is quite hard to get back to the true value after we get the response $\underline{z}$.

If we assume that the database entries x_i are independent as well as the Laplace noise addition terms η_i, the likelihood ratio becomes

$$
\begin{aligned}
L &= \frac{f_{x_1}(z_1) \cdot f_{x_2}(z_2) \cdots f_{x_{n-1}}(z_{n-1}) f_{x_n}(z_n)}{f_{x_1}(z_1) \cdot f_{x_2}(z_2) \cdots f_{x_{n-1}}(z_{n-1}) f_y(z_n)} \\
&= \frac{f_{x_1}(z_1) \cdot f_{x_2}(z_2) \cdots f_{x_{n-1}}(z_{n-1}) l(z_n - x_n)}{f_{x_1}(z_1) \cdot f_{x_2}(z_2) \cdots f_{x_{n-1}}(z_{n-1}) l(z_n - y)} = \frac{l(z - x)}{l(z - y)},
\end{aligned}
\tag{6}
$$

where we have dropped the n subscript for simplicity, so that we refer to the database entry of interest as $x_n = x$, while the corresponding query output is $z = z_n$, and $l(\cdot)$ denotes a Laplace density function. For the time being we do not make any assumption on the distribution of the population, so that we consider a general probability density function $f(\cdot)$, but we know that, for any specific couple (x, y), the marginal density of z equals that of the added noise.

Since the general form of a Laplace probability density function is

$$
l(w) = \frac{\lambda}{2} e^{-\lambda |w|},
\tag{7}
$$

the likelihood ratio takes the following form:

$$
L = \frac{\frac{\lambda}{2} e^{-\lambda |z - x|}}{\frac{\lambda}{2} e^{-\lambda |z - y|}} = e^{\lambda(|z - y| - |z - x|)}.
\tag{8}
$$

The likelihood ratio just depends therefore on the quantity x to be hidden, the quantity y introduced to hide x and the observed quantity z. In order to solve the modulus function involved in the likelihood ratio, we must consider the following four different cases, which account for the position of z relative to x and y:

1. $z > \max(x, y)$;
2. $z < \min(x, y)$;
3. $x < z < y$;
4. $y < z < x$.

Let's consider each case separately.

In Case 1, the likelihood ratio becomes

$$
L = e^{\lambda(z - y - z + x)} = e^{\lambda(x - y)},
\tag{9}
$$

which is independent of the observed response z.

For Case 2, we likewise find

$$
L = e^{\lambda(y - z - x + z)} = e^{\lambda(y - x)}
\tag{10}
$$

In Case 3 we have instead

$$
L = e^{\lambda(y - z - z + x)} = \frac{e^{\lambda(x + y)}}{e^{2\lambda z}}
\tag{11}
$$

which is a decreasing function of z.

And finally in Case 4 we have

$$L = e^{\lambda(z-y-x+z)} = \frac{e^{2\lambda z}}{e^{\lambda(x+y)}},$$ (12)

which is an increasing function of z.

In order to get a grasp of the impact of the observed response z, we must build the picture piecewise. Let's consider for example two opposite cases, where $x = 1$, $y = 3$, and viceversa (for simplicity, we set $\lambda = 1$). When $x = 1$ and $y = 3$, the L vs z curve is piecewise made of Cases 2, 3, and 1 (in that order, as z grows), and is plotted in Fig. 7.

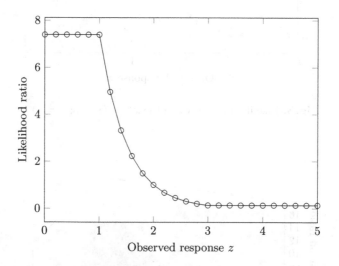

Fig. 7. Likelihood ratio when the $x < y$ ($x = 1$; $y = 3$)

If we reverse the values of x and y, we get instead Fig. 8 by crossing Cases 2, 4, and 1 as z grows.

In the end, the likelihood ratio varies in the range

$$e^{-\lambda|x-y|} \le L \le e^{\lambda|x-y|}$$ (13)

which sets an upper bound for the likelihood ratio that depends on the relative position of x and y, as well as on the amount of Laplace noise added. That upper bound is plotted in Fig. 9 for $\lambda = 1$.

Rather than looking at the upper bound on the likelihood ratio (and the resulting minimum guaranteed level of differential privacy), we can look at the average likelihood ratio, i.e. the average value of Eq. (8). Again, that ratio depends on the actual values of x (to be hidden), y (the data to be inserted in place of x to hide it), and z (the noisy value output by the database). For any

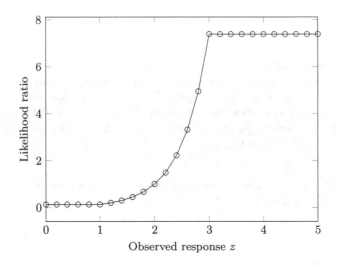

Fig. 8. Likelihood ratio when the $x > y$ (x = 3; y = 1)

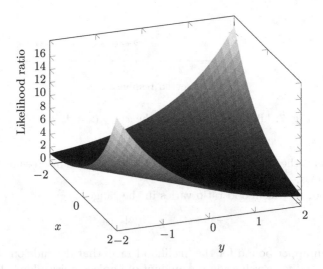

Fig. 9. Upper bound on the likelihood ratio

x, z is a random variable determined by the addition of Laplace noise η, and y is likewise a random variable drawn from the same distribution as the database population. Averaging is conducted with respect to both η and y through MonteCarlo simulation. Hereafter we assume that y follow a normal distribution $N(0, \sigma)$, and indicate the ratio of the standard deviations of the Laplace noise and y as r

$$r = \frac{\sqrt{2}}{\lambda \sigma}. \tag{14}$$

The likelihood ratio is therefore a function of x, λ, and σ. In Fig. 10 we plot the resulting average likelihood ratio (as averaged for both y and Laplace noise) when $\sigma = 1$ and for a range of values x of width 1σ around the central value $x = 0$. We see that the average likelihood ratio increases as x moves towards eccentric values, and increases faster as the amount of Laplace noise lowers. In order to get a likelihood ratio reasonably close to 1, we see that the amount of Laplace noise must be larger than twice the standard deviation of the database population, which may make the resulting output query useless. The resulting differential privacy level ϵ likewise worsens (its numerical value increases), as shown in Fig. 11.

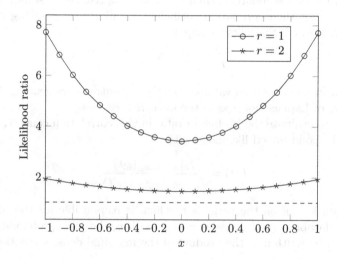

Fig. 10. Average likelihood ratio (uncorrelated database entries)

Let's consider instead the case of correlated database entries. We describe their correlation through a special case of the factor model introduced by Glasserman and Li [9], often named a Gaussian copula:

$$x_i = \sqrt{1 - \rho^2} v_i + \rho t \qquad i = 1, 2, \ldots, n \tag{15}$$

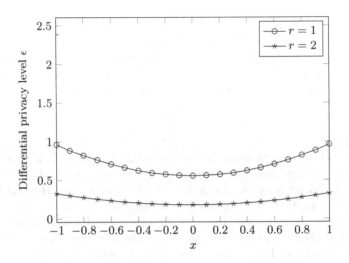

Fig. 11. Average differential privacy level (uncorrelated database entries)

where v_i are n i.i.d standard normal variables, t is likewise a standard normal variable, and ρ is their correlation coefficient. Similarly the masking variable y is generated through the following equation

$$y = \sqrt{1 - \rho^2}u + \rho t, \tag{16}$$

where u is a standard normal variable. The query outputs are generated through the addition of Laplace noise as in the uncorrelated case.

In order to evaluate the likelihood ratio in this correlation context, we introduce first the conditioned likelihood ratio

$$L(t) = \frac{f_{x_1, x_2, \ldots, x_n}(\underline{z}|t)}{f_{x_1, x_2, \ldots, x_{n-1}, y}(\underline{z}|t)}. \tag{17}$$

Due to conditioning on the variable t, which is responsible for the correlation among the database entries x_i's as well as with y, the joint probability density function can be written as the product of the marginal density functions:

$$\begin{aligned}
L(t) &= \frac{f_{x_1}(z_1|t), f_{x_2}(z_2|t), \ldots, f_{x_{n-1}}(z_{n-1}|t) f_{x_n}(z_n|t)}{f_{x_1}(z_1|t), f_{x_2}(z_2), \ldots, f_{x_{n-1}}(z_{n-1}|t) f_y(z_n|t)} \\
&= \frac{f_{x_1}(z_1|t), f_{x_2}(z_2|t), \ldots, f_{x_{n-1}}(z_{n-1}|t) l(z_n - x_n|t)}{f_{x_1}(z_1|t), f_{x_2}(z_2), \ldots, f_{x_{n-1}}(z_{n-1}|t) l(z_n - y|t)} = \frac{l(z - x|t)}{l(z - y|t)}.
\end{aligned} \tag{18}$$

In order to obtain the likelihood ratio, we now have to saturate with respect to the variable t

$$L = \int_{-\infty}^{+\infty} L(t)f(t)dt = \int_{-\infty}^{+\infty} \frac{l(z-x|t)}{l(z-y|t)}f(t)dt$$

$$= \int_{-\infty}^{+\infty} \frac{\frac{\lambda}{2}e^{-|z-x-t|}}{\frac{\lambda}{2}e^{-|z-y-t|}} \frac{1}{\sqrt{2\pi}} e^{-\frac{t^2}{2}} dt \tag{19}$$

$$= \frac{1}{\sqrt{2\pi}} \int_{-\infty}^{+\infty} e^{-\lambda(|z-x-t|-|z-y-t|)} e^{-\frac{t^2}{2}} dt$$

We can now exploit the relationship between the variables involved in Eq. (19):

$$z - x - t = x + \eta - x - t = \eta - t$$
$$z - y - t = x + \eta - \sqrt{1-\rho^2}u - \rho t - t = x + \eta - \sqrt{1-\rho^2}u - t(1+\rho) \tag{20}$$

The likelihood ratio can be finally written as

$$L = \frac{1}{\sqrt{2\pi}} \int_{-\infty}^{+\infty} e^{-\lambda(|\eta-t|-|x+\eta-\sqrt{1-\rho^2}u-t(1+\rho)|)} e^{-\frac{t^2}{2}} dt, \tag{21}$$

which is a function of the random couple $\{\eta, u\}$ taking values over $\mathbf{R}^2$.

We can average its value over the whole range of values taken by u and η. The resulting average likelihood ratio, obtained through MonteCarlo simulation with 100,000 instances, is shown in Figs. 12, 14, and 16 respectively for $\rho = 0.2, 0.5, 0.8$. The associated differential privacy levels are shown in Figs. 13, 15 and 17. As can be seen, correlation increases the average likelihood ratio, therefore lowering the level of differential privacy that can be achieved. This is clearly shown in Figs. 18 and 19, which are plotted for an eccentric value of x.

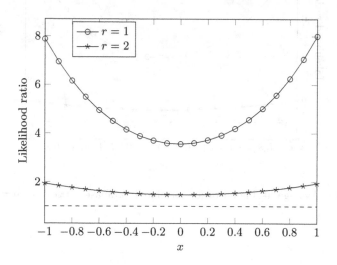

Fig. 12. Average likelihood ratio (correlated database entries) for $\rho = 0.2$

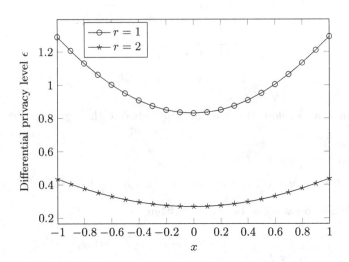

Fig. 13. Average differential privacy level (correlated database entries) for $\rho = 0.2$

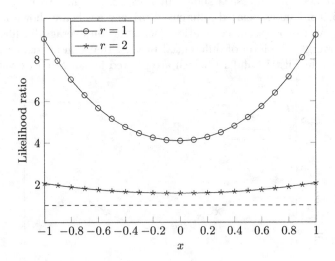

Fig. 14. Average likelihood ratio (correlated database entries) for $\rho = 0.5$

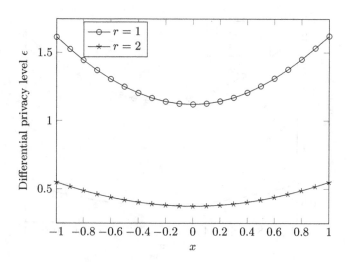

Fig. 15. Average differential privacy level (correlated database entries) for $\rho = 0.5$

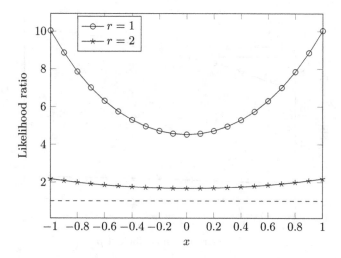

Fig. 16. Average likelihood ratio (correlated database entries) for $\rho = 0.8$

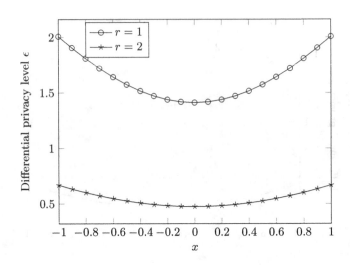

Fig. 17. Average differential privacy level (correlated database entries) for $\rho = 0.8$

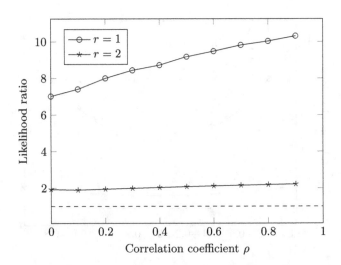

Fig. 18. Average likelihood ratio for $x = 1$

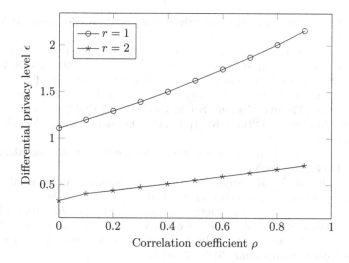

Fig. 19. Average differential privacy level for $x = 1$

5   Conclusions

Both the cases of independent and correlated data base entries show that the privacy level ϵ is a feature of the population statistical characteristics rather than the result of a social choice. In addition, it depends on the specific data subject whose data we want to protect. A natural consequence is that the population's statistical characteristics have to be investigated to determine the level of privacy that can be achieved (and if it can be achieved for all the subjects or just some).

As to the measures that can be implemented to obtain the desired level of privacy, the addition of noise is a valid tool, but determining the right amount of noise level is a critical task. Again, we may not have a good-for-all value, but it has rather to be determined specifically for each data subject, with the presence of correlation playing a role as well. It is anyway a tool that cannot be overused, since adding too much noise would make the query output useless.

References

1. Adam, N.R., Worthmann, J.C.: Security-control methods for statistical databases: a comparative study. ACM Comput. Surv. (CSUR) **21**(4), 515–556 (1989)
2. Agrawal, R., Srikant, R.: Privacy-preserving data mining. ACM Sigmod Rec. **29**(2), 439–450 (2000)
3. D'Acquisto, G., Domingo-Ferrer, J., Kikiras, P., Torra, V., de Montjoye, Y., Bourka, A.: Privacy by design in big data: An overview of privacy enhancing technologies in the era of big data analytics. CoRR, arXiv Preprint Series abs/1512.06000 (2015). http://arxiv.org/abs/1512.06000
4. Dwork, C.: Differential privacy: a survey of results. In: Agrawal, M., Du, D., Duan, Z., Li, A. (eds.) TAMC 2008. LNCS, vol. 4978, pp. 1–19. Springer, Heidelberg (2008). doi:10.1007/978-3-540-79228-4_1

5. Dwork, C.: A firm foundation for private data analysis. Commun. ACM **54**(1), 86–95 (2011)
6. Dwork, C., McSherry, F., Nissim, K., Smith, A.: Calibrating noise to sensitivity in private data analysis. In: Halevi, S., Rabin, T. (eds.) TCC 2006. LNCS, vol. 3876, pp. 265–284. Springer, Heidelberg (2006). doi:10.1007/11681878_14
7. Dwork, C., Roth, A., et al.: The algorithmic foundations of differential privacy. Found. Trends Theoret. Comput. Sci. **9**(3–4), 211–407 (2014)
8. Elliot, M., Mackey, E., O'Hara, K., Tudor, C.: The anonymisation decision-making framework (2016)
9. Glasserman, P., Li, J.: Importance sampling for portfolio credit risk. Manage. Sci. **51**(11), 1643–1656 (2005)
10. Hsu, J., Gaboardi, M., Haeberlen, A., Khanna, S., Narayan, A., Pierce, B.C., Roth, A.: Differential privacy: an economic method for choosing epsilon. In: 2014 IEEE 27th Computer Security Foundations Symposium (CSF), pp. 398–410. IEEE (2014)
11. Liu, C., Chakraborty, S., Mittal, P.: Dependence makes you vulnerable: Differential privacy under dependent tuples. In: Proceedings of the Network and Distributed System Security Symposium (NDSS 2016) (2016)
12. Naldi, M., D'Acquisto, G.: Option pricing in a privacy-aware market. In: 2015 IEEE Conference on Communications and Network Security (CNS), pp. 759–760, September 2015
13. Naldi, M., D'Acquisto, G.: Differential privacy for counting queries: can bayes estimation help uncover the true value? arXiv preprint arXiv:1407.0116 (2014)
14. Naldi, M., D'Acquisto, G.: Differential privacy: An estimation theory-based method for choosing epsilon. CoRR, arXiv Preprint Series abs/1510.00917 (2015). http://arxiv.org/abs/1510.00917
15. Sankar, L., Rajagopalan, S.R., Poor, H.V.: Utility-privacy tradeoffs in databases: an information-theoretic approach. IEEE Trans. Inform. Forensics Secur. **8**(6), 838–852 (2013)
16. Sarathy, R., Muralidhar, K.: Evaluating laplace noise addition to satisfy differential privacy for numeric data. Trans. Data Priv. **4**(1), 1–17 (2011)
17. Shoshani, A.: Statistical databases: characteristics, problems, and some solutions. In: Proceedings of the 8th International Conference on Very Large Data Bases, pp. 208–222. Morgan Kaufmann Publishers Inc. (1982)
18. Wasserman, L., Zhou, S.: A statistical framework for differential privacy. J. Am. Stat. Assoc. **105**(489), 375–389 (2010)

Diffix: High-Utility Database Anonymization

Paul Francis[1(✉)], Sebastian Probst Eide[2], and Reinhard Munz[1]

[1] Max Planck Institute for Software Systems, Kaiserslautern, Saarbrücken, Germany
{francis,munz}@mpi-sws.org
[2] Aircloak GmbH, Kaiserslautern, Germany
sebastian@aircloak.com

Abstract. In spite of the tremendous privacy and liability benefits of anonymization, most shared data today is only pseudonymized. The reason is simple: there haven't been any anonymization technologies that are general purpose, easy to use, and preserve data quality. This paper presents the design of Diffix, a new approach to database anonymization that promises to break new ground in the utility/privacy trade-off. Diffix acts as an SQL proxy between the analyst and an unmodified live database. Diffix adds a minimal amount of noise to answers—Gaussian with a standard deviation of only two for counting queries—and places no limit on the number of queries an analyst may make. Diffix works with any type of data and configuration is simple and data-independent: the administrator does not need to consider the identifiability or sensitivity of the data itself. This paper presents a high-level but complete description of Diffix. It motivates the design through examples of attacks and defenses, and provides some evidence for how Diffix can provide strong anonymity with such low noise levels.

Keywords: Privacy · Anonymity · Analytics · Database

1 Introduction

The General Data Protection Regulation (GDPR) makes a distinction between *anonymization* and *pseudonymization*. Anonymized data "are outside the remit of data protection" [10]: none of the provisions in the GDPR for protecting personal data need apply. When data is anonymized, individuals cannot be "singled out", at least not without undue cost and effort. Pseudonymization—replacing Personally Identifying Information (PII) with irreversible identifiers—still allows for identifying individuals, typically through the use of external knowledge about those individuals [1]. The GDPR considers pseudonymized data to be personal data that must be protected, thus limiting its legal use.

The GDPR strongly encourages the use of anonymization, and wants to make it clear that pseudonymization is not enough. The problem is that anonymization renders data useless for most analytic needs. At best, substantial expertise and effort is required to anonymize data, and even then it is extremely difficult to

© Springer International Publishing AG 2017
E. Schweighofer et al. (Eds.): APF 2017, LNCS 10518, pp. 141–158, 2017.
DOI: 10.1007/978-3-319-67280-9_8

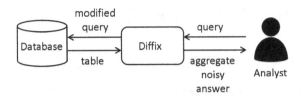

Fig. 1. Diffix acts as an SQL proxy to an unmodified database

determine whether data has been adequately anonymized or not[1]. Organizations that wish to share data are caught in a no-win situation: they can't share the data either because anonymization destroys the data, or because they are prevented from doing so because of concerns over legal liability.

This paper presents Diffix, a new approach to anonymization that substantially increases the utility of anonymized data while at the same time requiring no specialized expertise to configure. As Fig. 1 illustrates, Diffix operates as an SQL proxy between the analyst and an unmodified database (which does not have to be a database with an SQL interface). Analysts submit standard SQL queries to Diffix, which in turn queries the database and computes a noisy answer that it returns to the analyst. The amount of noise is minimal (Sect. 7): typically Gaussian with a standard deviation of two for counting queries (those that count distinct users). Analysts may make an unlimited number of queries to the database. There is no restriction on the data types in the database, including for instance free text and event sequences.

Sections 2 through 4 describe the problem, state assumptions, and give related work. Sections 5 and 6 describe Diffix. Section 7 presents evidence to justify Diffix's low noise levels. Finally, Sect. 8 states the limitations of this work, and outlines the future research agenda for Diffix.

2   Why Is Anonymization so Difficult?

For many decades before the advent of computers, census bureaus had the mandate to release statistical data while protecting privacy. This was historically done by releasing aggregate statistics—numbers that pertain to at least K individuals. Computer technology opened the possibility of releasing far more statistics, indeed of letting the public query data directly to produce whatever statistics might be of interest. As early as 1972, however, it was understood that simply withholding answers that pertain to fewer than K individuals does not adequately protect privacy [8].

---

[1] For example, a state-of-the-art anonymization tool is ARX [9]. Usage of this tool requires among many other things that the user is able to classify data as identifying, quasi-identifying, sensitive, and insensitive; can create masking-based, interval-based, or order-based generalization hierarchies; and can understand and configure privacy models such as δ-presence, l-diversity, t-closeness, δ-disclosure, k-Anonymity, k-Map, (ϵ,δ)-differential privacy, and risk-based privacy models for prosecutor, journalist and marketer risks.

The central problem is the *intersection attack*. By way of example, imagine a database that only returns answers that pertain to more than $K = 4$ individuals. Suppose that an analyst makes two queries, one for the number of people in the CS department, and one for the number of men in the CS department:

SELECT count(*) FROM table WHERE dept = 'CS' AND gender = 'M'	SELECT count(*) FROM table WHERE dept = 'CS'

Suppose that there are 34 people in the CS department, and 33 men. Since both of these numbers are greater than 4, the database returns the answers. The analyst can trivially conclude that there is one woman in the CS department even though the database would have refused to provide that answer directly. Armed with this knowledge, the analyst can then learn more about the woman. For instance, the analyst can query for the sum of salaries of all people in the CS department and the sum of salaries of all men in the CS department, and by taking the difference determine the salary of the woman:

SELECT sum(salary) FROM table WHERE dept = 'CS' AND gender = 'M'	SELECT sum(salary) FROM table WHERE dept = 'CS'

In 1979, it was shown that an analyst with no prior knowledge about the contents of a K-limiting database that gives exact answers can infer substantial information about individual users using the intersection attack [3]. It was also shown that one way to prevent the intersection attack is to distort answers unpredictably, for instance by randomly rounding user counts up or down to a value divisible by five [7,8] or removing random rows from the set of matching rows [2].

The problem of course is that random noise can be eliminated through averaging: causing a given answer to be repeated and taking the average value. In [2], Denning et al. make the following statement:

> Rounding by adding a zero-mean random value (noise) is insecure since the correct answer can be deduced by averaging a sufficient number of responses to the same query. Rounding by adding a pseudorandom value that depends on the data is preferable, because then a given query always returns the same response.

Contrary to their own advice, Denning et al. proposed using a pseudo-random value that depends not on the data, but rather on the query syntax. In this way, repetitions of a given query produce the same random sequence and therefore the same noisy answer. The problem with this solution, which the authors recognized, is that the analyst can still average out the noise by generating multiple different queries that all produce the same result, for instance by adding non-affecting conditions like "age < 1000".

Since 2003 [4] there has been renewed interest from the CS research community in the idea of adding random noise to answers, especially in the context of differential privacy [5]. With the exception of Rappor [6], however, to our knowledge all differential privacy proposals are susceptible to the averaging attack[2]. This inevitably leads to large amounts of noise and/or restrictions on the number of queries an analyst can make. Arguably these shortcomings are responsible for the overall lack of practical uptake of differential privacy.

Rappor, which we understand to be deployed by Google, is a distributed system whereby queries are sent to clients, each of which holds purely local information nominally about one user. Noise is derived from the fact that clients may lie about their data (randomized response). Rappor allows repeated answers without additional loss of privacy through a memoization feature: clients return the same randomized response to the same query as long as the true answer hasn't changed. The randomized response approach however results in a substantial amount of noise—distinct counts may be off by several hundred.

3   Measure of Anonymity

This paper measures anonymity in terms of the confidence with which the analyst can single out a user; that is determine that a single user has one or more given attribute values. With an intersection attack, an analyst can single out a user with a set of exact answers. Therefore, from the point of view of Diffix, anonymity is defined in terms of the confidence with which an analyst can determine the exact number of users that have one or more given attribute values. For instance, in the context of the intersection attack example in Sect. 1, the analyst wants to determine the exact number of people in the CS department and the exact number of men in the CS department. We refer to each such determination as a *guess*. We consider Diffix's anonymity to be strong when:

- The confidence the analyst has in a guess is not substantially higher than a guess the analyst could have made purely with external knowledge, or
- The probability of a substantially higher-confidence guess is very low.

This definition of privacy is similar to that used by Denning [3] as well as by the European Union Article 29 Data Protection Working Party Opinion on Anonymization [1]. Both of these focus on the ability to single out a user. In the case of Denning; the ability to identify that a given user has (or doesn't have) a given attribute value. In the case of Article 29; by identifying a user's records in a database. Diffix differs from these in that it incorporates the analyst's confidence and the probability of obtaining that confidence.

4   Assumptions and Terminology

Our system setup consists of an *analyst* that queries a *database* via Diffix (Fig. 1). The database is conceptually a single table organized as rows and columns. The

---

[2] Despite the thousands of papers on anonymity we could only find two that try to add noise in a way that depends on the data [2,6]. This is why the paper cites so little related work.

columns may be of any type, so long as there are equalities and inequalities defined for the type (e.g. *column = value* or *column < value*) returning TRUE or FALSE. The database holds "raw" data: no perturbation on the values in the database is required, and no columns need be removed, for instance those containing personally identifying information like names.

We refer to the entity whose privacy is being protected as the *user*. The user may well be a device like a smartphone or a vehicle or even an organization. We require that each database table with individual user data has a column containing user identifiers. This is typically nothing more than the Primary Key or Foreign Key in the relational database. By convention we call this column the *uid*. We assume that every distinct user has one and only one distinct uid. A user may of course have more than one row.

The database may change over time. However, to protect anonymity in the face of changes, all changes to the database must be timestamped.

Diffix must be configured to know (1) which column contains the timestamps, and (2) which column contains the uids. No other data-specific configuration is required. Critically, the system operator need not understand the semantics of any other columns.

The amount of noise proposed in this paper assumes no strong correlations between columns among groups of users. If such correlations exist, and there is a risk that an analyst knows of the correlation, then the amount of noise must be increased in proportion to the size of the correlated group.

An analyst may make an unlimited number of queries.

Analysts may have substantial knowledge about the contents of the database, including full knowledge of most columns and full or nearly full knowledge of most rows.

This paper does not address timing or other side-channel attacks.

5 Diffix: A New Approach to Anonymization

As stated earlier, Diffix is deployed as an SQL proxy sitting between the analyst and a live database (Fig. 1). The analyst could be a human or an application. The database could have an SQL interface or some other interface. In principle, Diffix does not have to be SQL-based, but as we discuss later Diffix needs to understand certain semantics of the query, so the query language should at least be simple, or composed of a simple subset of a more complex language like SQL.

5.1 Query Syntax

For the purposes of this paper we assume a simple SQL structure as follows:

```
SELECT columns, stat_functions()
FROM table
WHERE condition AND condition [ AND ... ]
GROUP BY columns
```

Here *stat_functions()* refers to statistical functions executed by Diffix that add noise to answers. The current implementation has the statistical functions count, sum, average, standard deviation, min, max, and median, but in principle Diffix could compute a wide variety of statistical functions.

The syntax for a condition is limited to 'column operator constant', where the operator includes equalities '=' and '<>' (not equal), inequalities '>=' and '<'. Inequalities must define a *range*, with '>=' on the left and '<' on the right.

Our implementation in fact supports a richer though still not complete subset of SQL. Notably, it allows JOIN operations, sub-queries (nested SELECT statements), a variety of math, string, and date functions, and SQL aggregate functions with GROUP BY. Diffix also places some limitations on the SQL. With the exception of the IN statement, the implementation prevents union semantics: OR for instance is disallowed. The implementation also places limits on the granularity of inequalities (greater than or less than), described further in Sect. 5.5.

Ensuring that the analyst cannot bypass these and other limitations entails considerable complexity and is outside the scope of this paper.

5.2   Key Insights

Our work on Diffix essentially picks up where Denning left off in 1980: that is, to *add noise, but make the noise dependent on the data*. In this paper, we refer to this general idea as *sticky noise*. Because the intersection attack depends on the analyst controlling the set of users that comprise a query answer, a natural design choice would be to make the noise dependent on the set of users that comprise a given answer. For instance, we could derive the seed for the Pseudo-Random Number Generator (PRNG) that produces the noise from the distinct set of users. This would defeat a naive averaging attack because the same answer would always have the same noise.

There are, however, two classes of attack against which this simple notion of sticky noise does not defend. The underlying problem is that this simple sticky noise defends against single repeated answers, but does not defend against combinations of answers. One class of attack is averaging attacks that exploit groups of answers. The other class is difference attacks. These exploit the mere fact that a pair of answers differ. In the following we give one example of each.

Split Averaging Attack. Consider the following attack, which we call the *split averaging attack*. The analyst produces the pair of queries shown in Fig. 2.

The sum of the counts of the two queries gives the number of users in the CS department, plus noise (here assuming that there is one row per distinct uid). Now repeat the pair of queries, this time using age=21 and age<>21. This produces the same sum, but with a different noise sample because each individual answer is different. The pairs can be repeated with age=22, 23, 24, and so on. With enough samples, the noise can be averaged away and a high-confidence exact count produced. Given exact counts, the analyst could then for instance carry out an intersection attack [3].

```
SELECT count(*) FROM table        SELECT count(*) FROM table
WHERE dept = 'CS' AND             WHERE dept = 'CS' AND
       salary = 100000 AND               salary = 100000
       gender = 'M'
```

Fig. 2. One pair of queries from a split averaging attack to learn exact count of people in the CS dept. Subsequent query pairs use `age=21, 22, ...`

Difference Attack. For this attack, suppose that an analyst happens to know that there is only a single woman in the CS department. Let's call her the victim. The analyst could form the two queries shown in Fig. 3.

```
SELECT salary, count(*)           SELECT salary, count(*)
FROM table                        FROM table
WHERE dept = 'CS' AND             WHERE dept = 'CS'
       gender = 'M'               GROUP BY salary
GROUP BY salary
```

Fig. 3. Difference attack to learn the woman's salary

Both queries produce a histogram of salary counts. The left query definitely excludes the victim from all answers. The right includes the victim only in the bucket that matches her salary. If there is any pair of answers whose values differ, regardless of the values of the reported noisy counts, then the analyst knows that the victim is included in the right-side bucket and therefore knows her salary.

We call this a *difference attack*, because analysts need only detect a difference in two answers—they don't care what the values are.

Key Insight: Noise Layers. Looking at both attacks, we observe that the analyst must modify *conditions* (e.g. `dept='CS'` or `gender='M'`) to carry out the attack. Suppose that, rather than add a single noise value for a single answer, we additionally add a noise value *per condition*?

For the moment, let's assume that these per-condition noise values are sticky in that the same condition produces the same noise value. Looking at the split averaging attack of Fig. 2, we see that each query would have three noise values: one based on the set of users, one based on the condition `dept='CS'`, and one based on the age condition (`age=XX` or `age<>XX`). The `uid`- and `age`-based noise values would change with each query, and so could be averaged away. The `dept='CS'` noise, however, would always be the same and could not be averaged away. The final averaged count would be perturbed by the `dept='CS'` noise layer. Let's refer to this noise layer as the *static condition* noise layer (or just *static* noise layer for short).

The static noise layer prevents the difference attack *as executed above*: the queries on the left would have the `gender='M'` noise layer, while the queries on the right would not. Therefore the right and left answer would vary for every pair, not just the pair matching the woman's salary. The analyst, however, could simply observe that for every pair but one, the difference between the left and the right is the same. By way of example, suppose that the `gender='M'` layer always adds 2 to the count. For the buckets not matching the woman's salary, the `uid`- and `dept`-based noise layers are the same. The only difference is from the `gender='M'` layer and so for all these buckets the left answer is exactly 2 greater than the right answer. If this is not the case for one of the bucket pairs, then it can only be because the woman is in the right-hand bucket. Thus the analyst learns her salary. We call this the *first-derivative difference attack*, because the analyst is looking for a difference in the difference.

The first-derivative difference attack can be solved with one more per-condition noise layer. This noise layer is dependent on the combination of condition and distinct set of users. We call this the *dynamic condition* noise layer, or just *dynamic* noise layer for short. Now, because every bucket has a different set of users, the dynamic noise layer for `gender='M'` changes with each bucket. This forces a pseudo-random difference in the count of each bucket pair, thus preventing the attack.

5.3 Details of Layered Sticky Noise

Figure 4 illustrates the overall anonymization process in Diffix.

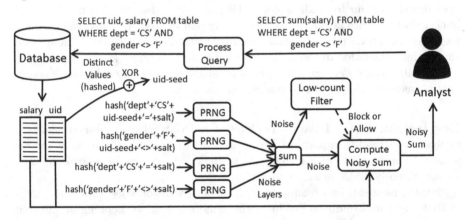

Fig. 4. Sticky noise layers and sticky noisy threshold.

Each static noise layer is generated by seeding a PRNG with a hash of the following parameters concatenated together:

1. The column name (normalized, e.g. all lower case, unicode).
2. One of the following:
   (a) If the condition is an equality (= or <>), the value of the constant in the condition.
   (b) Otherwise if the condition is the result of a GROUP BY clause, the corresponding reported value,

(c) Otherwise if the condition is a range, then the values of the two constants that define the range.

3. The condition operator (= or <> or 'range').

4. A secret salt that does not change from query to query.

Each dynamic noise layer additionally includes a value generated from the XOR of the hashes of the distinct uid's.

The PRNG, so seeded, then generates a zero-mean value from a Gaussian distribution[3] with a standard deviation appropriate to the required amount of noise (see Sects. 6 and 7). Note that all but the first of any repeated condition is removed from the query, and does not result in a new noise layer. In our current implementation, the standard deviation for each noise layer is $\sigma = 1$ for counting queries (counting distinct users). The standard deviation of the summed noise layers is then $\sigma = \sqrt{N}$, where N is the number of layers.

This is illustrated in Fig. 4. The query requests the sum of salaries for men in the CS department. Diffix modifies the query to obtain the uid and salary columns from the database. The query has two conditions, dept='CS' and gender<>'F'. These are used to generate the seeds for each condition's corresponding static and dynamic noise layers. The four resulting noise layers are summed to produce a final noise value, which is in turn used by two functions: one that computes the noisy sum of salaries, and the low-count filter, described next.

5.4   Sticky Noisy Threshold

A valuable feature of any database system is the ability to discover the contents of columns. For instance, suppose a database contains the search strings that users submitted to a search engine. An analyst cannot know in advance the searches that have been made, and so would like to discover what the strings are. Diffix supports this feature through the GROUP BY clause, but only reports a given column value or combination of column values when at least some small number of distinct users have that value or combination of values. This feature is called *low-count filter*: any response is silently suppressed if fewer than some small number of distinct users have that value.

This "small number" is not a hard-coded constant, but rather a *sticky noisy threshold*. Specifically, the threshold is sticky noise with mean K. Only if the number of distinct users that share a value exceeds the noisy value with mean K is the value reported.

In our implementation, $K = 4$, and the standard deviation of each noise layer is $\sigma = 1/2$. For example, if there are four noise layers (i.e. two each from two conditions), then the standard deviation is $\sigma = 1$. In addition, any bucket with two or fewer users is always filtered.

The reason we use a noisy threshold instead of a hard-coded threshold is that a hard-coded threshold K_h would allow an analyst to make a 100% confidence

---

[3] Distributions other than Gaussian may serve better, but in any event the noise is small and so we haven't yet explored this question.

guess in those cases where the analyst knows that a given count of distinct users is either K_h or $K_h + 1$. The noisy threshold lowers an analyst confidence with high probability even when an analyst has this knowledge.

5.5   Layered Sticky Noise with Range Shifting Attacks

The layered noise mechanism described so far defends against difference attacks that remove conditions from a query. Ranges allow difference attacks that don't require removing a condition, but rather that simply adjust the range.

As an example, suppose that the analyst has access to a company database that includes entry and exit times for all employees. The analyst knows an employee (the victim) that left the building at 14:26 on a given day, that no other employees left 2 min before and after, and that the employee didn't again exit the building until the next day around 17:00. The analyst could then learn the salary of the victim with pairs of queries like the following (Fig. 5):

SELECT count(*) FROM table
WHERE salary = 100000 AND
    exit >= '2015-06-17 14:27:00' AND
    exit < '2015-06-18 16:00:00' AND
	SELECT count(*) FROM table
	WHERE salary = 100000 AND
	    exit >= '2015-06-17 14:25:00' AND
	    exit < '2015-06-18 16:00:00' AND

Fig. 5. Range-based difference attack to learn the victim's salary. Subsequent pairs of queries would modify the range a small amount (14:25:01, 14:25:02, ...) so as to average away the range noise layers.

The query on the left excludes the victim while the query on the right includes the victim only if the salary is \$100K. Note that the time ranges are large enough that the analyst is confident that there are enough users with that salary to ensure that the low-count filter is bypassed. With only a single pair of queries, the noise layers associated with the ranges cause the two queries to (probably) differ whether or not the victim is present. The analyst, however, can average away the range noise layers by incrementally modifying the range (e.g. '14:25:01', '14:25:02', etc.) so that the noise is different but the set of users included in the range remains the same.

To defend against this, Diffix limits the granularity of ranges by "snapping" ranges into pre-defined sizes and offsets. Analysts are limited to these pre-defined *snapped alignments*. Diffix then adds static and dynamic noise layers based on the constants that define the boundaries of the range.

The basic idea of snapped alignment is that sizes are confined to an exponentially growing and shrinking set of values, and offsets fall on multiples of the size. For natural numbers, in our implementation we have chosen sizes from the set of values $\pm 1x10^N$, $\pm 2x10^N$, and $\pm 5x10^N$ where N is any positive or negative integer. This defines the sequence $[..., 0.1, 0.2, 0.5, 1, 2, 5, 10, 20, 50, ...]$ along with the corresponding negative numbers. Offsets are set at even multiples of the size, and are allowed to be shifted left or right by 1/2 the size.

Resulting valid ranges include $[1, 2)$, $[20, 40)$, and $[0.01, 0.015)$. These can be shifted by $1/2$ to create valid ranges $[1.5, 2.5)$, $[30, 50)$, and $[0.0125, 0.0175)$. Invalid ranges include $[1.1, 2.1)$, $[30, 49)$, and $[0.01, 0.014)$.

There is nothing special about this specific choice of snapped alignment. They could just as well have been defined as powers of 2. We choose this "125" sequence because we believe that analysts will find it more natural than powers of 2. (Money typically comes in these denominations for the same reason.)

For datetimes, it is convenient to use the natural boundaries of for instance years, months, days, hours, minutes, and seconds. Within these units, we specify additional natural ranges. For instance, within years we further define 2, 3, 4, and 6 month intervals, and within days, we define 2, 4, 6, and 12 h intervals.

In addition, Diffix imposes a maximum allowed range. The purpose is to prevent the analyst from averaging away the noise layers associated with a range by using a sequence of queries that grow the range. Diffix computes the maximum range by executing the anonymized min and max functions (Sect. 6.2), and then computing the smallest snapped range that encompasses this max and min. Any query whose range exceeds the maximum allowed range is rejected.

With snapped alignment, the above attack no longer works because the analyst cannot make a pair of ranges that on the one hand includes and excludes the victim, but on the other hand includes enough other users that the queries are not low-count filtered.

Of course there may well be cases where attacks with snapped ranges can in principle be formed. For instance, suppose that the victim happened to be the only employee to work on a given Sunday and didn't work on the following Monday. The analyst could then generate a query with a 2-day range of Sunday and Monday, and a second query only covering Monday. Both of these ranges adhere to snapped alignment, but nevertheless constitute a difference attack.

The noise layers associated with the range defends against this attack. The two queries would have a differently seeded noise layers, and so the answers may differ whether or not the victim is present.

5.6   Time Epochs for Difference Attacks on Changing Databases

All of the difference attacks described so far assume that the pair of queries operates on the same data. If the database changes (data is added, removed, or modified), and the analyst knows that the change is for only a single user, then the analyst can potentially execute a difference attack merely by executing the same query before and after the change.

To deal with this, Diffix defines a hierarchy of time epochs. Updates to the database after the last complete epoch are not included in answers. If for instance the smallest epoch is one day, then on any given day, only the database updates to the end of the previous day can be queried. For example, in Fig. 6, a query made at the time labeled *now* would query the database as updated at the end of the day labeled y. For the hierarchy, each higher-level epoch may for instance double in length. So for instance the 1-day epochs $(r - z)$ may fall under 2-day epochs $(f - j)$, which fall under 4-day epochs $(c - e)$, and so on.

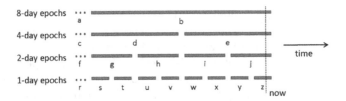

Fig. 6. Hierarchy of time epochs

One way to protect against this difference attack is to add two layers of noise for every epoch within which the query falls. So for instance the query done *now* would have layers of noise seeded by the epochs z, j, e, and b. As a result, relative to a query made at any previous point in time, there is a level in the hierarchy where on one hand a noise value differs, while on the other hand there are not enough differing noise values that the analyst can average away the noise. For instance, suppose that a single user change occurs during epoch s, and no change occurs between then and *now*. Even if the analyst queries every day and averages away the noise from the 1-day epochs, the 4-day epochs d and e would force a different noise value without being averaged away. This approach has the advantage of simplicity, but can result in a substantial amount of noise.

Another approach that doesn't require noise layers, but is more complex, is to dynamically determine which is the latest update that may be safely used. This can be done by finding a pair of adjacent epochs, at any level of the hierarchy, whereby the difference in distinct users between answers exceeds a noisy threshold. The query is then answered from the first epoch of the pair.

For example, suppose that the difference in distinct users between 1-day epochs s and t exceeds the noisy threshold. Later repeats of the query all give the same answer, that of epoch s. Now suppose that the difference between epochs x and y exceeds the noisy threshold. Subsequent to this, answers may be given from epoch x. These answers will differ enough from the epoch s answers to hide changes due to any single user.

The use of higher-level epochs avoids the situation where the database changes slowly, but never enough to exceed the noisy threshold between adjacent epochs. Were this to happen, answers would become less accurate over time. Higher-level epochs captures these changes. For instance, suppose that a big enough change occurs between 1-day epochs s and t, but only small changes occurs afterwards. If the change between for instance 2-day epochs h and i exceeds the noisy threshold, then answers from epoch h may be released.

6 Anonymous Statistical Functions

To this point, we've described how we produce sticky noise, but not exactly how the noise is used in statistical functions. Currently our Diffix implementation can compute and add noise to the following statistical functions: count, sum, average, standard deviation, min, max, and median.

Of these, there are two types of statistical functions. One returns a value for an individual row (i.e. the value of a single user). These include min, max, and median, which (in the absence of noise) return the value of the single user with the min, max, or median value. We refer to these as *single-row* statistical functions. The other type of statistical function returns an answer that is a composite of all values. These include count, sum, avg, and stddev, and are referred to as *multi-row* statistical functions.

Stated informally, the goal of any anonymous statistical function in Diffix is to "hide" the presence or absence of any given user under the assumption that *the analyst knows all values except that of the given user*. For multi-row functions, Diffix uses two mechanisms: (1) masking outliers, and (2) adding enough noise so that there is substantial uncertainty as to the value for users with high values. For single-row functions, Diffix can return an exact value (i.e. the value of a row with no noise added). However, it does so only when there are enough distinct users with the same value. Otherwise, it returns a noisy value.

6.1   Anonymous Sum and Count

Because a count is simply the sum of rows, the same function is used for both sum and count. The function has two phases, a pre-processing phase and a summing phase. The input to the summing phase is:

1. A table with two columns, a *uid* column and a *value* column. The uid's are distinct, and the value contains each user's total contribution to the count or sum.
2. A "baseline" sticky noise value N_b derived from the noise layers. N_b has a standard deviation of $\sigma = \sqrt{N}$, where N is the number of noise layers (see Sect. 7). The actual noise is a multiplicative factor of N_b.

Depending on the function, the pre-processing phase produces the value as follows:

count(distinct uid): All values are '1'

count(*): Each value is the number of rows for the uid

count(column): Same as count(*), except rows with NULL values are not counted

count(distinct column): Same as count(column), except duplicate values are removed before counting each user's rows

sum(column): Each value is the sum of the values for the uid

sum(distinct column): Same as sum(column), except duplicate values are removed before summing each user's values

The summing phase consists of the following steps:

1. Generate two sticky thresholds T_1 and T_2.
2. Label the T_1 users with the highest values *group 1*.
3. Label the T_2 users with the next highest values *group 2*.
4. Define A_2 as the average of the values from *group 2*.

5. Replace the *group 1* values with A_2.
6. Sum the values, and add noise with magnitude $N_b * A_2$. Counts are rounded to the nearest integer.

If there are both positive and negative values, then the above computations are done separately for the positive and negative values, using lowest values instead of highest, and using a separate baseline noise N_b for the negative values. The actual added noise is the sum of the two noise values. Note that for count(distinct uid), $A_2 = 1$, and the noise has $\sigma = 2$.

This approach hides outliers both in terms of their direct effect on the true sum, and in terms of their effect on the added noise. By using groups of users from which to derive values, the effect of any one user is hidden in a crowd. By using noisy thresholds to select the groups of users, the uncertainty of the analyst is increased. Rounding adds uncertainty in rare cases where the analyst can learn and exploit the value of a single pair of noise layers.

Both the count(distinct column) and sum(distinct column) functions have a pre-processing step where duplicate values are removed. In this step, duplicates are removed in such a way as to maximize the resulting number of distinct uid's. This minimizes the contribution of any given user, allowing Diffix to minimize the noise.

Anonymous Average and Standard Deviation. Both the anonymous average and the anonymous standard deviation use the anonymous sum function. The anonymous average is computed simply as the anonymous sum divided by the anonymous count.

To compute the anonymous standard deviation, first the true average is computed. Then, the square of the difference between each value and the true average is computed. Then the anonymous average of these squared differences is computed. Finally, the final output is the square root of this anonymous average.

6.2   Anonymous Min and Max

To compute the max value, Diffix computes the following two values, and selects the maximum of these two.

The first value is simply the largest value that has enough distinct uid's associated with it to pass the low-count filter.

For the second value:

1. Compute A_2 the same as with the sum function in Sect. 6.1.
2. Compute σ_2 as the standard deviation of *group 2*.
3. The second max value is computed as A_2 with noise $(N_b * \sigma_2)/8$.

This noise effectively eliminates the possibility that the analyst can reverse engineer the exact values that produced A_2 in the case where the values in *group 2* differ from each other. The divisor of 8 is chosen to minimize noise while still providing strong protection against reverse engineering values. Note that if all the values in *group 2* are the same, then $\sigma_2 = 0$ and no noise is added.

The anonymous min is computed the same as the anonymous max, but substituting low values for high.

The anonymous min and max functions can output the exact value for a given user. This value might even be the true min or max (though the analyst does not know this from the output). This does not reveal any information that the analyst could not otherwise have discovered with a query of the form:

SELECT column, count(*) FROM table GROUP BY column

and taking the highest (lowest) returned value as the max (min). On the other hand, the anonymous min and max functions may return a more accurate value than could be discovered using this query.

6.3 Anonymous Median

A similar approach is taken to compute the anonymous median. Specifically, the values from groups of distinct users above and below the true median are selected, and the anonymous median is computed from these values. The details are omitted due to space constraints.

7 Amount of Noise

Because Diffix does not "leak noise" with repeated answers as most differential privacy mechanisms do, individual query answers need have only enough noise to anonymize that given answer. Recall that the system is relatively more anonymous when the probability of a higher confidence guess is lower. While the decision of how much noise to add is up to the data owner, we believe that for sticky noise, a per-layer standard deviation of minimum $\sigma = 1$ provides adequate anonymity for counting queries.

To support this claim, we provide the results of two simulations. The first simulates a difference attack on counting queries where the analyst has no a priori knowledge about the true count, and is able to exclude the victim with a single condition (as for instance with the example of Fig. 3). Results (Fig. 7) are given for between 4 and 6 noise layers for the query with the excluding condition, with a per-layer $\sigma = 1$. Answers are rounded to the nearest integer.

We define *confidence improvement* as $C_i = 100 * (C - P_a)/(100 - P_a)$, where P_a is the probability that a given attribute occurs in the population, and C is the analyst's confidence in a guess. For instance, if an attribute occurs in the population with $P_a = 60\%$ probability, and the analyst has $C = 80\%$ confidence in their guess, then the confidence improvement is $C_i = 50\%$.

In the simulation, if the answer for the query that conditionally includes the victim is greater than the answer for the query that excludes the victim, the analyst guesses that the victim has the attribute (i.e. a given salary). The results are shown in Fig. 7 for the cases where the attribute probabilities are $P_a = 1\%$, $P_a = 5\%$, and $P_a = 50\%$.

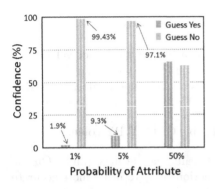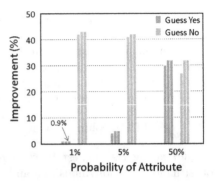

Fig. 7. Confidence C of an analyst's guess in a difference attack, and the improvement in confidence C_i over a statistical guess of the attribute probability P_a. Per-layer noise has $\sigma = 1$. Groups of four bars are for 4, 5, and 6 noise layers, left to right. Values are averages over 10^8 trials.

Starting with the $P_a = 50\%$ case, the difference attack improves the analyst's confidence to between $C = 62\%$ and $C = 66\%$. While somewhat better, the analyst's confidence remains acceptably low (in our opinion). Now consider the case where $P_a = 1\%$. In the case where the analyst guesses that the victim has the attribute, the analyst's confidence is $C = 1.9\%$, a 0.9% improvement. A guess that the victim does not have the attribute improves confidence by $C_i = 43\%$, from $P_a = 99\%$ statistical confidence to $C = 99.43\%$. Put into the perspective of the difference attack of Fig. 3, assuming that the probability of the victim having any given salary is 1%, the analyst could improve his or her confidence in what the victim's salary is not, but still has very little confidence in what the victim's salary is.

The second simulation examines the case where the analyst knows through external knowledge that a given count is one of two possible values, x or $x + 1$. In this case, the analyst's confidence in the correct answer is higher when the noisy answer is further from the two possible counts. For instance, suppose that the analyst knows that the only two possible answers are 20 and 21, and that they occur with equal probability. If the noisy answer is 21, then the analyst's confidence that the true answer is 21 is only $C = 53\%$ ($C_i = 6\%$). If the noisy answer is 26, however, the analyst's confidence that the true answer is 21 is $C = 79\%$ ($C_i = 59\%$). On the other hand, the probability of getting a noisy count of 26 is much smaller than getting 21 (0.06% versus 19%).

Figure 8 plots the confidence improvements and corresponding probability of improvement for the cases where the probability of the lower value (x) occurring is $P_a = 1\%$, $P_a = 10\%$, and $P_a = 50\%$. In this simulation, the analyst guesses x if the noisy count is x or smaller, and guesses x+1 otherwise. Each simulation tested 10^{11} trials. The left-most data points represent an average of a few 10's of trials, the right-most data points correspondingly more.

The data points on the lower right represent the case where the noisy count is either x or x + 1. This happens with a probability of roughly 36%. In these cases,

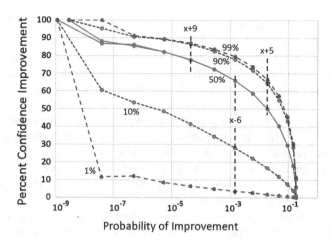

Fig. 8. Improvement in analyst's confidence C_i, and probability of getting that improvement, when analyst knows the true answer must be one of two possible known values (x and x + 1). Noise is 0 mean Gaussian with standard deviation 2. Three curves are for cases where lower value x occurs with 1%, 10%, and 50% probability. Points to the left represent more noise. Points where noisy count is x − 6, x + 5, and x + 9 are labeled.

the improvement in the analyst's confidence beyond the statistical probability of the expected outcome is very little.

Consider the point on the $P_a = 50\%$ curve where the noisy count is x + 9. Here the analyst's confidence improvement is $C_i = 78\%$, but this improvement happens in only 1 out of roughly 23 K trials. From the figure, we can see that noise with as low as $\sigma = 2$ provides good anonymity. Obviously more noise would provide still better protection, but we don't believe more noise is necessary. Note that, as a rule, an effective attack requires several conditions, and therefore we are not too concerned with queries that have noise less than $\sigma = 2$ (i.e. only one condition).

8 Summary, Limitations, and Future Work

This paper presents a description of Diffix, a database anonymization system that is easy to configure, is strongly anonymous, allows unlimited queries, adds minimal distortion to answers, and supports a variety of useful statistical functions.

In the process of describing Diffix, this paper shows how Diffix defends against certain basic attacks. Due to space limitations, this paper does not provide a thorough analysis of the attacks and defenses currently known to the authors. This is a limitation of the paper.

A major limitation of the work overall is the fact that we do not have a formal treatment of Diffix. As a result, while we are not aware of any attacks that break

Diffix's anonymity, we cannot make a positive statement that no such attacks exist. Moving forward, we hope to formalize and prove Diffix as much as possible. It is not clear how far we can get with a formal approach, so in parallel we plan to deploy an implementation of Diffix and make it available for attack, possibly with prizes for successful attacks. This exercise can lead to improvements to Diffix, a better understanding of how to evaluate risks (should some attacks be possible), and an overall increase in confidence in this new technology.

A big open question is whether Diffix provides enough utility to be used widely in practice, and if not, how it's utility may be improved. Is the accuracy adequate? Do analysts need richer query semantics? Do analysts need more statistical functions, and if so can these be provided? How much does the inability for analysts to "see the data" impede the analytic process overall?

We expect to research these and many other questions in the future, and hope that Diffix inspires the broader research community to pursue this and other new architectures.

References

1. Article 29 Data Protection Working Party Opinion 05/2014 on Anonymisation Techniques. http://ec.europa.eu/justice/data-protection/article-29/documenta tion/opinion-recommendation/files/2014/wp216_en.pdf
2. Denning, D.E.: Secure statistical databases with random sample queries. ACM Trans. Database Syst. (TODS) 5(3), 291–315 (1980)
3. Denning, D.E., Denning, P.J., Schwartz, M.D.: The tracker: a threat to statistical database security. ACM Trans. Database Syst. (TODS) 4(1), 76–96 (1979)
4. Dinur, I., Nissim, K.: Revealing information while preserving privacy. In: Proceedings of the Twenty-Second ACM SIGMOD-SIGACT-SIGART Symposium on Principles of Database Systems, pp. 202–210. ACM (2003)
5. Dwork, C.: Differential privacy. In: Bugliesi, M., Preneel, B., Sassone, V., Wegener, I. (eds.) ICALP 2006. LNCS, vol. 4052, pp. 1–12. Springer, Heidelberg (2006). doi:10.1007/11787006_1
6. Erlingsson, Ú., Pihur, V., Korolova, A.: RAPPOR: randomized aggregatable privacy-preserving ordinal response. In: Proceedings of the 2014 ACM SIGSAC Conference on Computer and Communications Security, pp. 1054–1067. ACM (2014)
7. Fellegi, I., Phillips, J.: Statistical confidentiality: some theory and application to data dissemination. In: Annals of Economic and Social Measurement, vol. 3, no. 2, pp. 399–409. NBER (1974)
8. Fellegi, I.P.: On the question of statistical confidentiality. J. Am. Stat. Assoc. 67(337), 7–18 (1972)
9. Prasser, F., Kohlmayer, F.: Putting statistical disclosure control into practice: the ARX data anonymization tool. In: Gkoulalas-Divanis, A., Loukides, G. (eds.) Medical Data Privacy Handbook, pp. 111–148. Springer, Cham (2015). doi:10.1007/ 978-3-319-23633-9_6
10. Kotschy, W.: The new General Data Protection Regulation - Is there sufficient pay-off for taking the trouble to anonymize or pseudonymize data? November 2016. https://fpf.org/wp-content/uploads/2016/11/Kotschy-paper-on-pseudonymisation.pdf

Privacy Policies in Practice

Towards a Principled Approach for Engineering Privacy by Design

Majed Alshammari[(✉)] and Andrew Simpson

Department of Computer Science, University of Oxford,
Wolfson Building, Parks Road, Oxford OX1 3QD, UK
{majed.alshammari,andrew.simpson}@cs.ox.ac.uk

Abstract. Privacy by Design has emerged as a proactive approach for embedding privacy into the early stages of the design of information and communication technologies, but it is no 'silver bullet'. Challenges involved in engineering Privacy by Design include a lack of holistic and systematic methodologies that address the complexity and variability of privacy issues and support the translation of its principles into engineering activities. A consequence is that its principles are given at a high level of abstraction without accompanying tools and guidelines to address these challenges. We analyse three privacy requirements engineering methods from which we derive a set of criteria that aid in identifying data-processing activities that may lead to privacy violations and harms and also aid in specifying appropriate design decisions. We also present principles for engineering Privacy by Design that can be developed upon these criteria. Based on these, we outline some preliminary thoughts on the form of a principled framework that addresses the plurality and contextuality of privacy issues and supports the translation of the principles of Privacy by Design into engineering activities.

1 Introduction

Privacy is subjective in nature: it is influenced by a variety of factors, including societal demands — which evolve over time — and technological developments. In the context of information and communication technologies, privacy and data protection laws and regulations alone are not sufficient in protecting the privacy of individuals [22]: they need to be accompanied with guidelines that aid software engineers in addressing the challenges of privacy-related issues in the early stages of the software development process.

Privacy by Design [4] has been advocated as a response to these challenges. The principles of Privacy by Design are based on the Fair Information Practice Principles (FIPPs) [26], and act as a universal framework for incorporating privacy into three main areas of application: information technologies, business practices, and physical designs and networked infrastructures [7]. In 2010 Privacy by Design was recommended as an international privacy standard by the participants of the 32nd International Conference of Data Protection and Privacy Commissioners in Jerusalem [5]. Subsequently, Privacy by Design has played a role in legislation such as the EU's General Data Protection Regulation [25].

E. Schweighofer et al. (Eds.): APF 2017, LNCS 10518, pp. 161–177, 2017.
DOI: 10.1007/978-3-319-67280-9_9

But Privacy by Design is no 'silver bullet'. Challenges in engineering Privacy by Design include a lack of holistic and systematic methodologies that address the complexity and variability of privacy issues and support the translation of its principles into engineering principles and activities. In some ways this is understandable, as the approach was developed to take into account a range of sources and standards. However, a consequence is that its principles are given at a high level of abstraction — meaning that there is a reliance on software engineers' expertise with regards to translating legal frameworks and standards into operational requirements. Consequently, *Privacy Engineering* has emerged as a means of applying engineering principles and processes in developing, deploying and maintaining systems in a systematic and repeatable way, with a view to achieving acceptable levels of privacy protection [11]. One might characterise Privacy by Design as being concerned with *What to do* with respect to achieving reasonable levels of privacy protection and Privacy Engineering as being concerned with *How to do it* [7].

We identify the main challenges of engineering Privacy by Design. In addition, we analyse three privacy requirements engineering methods to understand how these methods address the main challenges, from which we derive a set of criteria that have the potential to support the process of engineering Privacy by Design. These criteria are consistent with the principles of Privacy by Design, and are intended to aid software engineers in two ways: in identifying data-processing activities that may lead to privacy violations and harms in a comprehensive and concrete manner, and in specifying appropriate design decisions at an architectural level in a rational and positive-sum manner. We build upon these criteria to establish principles for engineering Privacy by Design.

2   A Set of Criteria to Address the Challenges of Engineering Privacy by Design

In this section we explore the main challenges of engineering Privacy by Design. We then analyse three privacy requirements engineering methods to understand how they address the identified challenges. Finally, we derive a set of criteria that address these challenges and support the process of engineering Privacy by Design.

2.1   The Challenges of Engineering Privacy by Design

Engineering systems according to the principles of Privacy by Design involves several challenges, including a lack of generalised methodologies that can be adopted to integrate the principles of Privacy by Design into systems engineering [13]. This integration requires: effective translation of abstract privacy principles, privacy risk models and privacy mechanisms into implementable requirements; integrating these activities into an appropriate process; and embedding such a process into the development lifecycle [20]. These can be decomposed into a number of concrete challenges.

1. *The complexity of privacy issues.* As privacy is a broad concept, encompassing legal, social and political aspects, it challenges software engineers to understand and translate its complex perceptions and concerns into operational requirements [13]. This 'plurality' requires specific expertise to map abstract definitions and principles of privacy, as well as the principles of Privacy by Design, to concrete requirements [13].

2. *The variability of privacy issues.* As privacy is subjective in nature and culturally variable [11], it challenges software engineers to understand and consider stakeholders' expectations and concerns, which, in turn, requires specific expertise, contextual analysis and resolution of stakeholders' conflict of security, privacy and utility interests [13].

3. *A lack of systematic methods that identify privacy concerns in a meaningful manner.* Privacy is a 'fuzzy' concept; consequently, it is difficult to protect [22]. This implies that privacy-related issues need to be identified in a contextual, comprehensive and concrete manner, as well as in relation to reasonable expectations of privacy [21]. This implies that an appropriate definition of privacy that considers the plurality and contextuality of privacy is required [12]. This challenges software engineers to holistically identify and systematically analyse potential privacy risks for eliciting explicit privacy requirements [13]. Further, privacy risk assessment needs to go beyond identifying technical risks; however, this requires an understanding of social perceptions and expectations that are derived from social norms [13]. The potential impact of privacy violations might be incorporeal, psychological, or emotional — meaning that the negative consequences of privacy violations may extend beyond affected individuals to society [21]. Such impact can be measured either financially or as personal and societal impacts [19].

4. *The degrees to which privacy is required.* The adequate levels of privacy protection need to be determined in a contextual manner without impacting functionality or usability. These levels could be specified by applying data minimisation as a fundamental step for engineering systems according to the foundational principles of Privacy by Design [13]. However, there are other considerations that need to be taken into account to determine the appropriate type of data minimisation, such as stakeholders' expectations and concerns, applicable regulations, technological capabilities, and appropriate privacy threat models [23]. Thus, there is a need for a technique that considers such factors and helps determine reasonable levels of privacy protection.

5. *A lack of means to address privacy concerns at an architectural level.* Many privacy-preserving solutions have a significant architectural impact [17] and are typically not accompanied by design guidelines to mitigate these impacts. There is a need for techniques that can be adopted to specify, implement and justify acceptable levels of privacy protection. This includes making appropriate design decisions that fulfil the elicited privacy requirements [13], specifying various levels of privacy protection, and determining appropriate architectural alternatives that support these levels [23]. In particular, there is a need for means to support the mapping of privacy requirements onto suitable software architectures.

6. *A lack of means to ensure and demonstrate privacy compliance.* Complying with applicable, complex legal frameworks and standards requires comprehensive approaches that manage personal data, together with involved actors, roles, responsibilities, business processes and their supporting systems, as well as organisational and technical controls. This implies that it is crucial to adopt a data management model that helps facilitate the manageability and traceability of the flow of personal data and supports the process of proactively identifying and addressing privacy concerns that arise in each stage of the personal data lifecycle, as well as ensuring and demonstrating privacy compliance with applicable legal frameworks and standards at each stage [6].

2.2   An Analysis of Privacy Requirements Methods

We now analyse three privacy requirements engineering methods against the challenges of Sect. 2.1. Specifically, we analyse the Framework for Privacy-Friendly System Design (PFSD) [23], LINDDUN [10] and the PriS method [16], which were previously analysed against a conceptual framework for privacy requirements engineering by Beckers [1].

We have chosen these methods as they have taken different approaches to Privacy by Design. PFSD is a hybrid approach that considers privacy by implementing the notice-and-choice model and by applying the data minimisation at an architectural level. LINDDUN is a risk-based approach that implements privacy requirements as accountability mechanisms. The PriS methods is a goal-oriented approach that defines privacy requirements as organisational goals.

The Framework for Privacy-Friendly System Design. The Framework for Privacy-Friendly System Design (PFSD) was developed by Spiekermann and Cranor to provide a comprehensive view of privacy engineering [23]. They translated common privacy definitions into engineering responsibilities in relation to three technical domains: the user sphere, the recipient sphere, and the joint sphere. The identified responsibilities are concerned with ensuring that users can exercise control over their personal data and mitigate potential privacy risks where personal data is not under their control. Consequently, a privacy responsibility framework was developed to serve as a basis for privacy requirements analysis.

PFSD identifies potential privacy risks by analysing system requirements, privacy expectations and concerns in relation to three sensitive system activities: data transfer, data storage, and data processing. This analysis is conducted in relation to an appropriate threat model to identify system activities that raise privacy concerns. The potential impact is estimated on the basis of several factors: types of personal data, involved parties, the ways in which these activities are performed, and the sphere of influence in which these activities execute. However, it does not explicitly adopt specific privacy risk analysis and assessment processes [23].

Spiekermann and Cranor emphasise the importance of understanding privacy expectations and concerns according to what is 'normal'. The resulting framework is based on a set of concerns identified as a result of empirical studies in relation to the three sensitive system activities. However, PFSD is not accompanied by guidelines on how to identify privacy expectations in a structured manner. Moreover, as perceptions of privacy are influenced by legal, social and economic changes, as well as by technological developments, a set of static activities that raise privacy concerns is not sufficient in considering the variability of privacy [23]. It may be argued that other considerations need to be taken into account, such as the adoption of a conceptual model that precisely specifies privacy-related concepts and distinguishes between the main operations that can be performed. Such a model needs to classify the various distinct processing activities for each operation instead of concentrating on three sensitive system activities. Such a model would aid in identifying and addressing activities that raise privacy concerns and in demonstrating compliance.

PFSD identifies a set of criteria for specifying the degree to which privacy is required: privacy expectations and concerns, legal requirements, business needs, appropriate threat models, and technological capabilities. Based on these, in addition to business and technical strategies, one can adopt one of two alternative approaches. The first is privacy-by-policy, which concentrates on enforcing privacy policies by implementing enforcement and compliance mechanisms. To achieve this, the approach implicitly adopts transparency and intervenability as privacy protection goals to implement, enforce and audit compliance [23]. However, for the purpose of developing a generic approach, universal privacy principles can be adopted, rather than sector-specific principles and guidelines. The second approach is privacy-by-architecture, which focuses on identifying architectural choices that specify various levels of privacy protection by minimising data collection, and emphasising anonymisation and client-centric data processing. These approaches are accompanied by implementation guidelines that aid in specifying different levels of privacy protections based on the degree of identifiability and linkability of personal data. These levels reflect the degree to which privacy is required in a four-stage scale: from identified and linked to anonymous and unlinkable [23].

LINDDUN. LINDDUN [10] is a privacy threat analysis framework for supporting the elicitation and fulfilment of privacy requirements. It provides a set of privacy threat types and a means for mapping these to Data Flow Diagrams (DFDs).

LINDDUN adopts a set of privacy protection goals, rather than utilising a particular characterisation of privacy. It considers seven privacy protection goals — unlinkability, anonymity and pseudonymity, undetectability and unobservability, plausible deniability, confidentiality, content awareness, and policy and consent compliance — which are consistent with the protection goals of [14]. LINDDUN emphasises the variability of privacy as a subjective concept;

however, it does not explicitly illustrate how to address this variability in relation to specific contexts.

From threat tree patterns, potential privacy risks are identified, misuse cases are documented, and requirements are elicited. The identified threats are mitigated by adopting the principle of data minimisation as a fundamental step in privacy protection, which supports specifying various levels of privacy protection based on the protection goals. However, other factors need to be taken into consideration to specify various levels of privacy protection, such as applicable legal frameworks and standards, reasonable expectations, and legitimate objectives. Moreover, threat tree patterns and corresponding technical measures need to be continuously updated.

LINDDUN's agnosticism to privacy risk analysis processes gives its users the opportunity to adopt familiar approaches. While LINDDUN uses DFDs to aid in identifying where privacy threats may occur during the flow of personal data [10], DFDs do not consider other details that support privacy decisions, such as types of personal data along with the applicable legal frameworks and standards, involved parties, roles and responsibilities, business processes and their supporting systems, and other technical controls. To comprehensively identify potential privacy risks, a data management model needs to be considered to provide end-to-end protection from collection to destruction and help ensure privacy compliance.

Finally, LINDDUN supports interaction between privacy requirements and software architectures by providing a catalogue of threat tree patterns to aid in mapping appropriate Privacy-Enhancing Technologies (PETs) onto the identified threat types [10]. However, developing such a catalogue without conducting a contextual analysis that addresses the plurality and contextuality of privacy is not sufficient in terms of reasoning critically about architectural decisions, alternatives and corresponding technical measures.

The PriS Method. The PriS method aims to integrate privacy requirements into the early stages of the design process by modelling privacy requirements as organisational goals [16]. The method emphasises the complexity of privacy as a legal and social concept, and, rather than referring to specific privacy definitions, principles or guidelines, considers eight privacy requirements as privacy protection goals: identification, authentication, authorisation, data protection, anonymity, pseudonymity, unlinkability and unobservability. Some security goals may have implications on privacy; therefore, identification, authentication and authorisation are adopted as security services, together with privacy protection goals. The aim is to eliminate or minimise the collection and processing of personal data. In addition, the method considers stakeholders' expectations and concerns during the elicitation of privacy-related goals in relation to the system's environment. Each of the privacy protection goals has relevant stakeholders who may have different conflicts of interest; therefore, conflict resolution techniques may be utilised [16]. However, it is not accompanied with a structured approach that identifies users' reasonable expectations of privacy in a contextual manner.

Having elicited privacy-related goals, their potential impact can be analysed. This may lead to the identification of new goals, which, in turn, may lead to new processes or improve existing goals. Next, these processes are modelled using relevant privacy-process patterns. However, the method does not adopt specific risk identification, analysis or assessment processes.

The PriS method adopts goal models to address privacy concerns in each process. However, the method supports the analysis of business processes and their supporting software systems, rather than adopting a data management model that manages and evaluates the flow of personal data [16]. As a consequence, potentially harmful activities that arise in each stage of the data lifecycle are considered at a high level of abstraction. Ideally, a data model would capture other information to support privacy decisions, such as types of personal data, along with the applicable legal frameworks and standards, involved parties, roles and responsibilities, and other technical controls — providing end-to-end protection from collection to destruction and ensuring privacy compliance in each stage of the data lifecycle.

The PriS method supports the mapping of privacy requirements onto appropriate software architectures by providing privacy-process patterns. Each pattern illustrates privacy activities that need to be implemented, which, in turn, aids in deciding where privacy controls (manifested by, for example, PETs) need to be implemented to achieve an acceptable level of privacy protection. Furthermore, alternative architectural choices can be prioritised according to the degree to which privacy is required to provide various levels of privacy protection [16].

2.3   A Set of Criteria for Engineering Privacy by Design

By identifying the main challenges of engineering Privacy by Design, analysing three privacy requirements methods and reflecting on relevant privacy literature [6,9,15,18,21,24], we derive a set of criteria that can address these challenges and support the process of engineering Privacy by Design.

1. Adopting Universal Privacy Principles and Protection Goals. This criterion emphasises the importance of adopting a unified set of privacy principles — as derived from the FIPPs. As an example, the postulated Global Privacy Standard (GPS) [3] harmonises various sets of the FIPPs into universal privacy principles upon which the principles of Privacy by Design are based [8]. Since these principles are consistent with privacy legislation and data protection regulations, they can be adopted in the context of privacy engineering.

In order to meet privacy principles, a set of universal privacy protection goals need to be specified to identify the rights of data subjects and the obligations of entities with reference to the GPS principles [3]. Such protection goals need to be much broader than data minimisation to achieve all privacy principles and address the complexity and variability of privacy. Hansen *et al.* [14] emphasise six protection goals for privacy engineering as a basis from which one can derive privacy requirements, select appropriate technologies that fulfil these requirements, and assess the impact of privacy on a given software system. Three of these six goals are the security triad of confidentiality, integrity, and availability. While security is recognised as a means of supporting privacy engineering [14], we assume that security properties and services are taken into account during the design process to support privacy in achieving an adequate level of privacy protection. This means that we will leverage the three other goals — unlinkability, transparency and intervenability — as privacy protection goals. Specifically, we consider unlinkability (and its specific properties — anonymity, undetectability and unobservability, and pseudonymity) as a general goal.

2. Adopting an Appropriate Data Management Model as a Basis for Contextual Analysis. This criterion is concerned with identifying and addressing potential privacy risks that arise in each stage of the data lifecycle in relation to its privacy principles and their associated protection goals, reasonable expectations and concerns in a comprehensive, concrete and contextual manner. The data management model helps in evaluating the flow of personal data at each stage of the lifecycle [6], as well as in tracing privacy requirements throughout the development stages to ensure compliance with applicable legal frameworks and standards at each stage. In addition, it can be used as a means to facilitate communication between various stakeholders by providing a common language.

3. Interpreting Appropriately Stakeholders' Expectations and Concerns. This criterion addresses the complexity and variability of privacy by translating social, legal and political perceptions, expectations and concerns into operational requirements in a contextual manner. This emphasises the importance of adopting a structured approach that identifies reasonable expectations of privacy. Nissenbaum's contextual integrity framework [18] aids in understanding, identifying and modelling privacy expectations as context-relative informational norms. In addition, a bottom-up approach that identifies activities that may compromise these expectations is required. Solove's taxonomy of privacy [21] aids in identifying potential privacy risks in relation to the activities of the system being developed in a concrete manner. In respect of the methods of Sect. 2.2, PFSD considers a set of static concerns as a result of empirical studies. However, these concerns vary between contexts and may change over time. To achieve compliance and achieve a better acceptance of a given software-based system, the concerns of other stakeholders (such data protection authorities, policy-makers, and senior management) need to be considered.

4. Adopting a Systematic Method that Considers the Plurality and Contextuality of Privacy to Identify Potentially Harmful Activities. This criterion pertains to the identification of privacy concerns in a contextual, comprehensive and concrete manner. This emphasises the importance of synthesising approaches (such as, for example, the aforementioned taxonomy of privacy [21] and contextual integrity framework [18]) to use reasonable expectations as a baseline during analysis. In addition, the data management lifecycle can be used to aid in addressing privacy concerns that may arise in each stage of the data lifecycle. In order to make rational decisions, appropriate impact analysis and assessment processes (such as the Privacy Risk Management (PRM) [6] and the Methodology for Privacy Risk Management [24], which are based on the ISO 31000 Risk Management Framework) can be adopted. Such a framework estimates the severity of materialised privacy risks according to causes of the identified privacy harms and their potential impacts. It follows that privacy risks can be holistically identified and systematically analysed to elicit concrete privacy requirements [13]. PFSD identifies privacy concerns by analysing three sensitive system activities in relation to its three spheres; LINDDUN identifies privacy concerns by mapping privacy threats into the main elements of a DFD; and the PriS method analyses the impact of privacy goals on business processes and their supporting software-based systems.

5. Specifying the Adequate Level of Privacy Protection in a Structured Manner. This criterion is concerned with determining acceptable levels of privacy protection required for the system being developed. These levels are based on a number of factors: stakeholders' expectations and concerns, appropriate threat models, applicable regulations, the context in which the system operates, technological capabilities, and appropriate types of data minimisation [23]. In particular domains, users' expectation may exceed related legal requirements; as such, this criterion aims to identify multiple levels of privacy protection, i.e. the default settings can be the maximum level of privacy protection [8] and other levels can be specified by considering data subjects' preferences [2]. This means that, to address the variability of privacy, reasonable expectations of various stakeholders need to be considered at an architectural level. Of our surveyed approaches, only PFSD explicitly defines four levels of privacy protection.

6. Identifying Appropriate Strategies for Mapping Privacy Requirements to Software Architectures. The aim of this criterion is to support the interaction between privacy requirements and software architectures. This emphasises the importance of identifying design strategies that aid in translating privacy requirements to software architectural decisions. In addition, strategies aid in implementing the adequate levels of privacy protection in a reasoned and effective manner, justifying applied technical measures, and arguing critically about design decisions. Such strategies can be used as a basis for identifying useful architectural patterns, associated design patterns, and their underlying PETs. Furthermore, strategies can be used as objectives or support for achieving privacy protection goals. PFSD applies the principle of data minimisation in relation to its three technical domains to specify appropriate architectural choices that fulfil privacy requirements; LINDDUN and the PriS method use catalogues and privacy-process patterns respectively to determine appropriate technical measures. However, catalogues and patterns alone are not sufficient to support reasoning critically about adopting particular technologies or making critical design decisions. This, in turn, requires identifying means that illustrate appropriate conditions for adopting each architectural pattern, design pattern and underlying technologies in relation to the adequate levels of privacy protection in each context.

3   An Analysis of Privacy by Design

We now analyse the identified criteria with respect to the principles of Privacy by Design to ensure their consistency.

3.1   The Principles of Privacy by Design

The principles of Privacy by Design are based on the GPS principles of [3], which harmonise various sets of the FIPPs into universal privacy principles [8]. These principles aim to meet legal obligations, achieve accountability, and enhance user trust [7,8].

Proactive Not Reactive; Preventative Not Remedial. This principle can be achieved by devising a principled approach that identifies and addresses potential privacy risks in a holistic and systematic manner [8]. To be holistic, there is a need to adopt universal privacy principles that provide high privacy standards [8] to meet stakeholders' expectations, which may exceed legal requirements in some jurisdictions [1]. The identification process needs to be undertaken in a comprehensive, concrete and contextual manner [21]. To be proactive and systematic, there is a need for complementary impact analysis and assessment processes to provide treatment strategies that prevent the occurrence of identified privacy risks.

The first, third and fourth criteria of Sect. 2.3 are consistent with this principle.

Privacy as the Default Setting. This principle refers to a subset of the FIPPs in respect of purpose specification, collection limitation, data minimisation, and use, retention and disclosure limitation [8]. Privacy as the default setting is considered as a system property [2]. 'Privacy by Default' implies that the default setting is considered to be an adequate level of privacy protection; in practice, however, users are not likely to restrict themselves to a default operational mode [2]. In addition, features need to be implemented in relation to the foundational principles, irrespective of the default operational mode [2]. Therefore, privacy features need to be 'hierarchically nested' in each component of a given system, to be stimulated by the 'informed consent' of the data subject [2]. Thus, multiple levels of privacy protection are needed to meet stakeholders' expectations.

The third, fourth and fifth criteria of Sect. 2.3 are consistent with this principle.

Privacy Embedded into Design. This principle can be achieved by integrating a principled approach into an appropriate software engineering process [8]. Such an approach needs to be holistic to consider the variability of privacy, integrative to consider stakeholders' participation, and creative to provide acceptable design alternatives. In addition, such an approach needs to be complemented by impact analysis and assessment processes to document and communicate the results of the analysis to stakeholders [8]. Furthermore, impact analysis and assessment processes need to be conducted at each stage or iteration of the engineering process [2].

The third, fourth and sixth criteria of Sect. 2.3 are consistent with this principle.

Full Functionality — Positive-Sum, Not Zero-Sum. This principle emphasises the need for privacy requirements to be embedded in a creative manner without affecting other system properties and attributes [8]. However, the adequate level of privacy protection and the functionality of a given software system need to be measured and prioritised in a systematic manner [2]. Moreover, such systems are increasingly large and complex; software architectures are considered to be effective means of managing such complexity.

The third, fourth, fifth and sixth criteria of Sect. 2.3 are consistent with this principle.

End-to-End Security — Full Lifecycle Protection. This principle refers to security as a principle of the FIPPs [8]. It is well understood that social factors need to be considered for providing adequate data protection [2]. However, measuring the level of security of complex software systems is a challenge [2]. To ensure full protection, a model that manages the flow of personal data, such as the personal data lifecycle [6], needs to be adopted as a basis for the identification of potential privacy risks, as well as the conduct of impact analysis and assessment.

The second, third, fourth and sixth criteria of Sect. 2.3 are consistent with this principle.

Visibility and Transparency — Keep It Open. The principle refers to a subset of the FIPPs in respect of accountability, openness and compliance, which, in turn, improve user satisfaction and trust [8]. Transparency is a prerequisite for accountability, and can be achieved by implementing compliance mechanisms, such as notice, access mechanisms and audit trails. In particular, privacy compliance polices that precisely define compliance rules need to be specified, documented and communicated to stakeholders [8]. This implies that compliance rules should be integrated with privacy requirements to achieve a satisfied level of accountability and user satisfaction. In addition, privacy protection goals need to be specified and documented to be used as a reference for all design decisions [2]. In addition, transparency can be achieved by the traceability of personal data throughout its lifecycle [2].

The first and second criteria of Sect. 2.3 are consistent with this principle.

Respect for User Privacy — Keep It User-Centric. The principle refers to a subset of the FIPPs in respect of consent, accuracy, access and compliance [8]. Privacy, however, is subjective in nature and depends on the culture and expectations of each society. This leads to the importance of considering the expectations of various stakeholders, including, specifically, data subjects [2]. To 'keep it user-centric', consent and privacy preferences need to be considered, and data avoidance needs to be an option rather than providing one level of privacy protection as a default setting. Accordingly, configurable privacy features need to be considered, and potential alternatives for implementing each privacy feature need to be interchangeable in a modular manner [2]. Further, these configurations need to be adaptable for each data subject [2].

The third, fourth, fifth and sixth criteria of Sect. 2.3 are consistent with this principle.

4   Principles for Engineering Privacy by Design

We now present a set of guiding principles to support embedding privacy into the system development lifecycle. The principles follow from our identified criteria and complement the principles of Privacy by Design.

4.1   Universal Privacy Principles and Protection Goals that Pertain to Global Infrastructures

To support the development of effective privacy-preserving solutions, the GPS principles of [3] can serve as a set of universal privacy principles that can be applied in a variety of contexts. In this regard, unlinkability, transparency and intervenability as proposed in [14] need to be adopted to complement the security protection goals of confidentiality, integrity and availability.

4.2   A Data Lifecycle Model that Supports Achieving Privacy Assurance and Transparency

A personal data lifecycle model would aid in managing the flow of personal data and associated metadata, together with relevant actors and supporting software systems. Typically, privacy principles derived from legislation and standards are written to govern and regulate the processing of personal data in five common stages: data collection, retention, use, disclosure, and destruction. On the one hand, each stage has a set of principles that govern the processing of personal data. For example, collection limitation and purpose specification are privacy principles that govern personal data at the collection stage. On the other hand, each stage has certain concerns that have implications on privacy. Therefore, it is important to adopt a management model that reflects how privacy principles and corresponding protection goals can be mapped to each stage to eliminate or at least mitigate potential harmful activities that may lead to privacy violations and harms. To assure privacy and demonstrate compliance, a personal data lifecycle needs to be adopted. The personal data lifecycle is considered to be a foundational means for supporting the identification of potential privacy risks, mitigation these risks and supporting traceability of privacy requirements throughout the development process, i.e. it is a basis for contextual analysis.

4.3 A Data-Centric Method that Identifies Privacy Concerns in a Comprehensive, Contextual and Non-reductive Manner

Privacy-related issues need to be understood in a non-reductive manner, not least to understand what to protect and by which means. This also requires a careful consideration of the context in which the given system operates to identify and meet reasonable expectations of privacy in a contextual manner. To identify privacy concerns in a comprehensive manner, the personal data lifecycle model needs to be adopted to support the identification of harmful activities that may compromise privacy protection goals in each stage of the lifecycle in relation to the applicable regulations and reasonable expectations of privacy.

The gap between policy-makers and software engineers can be bridged via a method that synthesises two existing frameworks to appropriately interpret privacy perceptions and meaningfully identify potential privacy risks: the taxonomy of privacy of [21] and the contextual integrity framework of [18]. By synthesising these frameworks, legal, social and political perceptions can be translated into operational requirements to be reconciled with system requirements in a structured manner.

Processing personal data may introduce various privacy risks that may impact upon data subjects and organisations, whether this impact is tangible or intangible. Therefore, a suitable framework should provide a rational process for identifying, analysing and evaluating potential privacy risks and their potential impact. This, in turn, can aid in determining the adequate levels of privacy protection, eliciting concrete privacy requirements, and specifying appropriate designs in a positive-sum manner.

4.4 Design Strategies that Translate the Principles of Privacy by Design into Design Objectives

Privacy by Design aims to achieve privacy assurance by meeting regulatory compliance requirements and mitigating potential privacy risks. In order to achieve this, the principles of Privacy by Design need to be appropriately translated into design objectives that help achieve privacy protection goals, which, in turn, achieve privacy principles.

The privacy design strategies of, for example, [15] and [9] specify architecture goals that realise a set of protection goals — which are derived from privacy principles and data protection regulations — to achieve a certain level of privacy protection; on the other hand, our strategies are a set of design objectives to achieve privacy protection goals. As such, our design strategies can be identified based upon the analysis and assessment of potential privacy risks and the principle of data minimisation. To be consistent with the principles of Privacy by Design, design strategies need to apply preventative measures, rather than remedial ones. These strategies support specifying, implementing and justifying the adequate level of privacy protection as the default setting. In addition, strategies are considered as means for mapping privacy requirement to suitable software architectures. In particular, they are intended to illustrate appropriate conditions for applying specific architectural patterns, associated design patterns and their underlying PETs (if any). These include aims, privacy concerns, privacy requirements, treatment options, privacy protection goals, privacy principles, and potential consequences. These, in turn, have the potential to help to reason critically about architectural alternatives.

5   A Way Forward

Integrating the principles of Privacy by Design into the system development lifecycle will be crucial in the next few years — not least because, as we have seen, Privacy by Design is now mandated by legislation such as the EU's General Data Protection Regulation.

The identified principles for engineering Privacy by Design have the potential to lay the foundations of a common and cohesive framework that addresses the plurality and contextuality of privacy issues by proactively addressing potentially harmful activities that may lead to privacy violations and harms. Further, they have the potential to support the translation of the principles of Privacy by Design into engineering activities. To this end, we now outline some preliminary thoughts on the form that such a framework might take.

We might consider four main elements: the personal data lifecycle to represent data processing activities in a way that is amenable to analysis; a data-centric method to identify privacy concerns; privacy design strategies that address these concerns at architectural levels; and a set of privacy-related artefacts that can be aligned with the system development lifecycle.

5.1   The Personal Data Lifecycle as an Instance of the Information Lifecycle

The data lifecycle model plays a crucial role in managing the flow of personal data, identifying potential privacy risks that arise in each stage of the lifecycle, addressing these risks in a proactive manner, and ensuring and demonstrating privacy compliance. In particular, the personal data lifecycle represents the typical stages along with their associated activities, types and sources of personal data (whether this data is collected, derived, or acquired from other sources), privacy principles (together with their relevant protection goals, involved actors, applied means and legitimate purposes), and potentially harmful activities that may lead to privacy violations and harms in each stage. This means that such a model must consider all stages of personal data — from collection to destruction. In addition, it facilitates compliance demonstration by tracing privacy requirements throughout development.

5.2 A Data-Centric Method that Identifies Privacy Concerns in a Meaningful Manner

This method aims to identify activities that may lead to potential privacy violations and harms in each stage of the personal data lifecycle in a meaningful manner. It should be *comprehensive* in that it should adopt the personal data lifecycle as a basis for contextual analysis. It should be *contextual* via the adoption of Nissenbaum's contextual integrity framework [18] and *non-reductive* via the adoption of Solove's taxonomy of privacy [21]. This method should also be accompanied by appropriate risk management process to assess the identified privacy risks.

5.3 Design Strategies to Translate the Principles of Privacy by Design into Design Objectives

Design strategies are sets of risk treatment decisions — based on the assessment of the identified privacy risks and their potential impact — at architectural levels. These strategies are mainly based upon the principle of data minimisation to achieve privacy assurance by meeting regulatory compliance requirements and mitigating potential privacy risks. In particular, they support the translation of the principles of Privacy by Design into design objectives for supporting the specified privacy protection goals in a particular context. These strategies can be used as means for mapping privacy requirement onto suitable software architectures to specify, implement and justify the adequate level of privacy protection as the default setting. These, in turn, support reasoning critically about architectural decisions, alternatives and associated privacy technical measures.

5.4 A Set of Privacy-Related Engineering Artefacts

These artefacts are models — derived from the principles of Privacy by Design — that help describe the main activities of making rational architectural decisions. In particular, they support the translation of the principles of Privacy by Design into privacy-preserving techniques or procedures, possibly with notation to accomplish specific engineering activities that can be integrated into or aligned with an appropriate software engineering process. The chosen process, in turn, can be embedded into the system development lifecycle with a view to: understanding how to identify the need for privacy and finding the places where it is needed during the analysis phase; determining what privacy aspects should be addressed and what degree of privacy must be achieved during the design phase; and specifying appropriate software architectural choices.

6 Conclusion

Engineering systems according to the principles of Privacy by Design involves several challenges, including: a lack of generalised methodologies that address the complexity and variability of privacy by identifying and addressing potential privacy risks in a comprehensive, contextual and non-reductive manner; ensuring and demonstrating privacy compliance; and supporting the translation of its principles into engineering activities.

We have identified the main challenges of engineering Privacy by Design. In addition, we have analysed three privacy requirements engineering methods from which we have derived a set of criteria that can address these challenges. To this end, we have presented a set of guiding principles developed upon these criteria that can be used as a means of complementing Privacy by Design. These principles support integrating privacy-related activities into an appropriate software engineering process and embedding that process into the system development lifecycle.

The identified principles have laid the foundations for a common and cohesive framework that addresses the plurality, contextuality and assurance of privacy by proactively identifying privacy concerns in a meaningful manner, ensuring and demonstrating compliance, and supporting the translation of the principles of Privacy by Design into design objectives and engineering artefacts, which, in turn, support identifying privacy-preserving techniques. Our next step will be to validate and refine the proposed framework via a series of case studies.

References

1. Beckers, K.: Comparing privacy requirements engineering approaches. In: Proceedings of the 2012 Seventh International Conference on Availability, Reliability and Security (ARES 2012), pp. 574–581. IEEE (2012)
2. Bier, C., Birnstill, P., Krempel, E., Vagts, H., Beyerer, J.: Enhancing privacy by design from a developer's perspective. In: Preneel, B., Ikonomou, D. (eds.) APF 2012. LNCS, vol. 8319, pp. 73–85. Springer, Heidelberg (2014). doi:10.1007/978-3-642-54069-1_5
3. Cavoukian, A.: Creation of a global privacy standard (2006). https://www.ipc.on.ca/images/Resources/gps.pdf
4. Cavoukian, A.: Privacy by design (2009). https://www.privacybydesign.ca/content/uploads/2009/01/privacybydesign.pdf
5. Cavoukian, A.: Privacy by design [leading edge]. IEEE Technol. Soc. Mag. **31**(4), 18–19 (2012)
6. Cavoukian, A., Monica, M., Fariba, A., Dan, R., Jeff, K.: Privacy risk management: building privacy protection into a risk management framework to ensure that privacy risks are managed, by default (2010). https://www.ipc.on.ca/images/Resources/pbd-priv-risk-mgmt.pdf
7. Cavoukian, A., Shapiro, S., Cronk, R.J.: Privacy engineering: proactively embedding privacy, by design (2014). https://www.privacybydesign.ca/content/uploads/2014/01/pbd-priv-engineering.pdf
8. Cavoukian, A.: Privacy by design: the 7 foundational principles implementation and mapping of fair information practices (2010). https://www.ipc.on.ca/english/Resources/Discussion-Papers/Discussion-Papers-Summary/?id=953
9. Colesky, M., Hoepman, J.H., Hillen, C.: A critical analysis of privacy design strategies. In: Proceedings of the 2016 IEEE Security and Privacy Workshops (SPW), pp. 33–40. IEEE (2016)

10. Deng, M., Wuyts, K., Scandariato, R., Preneel, B., Joosen, W.: A privacy threat analysis framework: supporting the elicitation and fulfillment of privacy requirements. Requirements Eng. **16**(1), 3–32 (2011)
11. Dennedy, M.F., Fox, J., Finneran, T.: The Privacy Engineer's Manifesto: Getting from Policy to Code to QA to Value. Apress, New York (2014)
12. Gürses, S., del Alamo, J.: Privacy engineering: shaping an emerging field of research and practice. IEEE Secur. Priv. **14**(2), 40–46 (2016)
13. Gürses, S., Troncoso, C., Diaz, C.: Engineering privacy by design. In: Proceedings of the 4th International Conference on Computers, Privacy & Data Protection (CPDP 2011), p. 25 (2011)
14. Hansen, M., Jensen, M., Rost, M.: Protection goals for privacy engineering. In: Proceedings of the 2015 IEEE Security and Privacy Workshops (SPW 2015), pp. 159–166. IEEE (2015)
15. Hoepman, J.-H.: Privacy design strategies. In: Cuppens-Boulahia, N., Cuppens, F., Jajodia, S., Abou El Kalam, A., Sans, T. (eds.) SEC 2014. IAICT, vol. 428, pp. 446–459. Springer, Heidelberg (2014). doi:10.1007/978-3-642-55415-5_38
16. Kalloniatis, C., Kavakli, E., Gritzalis, S.: Addressing privacy requirements in system design: the PriS method. Requirements Eng. **13**(3), 241–255 (2008)
17. Kung, A.: PEARs: privacy enhancing architectures. In: Preneel, B., Ikonomou, D. (eds.) APF 2014. LNCS, vol. 8450, pp. 18–29. Springer, Cham (2014). doi:10.1007/978-3-319-06749-0_2
18. Nissenbaum, H.F.: Privacy in Context: Technology, Policy, and the Integrity of Social Life. Stanford University Press, New York (2009)
19. Notario, N., Crespo, A., Martín, Y.S., Del Alamo, J.M., Le Métayer, D., Antignac, T., Kung, A., Kroener, I., Wright, D.: PRIPARE: integrating privacy best practices into a privacy engineering methodology. In: Proceedings of the 2015 IEEE Security and Privacy Workshops (SPW 2015), pp. 151–158. IEEE (2015)
20. Shapiro, S.S.: Privacy by design: moving from art to practice. Commun. ACM **53**(6), 27–29 (2010)
21. Solove, D.J.: A taxonomy of privacy. Univ. PA Law Rev. **154**(3), 477–564 (2006)
22. Spiekermann, S.: The challenges of privacy by design. Commun. ACM **55**(7), 38–40 (2012)
23. Spiekermann, S., Cranor, L.F.: Engineering privacy. IEEE Trans. Softw. Eng. **35**(1), 67–82 (2009)
24. The Commission Nationale de lInformatique et des Libertés (CNIL): methodology for privacy risk management (2016). https://www.cnil.fr/sites/default/files/typo/document/CNIL-ManagingPrivacyRisks-Methodology.pdf
25. The European Union: Official Journal of the European Union: General Data Protection Regulation (2016). http://eur-lex.europa.eu/legal-content/EN/TXT/PDF/?uri=OJ:L:2016:119:FULL&from=EN
26. United States Department of Health, Education, Welfare: Secretary's Advisory Committee on Automated Personal Data Systems: Records, Computers and the Rights of Citizens: Report. [Cambridge? Mass.]: [MIT Press], Cambridge (1973)

PrivacyScore: Improving Privacy and Security via Crowd-Sourced Benchmarks of Websites

Max Maass[1](✉), Pascal Wichmann[2], Henning Pridöhl[2],
and Dominik Herrmann[2]

[1] Secure Mobile Networking Lab, Technische Universität Darmstadt,
Darmstadt, Germany
mmaass@seemoo.tu-darmstadt.de

[2] Security in Distributed Systems Group, Universität Hamburg,
Hamburg, Germany
{wichmann,pridoehl,herrmann}@informatik.uni-hamburg.de

Abstract. Website owners make conscious and unconscious decisions that affect their users, potentially exposing them to privacy and security risks in the process. In this paper we introduce PrivacyScore, an automated website scanning portal that allows anyone to benchmark security and privacy features of multiple websites. In contrast to existing projects, the checks implemented in PrivacyScore cover a wider range of potential privacy and security issues. Furthermore, users can control the ranking and analysis methodology. Therefore, PrivacyScore can also be used by data protection authorities to perform regularly scheduled compliance checks. In the long term we hope that the transparency resulting from the published assessments creates an incentive for website owners to improve their sites. The public availability of a first version of PrivacyScore was announced at the ENISA Annual Privacy Forum in June 2017.

Keywords: Scanner · Tracking · Compliance · Security · Privacy · Data protection

1 Introduction

Setting up and running a website requires expert knowledge and a substantial amount of resources. Software systems have to be configured correctly, kept up-to-date and secured against attacks that are discovered during the lifetime of a site. The continuing flow of reports about security incidents on major websites indicates that many website operators are incapable of maintaining a sufficient level of security.

Vulnerabilities resulting from mistakes and negligence of website operators constitute a privacy risk for users. For instance, insecurely configured transport

---

A German version of this paper with a more detailed discussion of the legal considerations is available at [21].

© Springer International Publishing AG 2017
E. Schweighofer et al. (Eds.): APF 2017, LNCS 10518, pp. 178–191, 2017.
DOI: 10.1007/978-3-319-67280-9_10

encryption may be broken by eavesdroppers, and sensitive data on web servers may be stolen by criminals.

However, the privacy of users may also be under attack by the website operators themselves. Modern web design relies on third-party services: analytics services provide insights about visitors and ad networks generate revenue. Site owners commonly choose privacy-infringing third-party services, even though many typical requirements can be met with privacy-friendly alternatives, e. g., by running a local analytics tool such as Piwik [27].

The security and privacy risks resulting from (un)conscious decisions of site operators are complex and elusive. There is no straightforward way for end users to determine whether a site takes security seriously and whether it respects their privacy.

Existing website scanning services do not give a comprehensive impression of security and privacy features of a site. First, these services are mostly geared towards skilled administrators to assist with self-assessment. Secondly, most scanners focus on a very specific area: the properties of the encrypted connections from the browser to the web server. Thirdly, the interface of existing scanners makes it difficult to compare the results of different sites side-by-side. As a result, site operators have little incentive to improve security and privacy on their website beyond the status quo.

Our project PrivacyScore aims to fill this gap. Building on existing work, and in cooperation with data protection authorities DPAs and data protection non-governmental organization (NGOs), we are currently designing and implementing the **PrivacyScore Benchmarking Portal**[1] to assess both security and privacy measures of websites. The public availability of a first version of PrivacyScore was announced at the ENISA Annual Privacy Forum in June 2017.

The target audience of PrivacyScore are *end users* who want to know how a particular website ranks in its peer group, *researchers* who want to perform studies about security features of websites, and *NGOs and DPAs* that want to check the compliance of websites with data protection laws.

Our platform offers a scanning infrastructure and is built on the crowdsourcing paradigm. It offers the following distinctive features:

- Users can set up crowd-sourced lists of websites that belong to a certain category (e. g., all public schools in France). These site lists and their corresponding rankings are publicly visible and updated automatically on a regular basis to create an incentive for operators to improve their security and privacy compared to their peers or competitors. The results contain actionable advice for operators who want to improve their rating.
- Both list creators and ordinary users can adapt the rating and ranking of sites via customized ranking schemes. This allows list creators to create benchmarks that highlight particular checks, while giving users the opportunity to tailor the ranking to their personal privacy preferences.

---

[1] Available online at https://privacyscore.org/.

– PrivacyScore is released under an open-source license (GPLv3 or later) and the data collected on the platform is made available to the public in human-readable and machine-readable form.

The rest of the paper is structured as follows: After having reviewed related work in Sect. 2, we present the main features of PrivacyScore in Sect. 3. Section 4 provides details on our security and privacy checks, while Sect. 5 outlines the implementation. Finally, we discuss legal and ethical considerations in Sect. 6 before we conclude in Sect. 7.

2   Related Work

Most existing scanning services focus on *security issues* which may allow malicious adversaries to compromise a web server or to eavesdrop on encrypted traffic. Prominent examples are the SSL scanners by Qualys [28], High-Tech Bridge [14], and Mozilla [26]. Some of these services also check for the presence of relatively new HTTP headers [31], which protect against selected attacks.

On the other hand, there are only very few scanning services that focus on *privacy issues*, i. e., design decisions allowing site owners or third parties to track users. A popular service is "Webbkoll" [9], which is offered by *dataskydd.net*, a Swedish non-profit data protection organization.

Besides scanning services that allow users to scan arbitrary websites, there have been several efforts to scan pre-defined lists of websites and IP addresses. For instance, Helme regularly publishes a dataset containing an analysis of the HTTP security headers for the "Alexa Top 1 Million" list [30]. Many more scans are available in the *scans.io* repository.

Furthermore, there are numerous scientific studies that have analyzed security (e. g., [15,23]) and privacy aspects (e. g., [12]) of popular websites. These studies provide insights about the overall state of privacy and the adoption of security technologies on the web. However, as they typically focus on aggregate statistics, they do not create strong incentives for individual site owners to improve. Moreover, they rarely provide sector-specific insights ([12] is one of the few exceptions). And finally, as the published data is typically not updated after the publication, the results become outdated rather quickly. This is also true for the 2016 municipality survey [8] of *dataskydd.net*, that inspired us to create PrivacyScore.

More distantly related to our work are browser add-ons such as Lightbeam [25] and EFF's Privacy Badger [11]. These tools analyze visited sites on the fly and allow users to block dedicated tracking services. However, some add-ons have been shown to track their own users [16,32].

With the existing projects and tools checking sites for legal compliance and comparing multiple sites are tedious processes. At the moment these tasks involve substantial amounts of manual work, because various results have to be obtained from multiple sources. With PrivacyScore we want to unify and simplify this process so that it becomes easily repeatable.

3 PrivacyScore Overview

In this section we describe the main features of the PrivacyScore platform. Figure 1 provides an overview of the use cases and data structures.

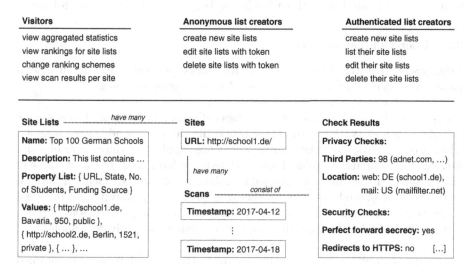

Fig. 1. Use cases and data structures

3.1 Main Use Cases

Like other website scanning services, PrivacyScore allows users to submit URLs of websites which are then analyzed in terms of security and privacy features. While one-off single-site scans are supported, the main purpose of PrivacyScore is the creation and publication of site lists that comprise multiple websites that share a common feature. For instance, a list could consist of the websites of all schools of a country, of major newspapers, or popular health portals.

Users can browse the database of existing site lists (using tags and a full-text search) or create new site lists. New site lists can be created by anyone at any time. A site list is created by supplying a *list of website URLs*. In addition, the creator of a site list can supply metadata such as a title for the list, a description of the methodology used to select the URLs, and a set of tags. Once all relevant data has been entered (or uploaded using a CSV file), it is submitted to the scanning engine, which retrieves each site and gathers a number of facts using multiple scan modules. The gathered facts are evaluated by checks that assess specific security and privacy properties (cf. Sect. 4). The results can be displayed at varying levels of detail, from aggregate statistics over a tabular ranking of all sites to detailed results for each individual check and site.

Site lists and results are retained in the system. All lists are *re-scanned on a regular basis* by default in order to document when site operators make changes to their sites (site list creators can disable automatic re-scans).

The system supports both incidental and professional use. Occasional users can create site lists or scan individual websites without registration. They receive a randomly generated *access token* that allows them to change and delete their site list at a later time. Professional users like DPAs can create a *user account* to manage their site lists without having to keep track of their access tokens.

3.2 User-Centric Results

PrivacyScore has two features that enable users to create meaningful assessments: *user-defined properties* and *user-defined ranking schemes.*

User-defined Properties. A set of properties defined by the creator of a list can be stored for each site within a list. These properties can provide additional insights. The set of properties and their initial values are supplied by the creator of a site list, but they can also be refined and updated at a later time. In the example of school websites, the following properties might be of interest: location (federal state), number of students, and whether it is publicly or privately funded. When users view the results of the assessment, they can use the properties to perform comparisons like "is there a difference between public and private schools?".

User-defined Ranking Schemes. The ranking of the scanned websites is obtained by aggregating the results of the individual checks using a user-defined ranking scheme. Most existing scanning services use predefined weights to model the fact that some vulnerabilities are more critical than others. In contrast to existing scanning services, where the scanning service imposes its ranking methodology on all scans, PrivacyScore gives its users more control. Our user-defined ranking schemes make the results useful for different audiences. For instance, DPAs may solely be interested in features indicating non-compliance with data protection law, while privacy activists may want a more strict rating for the purpose of "naming and shaming" websites with excessive data collection practices.

List creators can choose from a set of pre-defined ranking schemes. Moreover, users who view a site list can switch to a different ranking scheme or define their own on the fly. Our framework allows to calculate (potentially weighted) total scores or to define different types of ratings, for instance based on school grades (e. g., A$^+$ to F) or by color-coding the result (e. g., red, yellow, green).

In order to make the results more easily accessible, checks are organized in *check groups.* A ranking scheme defines how checks are organized into groups, how each possible outcome of a check is supposed to be rated, and which importance is associated to each check and group.

Rating and Ranking in the Beta. In the following we explain the ranking scheme that is available at the start of the beta phase (cf. Fig. 2). This is subject to change and we will provide a more comprehensive description of the methodology at a later time. For now the mapping of checks to check groups cannot be influenced by users and there are four check groups: *NoTrack, Attacks, EncWeb,* and *EncMail* (cf. Sect. 4).

#	URL	Name	Type	NoTrack	Attacks	EncWeb	EncMail	Rating
				»	« »	« »	«	
1	http://www.ibb.de/ (1 failure) / 2017-06-24 @ 18:29:42	IBB Berlin	public	✓	❶	❶	❓	❶
2	http://www.helaba.de/ / 2017-06-24 @ 18:26:12	Hessische Landesbank	public	✓	❶	❶	❶	❶
3	http://www.berlinhyp.de/ / 2017-06-24 @ 18:24:42	Berlin Hyp AG	public	✓	❶	✖	❶	✖
4	http://www.bayernlb.com/ / 2017-06-24 @ 18:24:26	Bayerische Landesbank	public	✓	⚠	❶	❶	⚠
5	http://www.bhw.de/ / 2017-06-24 @ 18:23:35	BHW Bausparkasse AG	private	❶	❶	❶	❓	❶
6	http://www.pfandbriefbank.com/ / 2017-06-24 @ 18:22:38	Deutsche Pfandbriefbank AG	private	❶	❶	❶	❓	❶
7	http://www.hypovereinsbank.de/ / 2017-06-24 @ 18:22:57	Unicredit Bank AG	private	❶	❶	❶	❶	❶

Fig. 2. Ranking for a site list that contains home pages of German banks

The currently implemented ranking scheme is based on the user-defined *order of the check groups*. Users can manipulate the order according to their personal preferences. Sites with a "good" (green) rating in the highest-priority check group (leftmost column) are pulled to the top of the table, followed by sites with a yellow and red rating in the first check group, respectively. All sites with the same rating (color) in the first check group are further sorted according to their rating in the next check group – and so on until all check groups have been considered.

The rating of a site in a specific check group is determined by the checks belonging to that group. In the beta phase, a *green* rating is obtained if all checks of a group succeed, while a *red* rating is obtained if one of the critical checks within a group failed. Otherwise the site obtains a *yellow* rating. The criteria for each check are documented on the PrivacyScore website (cf. Fig. 3).

Finally, the *overall rating* of a site is given by the rating of the worst group. For instance, a site that has only green group ratings gets a green overall rating, while a site with at least one yellow or red group rating gets a yellow or red overall rating, respectively.

3.3 Open Data Versus Privacy

We have designed PrivacyScore with the intention to improve transparency for end users by creating awareness for poor security and privacy practices of site operators. Therefore, all data that is generated on the platform is available publicly via an open RESTful API.

However, we recognize that some professional users have special privacy requirements. Therefore, all of the scan modules implemented on PrivacyScore run locally, i. e., the scanned URLs are not leaked to third parties. In addition, in order to support private investigations, site list can be marked as *private*.

http://www.bayernlb.com/

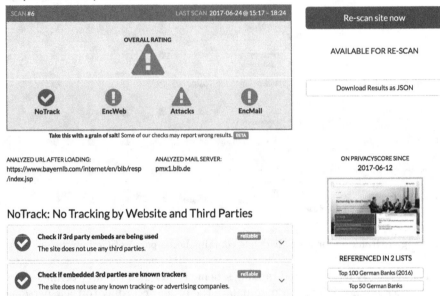

Fig. 3. Scan results for individual sites contain a list of all checks. (Color figure online)

This allows corporate users and DPAs to use PrivacyScore without disclosing this fact to the public. Furthermore, site lists can be deleted by the list creator or a system administrator upon request.

We also support users with even stricter privacy requirements, who can run their own (in-house) instance of PrivacyScore, as we release our source code under the GPLv3+ license.[2]

The open source nature also makes it easy to add additional scan modules, which are Python modules providing a specific interface. That way, scan modules can either be implemented directly in Python or just use a simple Python wrapper calling any external executable.

4 Privacy and Security Checks

PrivacyScore is designed to perform various checks on each website. In the following we describe our roadmap, i. e., the checks that we plan to support in PrivacyScore. We distinguish two types of checks: *Security checks* analyze whether site operators follow best practices that protect against malicious attacks by outsiders. These checks are relevant because successful attacks may infringe the privacy of users. We also perform various *privacy checks* that determine whether the owners of a site designed it in such a way that it infringes the privacy of users.

---

[2] See https://github.com/privacyscore.

4.1 Privacy Checks

The privacy checks are reported in the *No Track* check group in the beta phase (cf. Figs. 2 and 3). The most prevalent privacy problem on modern websites is the plethora of tracking, analysis, and advertising services. These services are usually embedded as JavaScript files that are retrieved from a web server run by the service provider (the so-called "third party"). The privacy and security implications of including third-party services in a website have been widely discussed [22]. Nevertheless, their use is ubiquitous on the modern web.

PrivacyScore enumerates the *hostnames of third parties* that are included when a website is visited. The hostname of every third party is checked against a list of known advertisers and trackers (extracted from the EasyList [4]) to determine which of them are trackers.

A common method for tracking users across multiple sites or over multiple visits to the same site are *HTTP cookies*. PrivacyScore measures how many cookies are being set, and how many of these are owned by third parties (which could use them for cross-page tracking of users). A more modern technique for tracking and re-identifying users is *browser fingerprinting*. Here, characteristics of the browser (e.g., installed plugins and their version) and the device (e.g., available fonts and screen resolution) are being measured to compute a fingerprint. Studies have shown that this fingerprint can often uniquely identify a browser [10,19]. PrivacyScore will check whether the source code of a website contains known patterns of browser fingerprinting.

Furthermore, many websites rely on content distribution networks (CDNs) or load balancing services run by third parties, either for the site itself or in order to include software libraries such as jQuery. CDNs reduce page load times and improve scalability. However, they also pose a risk to the privacy and security of the users because the CDN operators have full access to the unencrypted traffic. This was demonstrated by a recent vulnerability in the Cloudflare denial of service (DoS) protection service, which exposed private information from thousands of websites [6]. Additionally, the CDN companies themselves could track users on all websites that use their services. Therefore, PrivacyScore checks whether the website itself or content from third parties is served from popular CDNs.

Finally, the *geographic location of servers* may be of interest. If the server is hosted under a different jurisdiction than the company itself, additional data protection rules may apply. While the prevalence of CDNs with colocations in many countries makes determining the geographic location of servers and their associated jurisdictions complicated, a first approximation can be made using a GeoIP database. PrivacyScore checks the location of the web-, mail-, and nameservers used by a website.

4.2 Security Checks

Insecure websites are more likely to suffer from breaches, unintentional data leaks, or data monitoring by rogue hotspots or ISPs. PrivacyScore includes checks for security issues that may indicate privacy problems.

The most straightforward security feature a website can offer is to encrypt HTTP connections using TLS. PrivacyScore checks if the website offers TLS, and if yes, whether unencrypted connection attempts are automatically forwarded to the HTTPS version of the site. It also checks if the website follows established best practices for TLS deployment, if it is vulnerable to known attacks (such as Heartbleed and POODLE), and if the website contains unencrypted content on an encrypted page (*mixed content*). These checks are part of the *EncWeb* check group. Similar checks are run for the primary *mail server* that is listed in the MX domain record of the site, if one exists (*EncMail* check group).

We also check whether a website sets *HTTP security headers* like Content-Security-Policy and X-XSS-Protection that protect users from certain attacks. Together with the checks for unintended information leaks (described in the next paragraph) these checks make up the *Attacks* check group.

The checks for unintended information leaks try to retrieve content from various well-known locations on a web server. Leaks may occur at the locations */server-status/* and */server-info/*, where the Apache server software publishes details about recently served requests (including source IP address) and the current load. We also check whether the operators have forgotten to remove frequently used test scripts (*test.php* and *phpinfo.php*) in the root directory of the server. These scripts may disclose the version and configuration of the server. We also check for the presence of */.git/* and */.svn/* directories. Operators that use version control systems to manage their sites should prevent unauthorized access to these locations. Otherwise, adversaries could retrieve the data stored in these locations to inspect the source code of server-side scripts, which may contain sensitive information such as database access credentials. Finally, we check for the presence of *core dumps*, which are located at */core* and contain the memory of a process at the time it crashed. Core dumps can contain private information and should not be exposed publicly.

Another aspect that is often overlooked in practice is the security of the underlying Domain Name System (DNS) records. If the DNS entries can be compromised, sophisticated phishing attacks may be possible, regardless of all other security features of a website. Accordingly, PrivacyScore checks if the DNS records of a site are protected with *DNSSEC*. PrivacyScore also checks if the mail server of a site uses state-of-the-art authentication techniques by consulting Sender Policy Framework (SPF) and Domain-based Message Authentication, Reporting and Conformance (DMARC) records in the DNS [17,18].

The final building block in website security is keeping the software up to date. When PrivacyScore retrieves a website it searches for *outdated software* by looking at version banners in headers sent by a server ("Server" HTTP header, SMTP version banner string). It also tries to detect the version of the content management system (CMS) that is used to build the website ("generator" attribute in HTML, and potentially file fingerprinting). Finally, PrivacyScore attempts to detect outdated client-side JavaScript libraries, which has been shown to be a surprisingly prevalent problem today [20].

4.3   Incentives and Actionable Advice for Operators and Users

PrivacyScore increases the visibility of security and privacy issues found on the scanned websites. However, we also want to increase the incentive for operators to improve their systems. Therefore, we plan to enrich the checks with explanations of the resulting security and privacy risks. For instance, a missing or incorrectly set HSTS header means that malicious Wi-Fi access points can eavesdrop on traffic by performing an SSL stripping attack [24].

However, besides creating an incentive for site owners, our advice may also help attackers. For instance, we could create a tangible illustration of the risks resulting from outdated software by listing all relevant CVE entries [2] and reporting whether ready-to-run exploit modules for the Metasploit framework [5] are available. This example demonstrates that legal and ethical ramifications have to be considered to find an acceptable trade-off (cf. Sect. 6).

Furthermore, we want to support operators by offering actionable advice. This includes suggesting alternative software (e.g., using a self-hosted analytics platform like Piwik [27] instead of Google Analytics) and recommending specific configurations for popular operating systems, web servers, and CMSs.

Finally, we will support end users in protecting their privacy by suggesting protection strategies like installing browser add-ons such as PrivacyBadger [11] or uBlock Origin [29] that block advertisements and trackers.

5   Implementation

At the time of writing PrivacyScore is in a public beta phase and under active development (the benchmarking portal is available at https://privacyscore.org/). We are implementing the system using a multi-tier software architecture (cf. Fig. 4). Data is collected by a number of dedicated scanning machines (workers), each running a scanning system implemented in Python. Scanning jobs are managed using the distributed task queue Celery [1].

This architecture allows us to scan multiple websites concurrently and to delegate individual scan modules to different machines, making the system horizontally scalable. New machines can be dynamically added to decrease the time that is needed to collect the data for a scan of a site.

New scanning tasks are queued by the front-end server (written in Python), while the results are aggregated and stored in a PostgreSQL database by a back-end server. For security reasons, the database is not publicly accessible. Instead, the back-end offers selective access to the data via a RESTful API. The front-end views are implemented in Python using the Django web framework [3].

Implemented Checks. At the time of writing, we have implemented four scan modules. The first scan module uses the *OpenWPM* [12] framework to collect information directly from a website by visiting it with a remote-controlled Firefox browser (we plan to support different browsers as well as browsers running on mobile operating systems in the future). OpenWPM allows us to observe requests

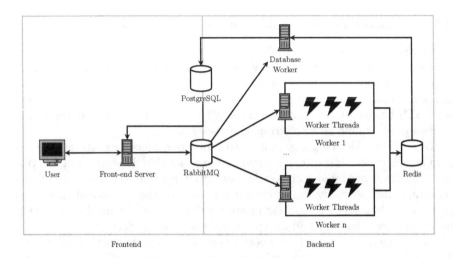

Frontend   Backend

Fig. 4. System architecture of PrivacyScore

to third-party hosts as well as the cookies they set. We also check whether the web server sent any HTTP security headers.

The second scan module analyzes the security of the encrypted connections to the web server and (if available) to the mail server of a website using the *testssl.sh* script developed by Dirk Wetter [7].

The third scan module performs GeoIP lookups to determine the geographic location of the web and mail servers and the fourth scan module checks whether a website leaks information about its internal configuration.

The remaining checks mentioned in Sect. 4 are currently in development. Furthermore, only the supplied URLs (or the final URL, if the browser is redirected) are checked at the moment. In the future, we may instruct the browser to click on a few random internal links to get a more comprehensive picture of each site.

6   Legal and Ethical Considerations

Automated scanning of websites on the internet poses a number of legal and ethical questions. In the following we will mention important issues, which we are currently discussing with legal academics and practitioners.

6.1   Legal Considerations

In some jurisdictions performing an automated security scan of a website without permission granted by its operators may be illegal or constitute a breach of its terms of service.

This issue can be tackled in various ways. We are currently operating with a manual "opt out" policy. Site operators can contact us and declare that they do not want their sites to be scanned in the future. The respective URLs will be added to a blacklist. However, the last known scan results remain visible on the PrivacyScore website, annotated with a note that the operator has disapproved further scanning.

In principle, the scanner could also be programmed to refrain from scanning a website if it encounters a "Disallow" entry in the file *robots.txt* on the web server, which is a commonly used method for site operators to indicate to search engine robots that some or all parts of their site should not be indexed. However, to the best of our knowledge, none of the existing website scanners respect the rules contained in the *robots.txt* file. Furthermore, the Internet Archive has recently announced to ignore *robots.txt* files on purpose [13]. A viable compromise for PrivacyScore might consist in delegating the question whether to honor statements from *robots.txt* to the list creator.

As executing certain scan modules may violate local laws, operators planning to run an instance of PrivacyScore are advised to evaluate applicable laws before deploying a scanner in their country. A more detailed analysis of the legal issues surrounding PrivacyScore is available in a German version of this paper [21].

6.2 Ethical Considerations

It is our intent to help site operators and users, but not adversaries. However, some of our checks and advice provide information that may be useful for attackers, i.e., PrivacyScore is a *dual-use tool*. Therefore, we are carefully designing what checks we implement and how we present the results to the user.

Scanning a website generates traffic (typically less than one megabyte) and temporarily increases its CPU load. Therefore, each scan incurs some cost for the owners of a website. We believe this to be ethically acceptable, because the purpose of having a publicly available website is to have visitors that download it. Furthermore, we consider the public good of providing assessments to outweigh the typically negligible costs of each scan for the website operators.

However, we have to ensure that we do not induce a critical load on a website, which might result in denial of service. This is especially relevant for the SSL checks, which generate a large number of connections. To prevent too frequent scans we implement rate-limiting controls ensuring that the scanned sites cannot be overloaded maliciously.

7 Conclusion

Running a secure and privacy-respecting website has become a demanding task. On the one hand, website owners must constantly adapt their security measures to novel threats. On the other hand, they have to make the right decisions during the design and operation of their site in order to safeguard the privacy of their users. Today, many sites offer poor security and privacy, either because site owners are unwilling to cover the additional costs or because privacy measures are in conflict with their business model.

We believe that some site owners would make more privacy-conscious decisions if they had an incentive to do so. Our project PrivacyScore aims to create such incentives by generating transparency and publicity. It allows anyone to set up a benchmark for a peer group of websites. Security and privacy features of the sites in a group are automatically analyzed, resulting in a public, regularly updated, and user-controllable ranking.

PrivacyScore is open source software and we plan to release all collected datasets for research purposes. Besides running it as a public service, PrivacyScore can also be deployed in-house. We hope that it will become a useful tool for DPAs that are faced with the task of enforcing a large number of regulatory requirements specified in the General Data Protection Regulation (GDPR).

Acknowledgments. This work has been co-funded by the DFG as part of project C.1 within the RTG 2050 "Privacy and Trust for Mobile Users". The authors are grateful to Marvin Hebisch and Nico Vitt, who implemented a prototype, the attendants of the PET-CON 2017.1 workshop, and members of Digitalcourage e. V. for their valuable suggestions.

References

1. Celery: Distributed task queue (2017). http://www.celeryproject.org/
2. Common Vulnerabilities and Exposures (2017). https://cve.mitre.org/
3. Django web framework (2017). https://www.djangoproject.com/
4. EasyList (2017). https://easylist.to/
5. Metasploit Penetration Testing Software (2017). https://www.metasploit.com/
6. Cloudflare: Incident report on memory leak caused by Cloudflare parser bug (2017). https://blog.cloudflare.com/incident-report-on-memory-leak-caused-by-cloudflare-parser-bug/
7. Wetter, D.: testssl.sh (2017). https://testssl.sh/
8. dataskydd: Kommunundersökning (2016). https://dataskydd.net/kommuner-201611/
9. dataskydd: Webbkoll (2017). https://webbkoll.dataskydd.net/en/
10. Eckersley, P.: How unique is your web browser? In: Atallah, M.J., Hopper, N.J. (eds.) PETS 2010. LNCS, vol. 6205, pp. 1–18. Springer, Heidelberg (2010). doi:10.1007/978-3-642-14527-8_1
11. EFF: Privacy Badger (2017). https://eff.org/privacybadger
12. Englehardt, S., Narayanan, A.: Online tracking: a 1-million-site measurement and analysis. In: Proceedings of the 2016 ACM SIGSAC Conference on Computer and Communications Security (CCS 2016), pp. 1388–1401. ACM (2016)
13. Graham, M.: Robots.txt meant for search engines don't work well for web archives (2017). https://blog.archive.org/2017/04/17/robots-txt-meant-forsearch-engines-dont-work-well-for-web-archives/
14. High-Tech Bridge: SSL/TLS Server Test (2017). https://www.htbridge.com/ssl/
15. Holz, R., Amann, J., Mehani, O., Kâafar, M.A., Wachs, M.: TLS in the wild: an internet-wide analysis of TLS-based protocols for electronic communication. In: Proceedings of the 23nd Annual Network and Distributed System Security Symposium (NDSS 2016). The Internet Society (2016)

16. Khandelwal, S.: 'Web Of Trust' Browser Add-On Caught Selling Users' Data (2016). http://thehackernews.com/2016/11/web-of-trust-addon.html
17. Kitterman, S.: Sender Policy Framework (SPF) for Authorizing Use of Domains in Email, Version 1. RFC 7208 (2014)
18. Kucherawy, M., Zwicky, E.: Domain-based Message Authentication, Reporting, and Conformance (DMARC). RFC 7489 (2015)
19. Laperdrix, P., Rudametkin, W., Baudry, B.: Beauty and the beast: diverting modern web browsers to build unique browser fingerprints. In: Proceedings of Symposium on Security and Privacy (S&P 2016), pp. 878–894. IEEE (2016)
20. Lauinger, T., Chaabane, A., Arshad, S., Robertson, W., Wilson, C., Kirda, E.: Thou shalt not depend on me: analysing the use of outdated javascript libraries on the web. In: Proceedings of the 24th Annual Network and Distributed System Security Symposium (NDSS 2017). The Internet Society (2017)
21. Maass, M., Laubach, A., Herrmann, D.: PrivacyScore: Analyse von Webseiten auf Sicherheits- und Privatheitsprobleme - Konzept und rechtliche Zulässigkeit. In: INFORMATIK 2017 (to appear). https://arxiv.org/abs/1705.08889, Gesellschaft für Informatik, Bonn (2017)
22. Mayer, J.R., Mitchell, J.C.: Third-party web tracking: policy and technology. In: Proceedings of Symposium on Security and Privacy (S&P 2013), pp. 413–427. IEEE (2012)
23. Mayer, W., Zauner, A., Schmiedecker, M., Huber, M.: No need for black chambers: testing TLS in the e-mail ecosystem at large. In: Proceedings of the 11th International Conference on Availability, Reliability and Security (ARES 2016), pp. 10–20. IEEE (2016)
24. Moxie Marlinspike: sslstrip (2017). https://moxie.org/software/sslstrip
25. Mozilla: Lightbeam (2017). https://www.mozilla.org/en-US/lightbeam/
26. Mozilla: Observatory (2017). https://observatory.mozilla.org/
27. Piwik: Piwik Free Web Analytics Software (2017). https://piwik.org/
28. Qualys: SSL Server Test (2017). https://www.ssllabs.com/ssltest/
29. Raymond Hill: uBlock Origin (2017). https://github.com/gorhill/uBlock
30. Helme, S.: Publishing my daily crawler data for wider analysis (2017). https://scotthelme.co.uk/alexa-top-1-million-analysis-feb-2017
31. Helme, S.: SecurityHeaders.io (2017). https://securityheaders.io/
32. Starov, O., Nikiforakis, N.: Extended tracking powers: measuring the privacy diffusion enabled by browser extensions. In: Proceedings of the 26th International Conference on World Wide Web (WWW 2017). ACM (2017)

Privacy Data Management and Awareness for Public Administrations: A Case Study from the Healthcare Domain

Vasiliki Diamantopoulou[1]([✉]), Konstantinos Angelopoulos[1], Julian Flake[2], Andrea Praitano[3], José Francisco Ruiz[4], Jan Jürjens[2,5], Michalis Pavlidis[1], Dimitri Bonutto[6], Andrès Castillo Sanz[7], Haralambos Mouratidis[1], Javier García Robles[4], and Alberto Eugenio Tozzi[6]

[1] University of Brighton, Brighton, UK
{v.diamantopoulou,k.angelopoulos,
m.pavlidis,h.mouratidis}@brighton.ac.uk
[2] Fraunhofer-Institute for Software and Systems Engineering,
Dortmund, Germany
{julian.flake,jan.juerjens}@isst.fraunhofer.de
[3] Business-e, Rome, Italy
andrea.praitano@business-e.it
[4] Atos, Madrid, Spain
{jose.ruizr,javier.garciar}@atos.net
[5] University of Koblenz-Landau, Koblenz, Germany
[6] Ospedale Pediatrico Bambino Gesù, Rome, Italy
{dimitri.bonutto,albertoeugenio.tozzi}@opbg.net
[7] International University of La Rioja UNIR, Madrid, Spain
andres.castillo@unir.net

Abstract. Development of Information Systems that ensure privacy is a challenging task that spans various fields such as technology, law and policy. Reports of recent privacy infringements indicate that we are far from not only achieving privacy but also from applying Privacy by Design principles. This is due to lack of holistic methods and tools which should enable to understand privacy issues, incorporate appropriate privacy controls during design-time and create and enforce a privacy policy during run-time. To address these issues, we present VisiOn Privacy Platform which provides holistic privacy management throughout the whole information system lifecycle. It contains a privacy aware process that is supported by a software platform and enables Data Controllers to ensure privacy and Data Subjects to gain control of their data, by participating in the privacy policy formulation. A case study from the healthcare domain is used to demonstrate the platform's benefits.

Keywords: Privacy management · Data protection · Privacy level agreement · eHealth · Telemedicine · VisiOn Privacy Platform

© Springer International Publishing AG 2017
E. Schweighofer et al. (Eds.): APF 2017, LNCS 10518, pp. 192–209, 2017.
DOI: 10.1007/978-3-319-67280-9_11

1   Introduction

The rapid development and the advances in Information and Communication Technologies (ICT) have led to their adoption by organisations, enabling them to transform their services to e-services, increasing their efficiency, productivity and growth [12]. Emphasis is given on security and privacy of the Information Technology (IT) systems when they are used for the management of personal data. During the development and operation of IT systems, security and privacy properties should be satisfied. This is even more imperative when IT systems are used by data controllers who work and manage critical types of personal data (i.e. sensitive data), for example, health-related ones.

The adoption of IT systems by the healthcare sector can also demonstrate substantial benefits, e.g., cost reduction, improved quality of care, promotion of evidence based medicine, record keeping, mobility [15], offering of efficient and real-time services to patients, flexibility, and patient safety [22]. However, the transition from paper-based health records to Electronic Health Records (EHR) lurks new challenges related to the secure transmission and privacy-handling of data, since health information is considered to be one of the most confidential types of personal information [14]. Health data exposed in the electronic environment is vulnerable to security and privacy threats [13].

The necessity for the privacy-enabled management of personal data is also reflected in the General Data Protection Regulation (GDPR) [5], which aims to protect the data subjects' interests, imposing data controllers to ensure data subjects' privacy and providing them the ownership and control of their data. Moreover, a recent research [4] regarding the European citizens' opinion for their attitude to data protection revealed that 69% of them are concerned that their personal data may be used for a purpose other than the one it was collected for. Other studies [19] have indicated that patients are reluctant to share their health information but for direct clinical care.

Data controllers should ensure secure management of their IT systems but also this should be communicated to the data subjects who are obliged to provide their personal data to use the provided e-services. Additionally, data subjects should be aware of their privacy rights so they can decide and declare their preferences regarding the management of their personal data.

This paper proposes the VisiOn Privacy Platform (VPP), an outcome of a H2020 European Project that provides privacy protection for electronic provided services by Public Administrations, which can be adequately applied in the healthcare domain. The adoption of this holistic, platform-supported approach improves privacy regarding the e-services in the following perspectives: (a) it enhances user's trust and confidence when using e-services, by exploiting existing software engineering approaches and combining them with modelling languages to analyse trust relationships between data controllers and data subjects (i.e. hospitals and patients), which could negatively affect the adoption of such services that the data controllers provide; (b) it improves transparency, by imposing accountability to data controllers, regarding protection of data subjects' information; (c) it builds confidence between the data controllers and subjects, since it provides a new type of Privacy Management system that allows the latter to take control over the data they provide in order to take advantage of the e-services; (d) it adapts data controller's privacy protection policies to each data subject's privacy preferences and introduces the concept of Privacy Level Agreement (PLA), a formal digital contract between data controllers and data subjects. A PLA presents the results of the analysis of the privacy threats, vulnerabilities and trust relationships of data controllers' IT systems, whilst complying with laws and regulations. Moreover, the structure of the PLA allows data controllers to elicit data subjects' privacy requirements, and eventually provides feedback regarding the data sharing policies of the data controllers.

The remainder of the paper is structured as follows: Sect. 2 discusses the state of the art while Sect. 3 presents the functionalities and the architecture of VPP. Section 4 illustrates our work with a real-world case study. Finally, Sect. 5 concludes the paper and raises issues for further research.

2   State of the Art

The concept of VPP encapsulates various aspects, namely the protection of privacy issues, the privacy awareness that arises to data subjects, the identification of privacy and security requirements from multiple perspectives and the customisation of privacy policies, based on individuals' privacy preferences.

The idea of an agreed, standardised way for web sites to communicate with users regarding their privacy policies presented in a standard machine-readable format has been introduced by the Platform of Privacy Preferences (P3P) Project [24]. This standard facilitates web browsers and other user agents to interpret privacy policies on behalf of their users, providing them directions in order to decide when to exchange data with web sites. The limitation of P3P lies on the fact that it was designed for static environments where users' privacy preferences are not expected to change. Furthermore, P3P does not provide sufficient support for specifying privacy threats and vulnerabilities that might endanger the privacy needs. In [10] the authors propose an architecture that promotes the employment of privacy policies and preferences. They define and introduce the concept of the Privacy Controller Agent for collecting, storing and comparing service providers' privacy policies with the preferences specified by the users. However, this work, as opposed to VPP, does not provide an agreement between two entities (e.g., citizen and PA, patient and hospital) but rather an architecture to define privacy policies.

In the literature multiple approaches have been proposed for capturing privacy requirements systematically. The Privacy Safeguard (PriS) [18], a privacy requirements engineering methodology, incorporates privacy requirements into the system design process, where privacy requirements are modelled as organisational goals. Next, the Modelling and Analysis of Privacy-aware Systems (MAPaS) framework [7] models requirements for privacy-aware systems. The authors in [23] adopt the concepts of privacy-by-policy and privacy-by-architecture, and propose a three-sphere model of user privacy concerns, relating

it to system operations (i.e. data transfer, storage and processing). The authors
in [11] propose a framework for privacy management and policies that addresses
various organisational perspectives, focusing on how organisations should evaluate their own privacy policies. Differently than those works, VPP provides a
holistic privacy management approach which is based on the Privacy by Design
(PbD) principles, since it starts with the elicitation of the user privacy requirements and it ends with the provision of Public Administration online services.

   The concept of PLA has been recently adopted by the research community as a standardised way for cloud providers to describe their data protection
practices. More specifically, the Privacy Level Agreement Working Group of the
Cloud Security Alliance has defined a PLA in the context of cloud services [8]. In
the same direction, the authors in [9] have presented the concept of PLA focusing on the cloud environment while the PLA is considered as a formal way for
the cloud providers to ensure that their privacy policy is communicated to the
service consumers. However, these works are limited to privacy aspects of cloud
provision without providing any support for the specification of user's (e.g., citizen, patient) preferences or the definition of privacy threats and vulnerabilities.

   Finally, the recent development of quite a few commercial products highlights
the need regarding the individuals' data protection. A repository provided by the
Information Shield[1] contains all the necessary material to support companies and
organisations in formalising or updating their privacy policies while maintaining
them compliant with relevant laws and regulations, at national and international level. Nymity[2] supports organisations enabling them to demonstrate data
privacy compliance, based on an accountability approach. 2B Advice[3] is a consulting services organisation, consisted of a group of companies which aims to
offer data privacy advice, software solutions and certifications. Another software
solution dedicated to data protection management is called Otris privacy[4]. This
tool focuses on the planning, setting-up, operation and decommissioning of data
processing methods. OneTrust[5] platform assists service providers to guarantee
the data privacy compliance with the relevant regulations, laws and privacy
policies to their clients. Contrary to these products, VPP conducts security and
privacy analysis of the information systems of each service provider, which is
reflected to each PLA, ensuring that the processes followed by the organisations
are law compliant. This is achieved by including in our proposed platform a tool
that allows to encode privacy laws and automates the law-compliance checks
of the composed privacy management policies. Additionally, the aforementioned
approaches compose privacy management policies ad-hoc, whereas in VPP are
composed by the preferences of the service consumers.

---

[1] https://informationshield.com/.

[2] https://www.nymity.com.

[3] https://www.2b-advice.com.

[4] https://www.otris.com/products/data-protection-management/.

[5] https://onetrust.com.

Another commercial solution for data protection is the TRUSTe[6] platform, which directs on Data Privacy Management (DPM), enabling users to control a set of provided technology-driven solutions in order to manage potential privacy challenges. Similarly, Disconnect[7] is a commercial software that facilitates users to easily understand the websites' privacy policies and realise how websites are handling their data. The common characteristic of the aforementioned two commercial solutions is that they focus on the better analysis and comprehension of each privacy policy, protecting user from actions that will put their personal data in danger. The approach that the VPP follows is based on the privacy preferences elicitations from both sides - service providers and service consumers - allowing the development of personalised PLAs, according to them.

3   The VisiOn Privacy Platform

3.1   The VisiOn Privacy Platform Functionalities

VPP supports the analysis of privacy issues from different perspectives (i.e. organisational, business-process, threat, and trust). It provides a holistic approach, covering all the potential aspects that influence and, consequently, shape the relationship in terms of trust between data subjects and online services provided by a data controller. VPP distinguishes two roles: data controller and data subjects. The data subject uses VPP's functionalities during run-time only, i.e. while using a service carried out by the data controller. The data controller uses VPP's functionalities during both, design-time and run-time of a system.

Data Controller's Functionalities. During design-time, the data controller/ data processor uses VPP to capture security and privacy requirements of their systems by modelling and analysing the data controller's/data processor' system or service under planning, from different perspectives: (i) potential threats to the data controller's systems and its environment that lead to security and privacy issues are captured and countermeasures to mitigate these risks are identified; (ii) trust relationships between the data controller and third party providers are modelled and analysed in order to realise whether these relationships endanger transparency and accountability from data subjects' perspective; (iii) the socio-technical environment of the data controller's/data processor's systems is captured by models of interactions between human and non-human actors. These models capture goals the actors try to achieve and information that is processed to achieve the goals; (iv) procedural models of business processes, enriched with security related information, which can act as blueprints to define executable business process models containing supplementary security related information; (v) once the requirements, with a special focus on the security and privacy aspect, are captured, the data controller's/data processor's system designer can

---

[6] https://www.truste.com.

[7] https://disconnect.me/icons.

specify the details of the system under planning, by using a standard modelling language. The resulting specification models can be complemented with privacy and security related constraints the models have to comply with, while identified non-compliances are reported. The reports can be used by the system designers to refine their system specifications to finally meet the privacy specifications.

All models and analysis results enhance the data controller's/data processor's comprehension of the privacy and security issues, regardless of the expertise level and the technical knowledge of the data controller's employee, supporting the visual analysis of privacy and security issues at different levels and perspectives.

In addition to this design cycle support, VPP offers functionalities that prepare the actual use of VPP during run-time. The data controller/data processor uses VPP to create questionnaires that are filled by data subjects once the system is in production. This allows the data controller to capture each data subject's privacy preferences, which are used to create data access policies and, finally, the PLA. VPP supports the data controller/data processor in creating questionnaires, by suggesting suitable questions, automatically derived from system models. Furthermore, machine-readable representations of data protection legislations are fed into the system by the data controller/data processor, in order to specify policies that must be fulfilled by the system. This, together with a checklist questionnaire, allows the data controller to self-assess its compliance with relevant laws and regulations. Non-compliance issues are reported and can be resolved before the system or service under planning is released. As an additional preparatory step before the system or service under planning is released, the data controller/data processor fills an additional questionnaire to provide information required for the evaluation of data subjects' personal data.

During run-time, the data controller's system uses VPP to evaluate data access requests against the privacy policies reflecting the data subjects' privacy preferences. The data controller's/data processor's system can use VPP for the actual enforcement of data access policies. The data controller/data processor uses VPP directly to monitor the system's compliance with the data processing policies that reflect the data subject's privacy preferences during run-time.

Data Subject's Functionalities. Data subjects are supported by VPP during run-time in different ways. In the first place, data subjects interact with VPP to define and update their privacy preferences related to their personal data, by answering the aforementioned questionnaire, where they define if and how they wish their data to be processed. These privacy preferences are input to data access policies and PLAs. Data subjects can view their personal PLA, which furthermore contains visual representation of the systems involved in the processing of the data subjects' data, and the results of system analysis and law compliance checks performed by the data controller. All information contained in the PLA aims to raise transparency of the data processing and therefore the trust in lawful processing of the data subjects' personal data. Moreover, VPP provides useful insights to the data subjects regarding the value of their personal data. Thus, realising the value of their data, data subjects are able to choose what data they wish to share and with whom, which might lead to the need to modify their personal privacy preferences. Finally, VPP enables data subjects to monitor issued access requests related to their personal data, the data access decisions and enforcements.

All the aforementioned functionalities aim to raise the data subjects' awareness of how their data is processed and of any potential threats, giving them all the necessary information to decide the level of data sharing. Moreover, VPP enables the interaction between data controllers and data subjects, respecting thus the latter's privacy rights, as the GDPR requests. Finally, VPP enables data controllers, and also data processors or data protection officers, to communicate - in a semi-automated way - the identified data breach(es) (Article 34 of [5]).

3.2   The Vision Privacy Platform Architecture

After defining the functionalities of VPP, the logical architecture of the platform is now presented. To this end, task categories that bundle similar functionalities were identified. In particular, (i) design and evaluation of system requirements with focus on privacy concerns, (ii) specification of system and service details with focus on privacy concerns, (iii) assessment of data subject's privacy preferences, (iv) enforcement and monitoring of system's compliance with data subject's privacy preferences at run-time, (v) visualisation of analysis results, system logs, system's compliance and, finally, the generation of the PLA.

Each of these five task categories are addressed by a functional component of VPP, integrating a powerful set of tools. More specifically, the five functional components of VPP are the following:

The *Privacy Requirements Component* supports the data controller to design and process privacy requirements. This is achieved by modelling the services and the system under development from several perspectives, covering different aspects, i.e. the socio-technical environment, trust relationships between actors, security threats and business processes' compliance with privacy and security requirements.

The *Privacy Specification Component* allows the specification of further system details (by e.g., UML models), based on the requirements captured by the Privacy Requirements Component. The detailed specifications are analysed in terms of privacy and security issues, value of personal data and compliance with relevant data protection laws and regulations. This analysis is based on established privacy and security properties, such as secure information flow [17].

The *Privacy Assessment Component* allows data subjects to define their privacy preferences for data sharing and management by the data controller. Their preferences are captured by answering simple and very clear questions presented in Privacy Visualisation Component. Moreover, answers to additional questions are used for the estimation of the value of the data subject's personal data that will be presented in the PLA. The data controller uses the Privacy Assessment Component to specify these questions and also to provide required information about the processing of data subject's personal data.

The *Privacy Run-time Component* monitors data access requests and enforces data access policies. These policies for automatic enforcement are generated automatically by deriving information from system models and interpretation of data subject's privacy preferences (as described in the questionnaires). This functionality is transparent to the end users and works in the back-end. The information provided to data subjects is done through the Privacy Visualisation Component, which shows the relevant requests, issues, etc. to their data. This component is key in the integration with the system under development, as the requests have to be done through the service it offers before accessing the data.

The *Privacy Visualisation Component* acts as a unified user interface during run-time for both, data controller and data subjects, by integrating the user interfaces of the different tools of the other four components. The PLA, as the manifestation and visualisation of the system's properties and data subject's preferences, is compiled and visualised by this component.

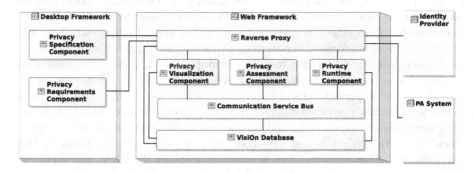

Fig. 1. VisiOn Privacy Platform: components and frameworks

Figure 1 depicts the five functional components described along with three supplemental components of VPP, responsible for connecting the functional components with each other and with external systems. These three supplemental components are left to describe.

Firstly, the *Reverse Proxy* component acts as a gateway to VPP for systems that are not part of VPP. Requests to access VPP are issued by human actors and by systems of the data controller (labelled *PA System* in Fig. 1). To avoid managing and storing sensitive account data like passwords, unauthorised access requests are redirected to an external Identity Provider, which performs users' and services' authentication. Upon successful authentication, the external Identity Provider issues a token which authorises the user or service to access VPP. Authorised access requests are passed to the appropriate internal functional component.

Secondly, the *Communication Service Bus* component integrates an Enterprise Service Bus and enables tools to directly exchange messages without persisting the exchanged information. This is used in situations where a tool has to directly react on certain events. To achieve this, the Communication Service Bus provides a message bus that supports messaging between one sender and one receiver and messaging between one sender and arbitrary many receivers. This allows for flexibility in the communication and selection of tools. New tools can be added or replace an existing one, without requiring to modify its communication partners. A tool sending information does not need to know which tool or tools actually receive the information, a tool receiving information does not need to know which tool actually sends the information.

Thirdly, the *VisiOn Database* is a common data store, used by the functional components to persist data that may be read and processed by other components. A tool writing data to the VisiOn Database does not need to know which other tool will read this data. A tool reading data from the VisiOn Database has to know at least the location and the format of the data.

Finally, the components of VPP are integrated in two complementary frameworks, the *Desktop Framework* and the *Web Framework*. The Desktop Framework is used by the data controller's administrators only. It is used during design-time to capture and analyse the privacy characteristics, requirements and properties of their systems. It contains the modelling tools of the Privacy Requirements Component and the Privacy Specification Component. The output of the modelling tools of these components is stored in the VisiOn Database for further processing by other tools, for example for the automatic generation of questions to be answered by data subjects. In addition, the Web Framework provides run-time privacy related functionalities and also configuration settings. It has as input the data controller's privacy requirements and, based on these, data controllers can create the questionnaire with the corresponding questions. Then, the data subject can specify their privacy preferences by filling in this questionnaire. Moreover, the Web Framework displays the PLA, informing the data subjects of how their data is used, by whom and for what purpose, and also enforces the corresponding privacy policies. It is also the main interface for both data controllers and data subjects, so it is integrated with the Identity Provider of the data controller, which allows users to easily access and use the functionalities of VPP.

4   Case Study

In this section we report our experience of applying VPP to a real-world case study in the healthcare domain. This case study involves two paediatric clinics, namely Ospedale Pediatrico Bambino Gesù (OPBG) and Hospital Infantil Universitario Niño Jesús (HIUNJ) that use a telemedicine platform to exchange medical information of patients.

4.1   Motivating Scenario

The procedure of obtaining a patient's consent during medical procedure is a key aspect for guaranteeing transparency in the treatment of personal healthcare data. For this reason, the consent form includes a written detailed document which patients should carefully read before signing. This process is due even when a patient seeks urgent healthcare, unless immediate medical treatment must be provided in order to prevent potential death or complications. Through the consent form, health professionals establish a formal relationship with patients or their legal guardian, who provides all the necessary information that facilitates the decision making on both medical and personal data processing.

The information included in the consent form is complementary to and should not substitute the information provided orally by the health personnel during a treatment. Moreover, the written consent form is part of the medical record. In particular, the responsibility of filling a medical record is bound by certain rules. Consent to medical and surgical treatment is personal and can be provided only by the patient. In case the patient is unable to give a consent, medical data and approval of informed consent is respectively provided by the person exercising parental responsibility or by a legal guardian. The exercise of parental or tutorial responsibility is implemented on the declaration. Note that consent cannot be delegated, so the person who legally represent the minor is the only one entitled to provide consent to medical treatment. Another mandatory condition is the state of necessity. If the patient is in a state of emergency, the physician can act without the acquisition of the consent form because of the need to save the patient from the danger of serious harm or a life threat.

In this scenario, a platform, such as VPP, that allows the patient to fully control their information through permitted and prohibited operations and consents is a massive breakthrough. Furthermore, VPP increases awareness and understanding of the importance of protecting their data, highlighting the benefits/risks of signing/not signing a consent form. These requirements are the most important but there is a full list of high level requirements to consider in the process of compiling an aware consent form for a telemedicine scenario. The patients should have a clearer picture of the benefits/risks for compiling it.

The processes in telemedicine services fall within the sensitive data being processed by electronic instruments, which are currently regulated by the provisions of Directive 2002/58/EC [2]. The methods and the solutions necessary to ensure confidentiality, integrity and availability of data should therefore be adopted in accordance with the security measures explicitly provided in the Directive 95/46/EC [1], covered under the GDPR [5] and the new regulation replacing the Directive 2002/58/EC [2], which can be found in [3].

The provision of a medical performance is historically connected to the physical presence of the patient in a hospital doctor's studio or of the doctor in the home of the patient. The eHealth services try to change this traditional approach. The new technology could help doctors to provide some medical performances by remote place. The major problem of medical services is related to the type of data exchanged. In each medical service, data is classified as sensitive data and this kind of data request a high level of protection of the three aspects of security (Confidentiality, Integrity and Availability) [16].

An important aspect of the eHealth is that the clinical record (totally or partially) has to move from one site to another. Consequently, this transfer aims to raise two important issues. First, who has the right to access this data and secondly, if the patient has given their consent to transmit their data.

Another important problem is related to how the patient's sensitive data is transmitted. In eHealth, data is transmitted by video, audio and files. For this type of data it is necessary to develop modular system that includes technical and/or organisational enforcement measures, able to balance the right to protect the sensitive data and the processing of this data necessary to protect the vital interests of the data subject or of another natural person, where the data subject is physically or legally incapable of giving consent [5].

4.2 Privacy Level Agreement for Hospitals

Patients, through Privacy Visualisation Component and Privacy Assessment Component of VPP, are able to define the privacy preferences concerning their data, defining what data they wish to share and how they expected to be managed. The questionnaire is a user-friendly way of defining the preferences, using natural language more simple and easy to understand by the patients. For the generation of PLAs that will capture the privacy preferences of the patients, the questionnaire provided by the Hospital and the answers given by the patients are required. In particular, the data processor accesses the Privacy Assessment Component, which guides them to create questions to the patients about the Hospital System and how they wish their data to be managed. Moreover, this component is responsible for collecting the relevant information that has been generated in the Privacy Requirements Component, regarding the access rights that are documented for each piece of data transmitted within the Hospital system. Thus, the data processor forms questions accordingly, responsible for capturing patients' preferences regarding these access rights. An instance of this questionnaire is depicted in Fig. 2.

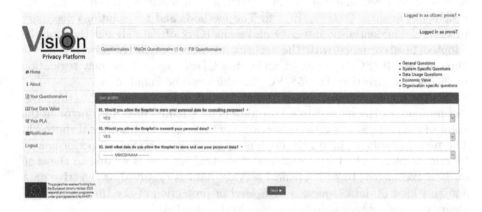

Fig. 2. A questionnaire for an eHealth service

After the development of the questionnaire, the data processor evaluates the sensitivity of the data mentioned in the questions. These values are inserted through the Privacy Specification Component and then, they are depicted in a web diagram form in the PLA. This diagram contains the value from the data processor perspective, the patient's perspective, and the average of the values of all the previously registered to the eHealth service patients. Next, the data processor is ready to publish the questionnaire where the patients can answer, providing also their values for the sensitivity of their data. For each patient's answer, the Privacy Visualisation Component collects the responses, the relevant laws, the information derived from the modelling of privacy information, which includes the security and trust analysis results and the data value of patients' data, and finally, composes the PLA. A PLA, as it is depicted in Fig. 3, describes a patient's personal privacy preferences, along with statistics, policies and laws applied by the hospitals. The structure and the design of the PLA is simple enough and easily understandable by each patient, including textual and visual information. This information is up-do-date, so patients can always find all their information compiled in a single place. This functionality is very useful as it provides a complete description of patients' privacy status.

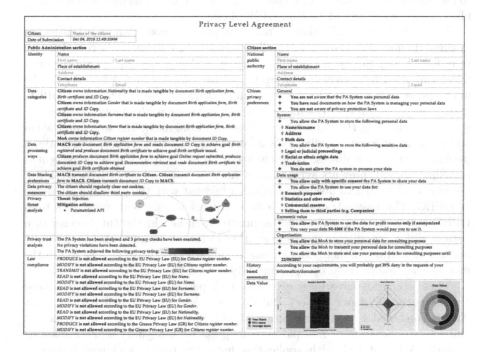

Fig. 3. A patient's PLA

4.3 Applying VPP in eHealth

Before deploying VPP at the premises of OPBG and HIUNJ, the physicians at each hospital were able to retrieve patient data from the hosting hospital's repository and send it through a telemedicine application, without any restriction. The application was extended by including the functionality of sending a request to VPP before querying to the repository of documents of patients. The aforementioned request contains information about the person or institution that asks for the health data, the identification of the patient concerned and the items that can be susceptible of privacy protection. VPP compares the fields in the request to the privacy preferences that are recorded in that moment.

There are two important points to be taken into account. First, before any data is required by the doctors, the parents or tutors of the minor should fill a questionnaire presented to them by VPP. That questionnaire is stored in the VisiOn Database and can be modified any time the parents/guardians wish to. Second, both hospitals must deploy an instance of VPP to protect the data stored in their premises. The parents/guardians must fill a questionnaire in each hospital in which data of their child is stored. As an example, if an Italian child on holidays in Spain goes to HIUNJ and the doctors there think they must see a report or a x-ray image created and stored in OPBG, supposing they have access to the corresponding application there (e.g., OBGclinico), the parents must have filled the questionnaire of VPP in OPBG before.

To monitor the application of rules for privacy protection, VPP is tested in three simulated scenarios. In the first scenario, a patient has a complex and rare disease and the medical staff in charge of their follow-up decide to ask a teleconsultation to a specialist group in another hospital in order to decide the most appropriate diagnostic procedures and therapy. The physicians at OPBG make a diagnosis, producing a medical report and some medical images, while the specialised group at HIUNJ retrieves these files from an OPBG web application and confirms whether the diagnosis is correct or not. In the second scenario, a patient has a chronic disease and is followed up by OPBG. While the patient is travelling abroad, presents symptoms of their disease and visits HIUNJ. Then, the physician in HIUNJ needs to perform a televisit with the patient's physician at OPBG. The first retrieves the patient clinical history and some data from OPBG system to perform a more accurate diagnosis. In the third scenario, a patient with a rare disease moves to another European country with their family and needs to transfer their clinical dataset, in order to allow the hospital in the new location follow them up appropriately.

These scenarios have been executed with patient data partially produced for the purposes of our project and do not belong to any real patient. This data is combined with a composition of real clinical data taken anonymously and retrospectively from real patients, to preserve anonymity while remaining realistic. A hospital eHealth application hosts the patient's clinical history, a computer tomography image, a histological and a surgical intervention report.

In this use case, technicians (hospitals personnel) are in charge of modelling the overall system and setting the infrastructure. Doctors (hospitals personnel) connect to a web application from another hospital to access the health data of a patient and parents (or tutors) of a patient that connect to VPP, to declare permissions to let the doctors of another EU country to access or not the health data of their child. For evaluating VPP, two trials were performed. In the first trial, the objectives and the functionalities of the VPP were explained to the parents/tutors of the patients. Next, the parents/tutors filled a consent form to authorise the use of their answers for the purpose of this case study. After their interaction with the VPP, i.e. after they fill the questionnaire related to their privacy preferences, and the creation of the PLA for each patient/tutor, they answered a questionnaire[8] in order to assess the usability and usefulness of VPP. In the second trial, the IT personnel was trained on how to use the Desktop Framework tools and how to create a questionnaire related to the e-Health service. Next, they were provided a questionnaire(see Footnote 8) similar to the one the parents/tutors, in order to evaluate VPP from the data processor's perspective.

The data processors, after the VPP installation and the integration with the hospital infrastructure, are able to model their systems and elicit privacy requirements, by using the Desktop Framework of VPP. After the data processors create a questionnaire on the VPP web portal, they attach the metadata for each question (metadata is basically keywords to add during the questionnaire building procedure). Then, when a patient registers on the eHealth service and compiles the questionnaire, this metadata are stored on the VPP back-end, according to the answers given. The models developed by the data processors are also stored on the VisiOn Database. The patients, after answering the questionnaire, can visualise their own PLAs and the attempts to access their resources, checking the notifications created by the Privacy Runtime Component. The data processors are also able to monitor these processes, for each patient, according to the level of authorisation that the organisation granted them for this information. When a physician from another hospital tries to retrieve the data from the web application integrated with the Web Framework of VPP, they receive feedback from VPP, according to the PLAs set up by the patients.

In a manner wholly transparent for users, the requests made by the clinicians to get the desired documents are converted to a XACML format, which is semantically very rich. These transformed requests are immediately sent to VPP that decodes and checks them against the policies derived from the preferences recorded by the patient, or the parents, or legal tutors of the patient. With the response of a simple PERMIT or DENY statement, the developed application proceeds to request data to the databases in the servers of the health system, or notifies the doctor that the data required cannot and should not be granted, because the patient does not wish so.

The contingency of an emergency or danger of death situation has been taken into account. The possibility that the doctor asserts that a situation of that extreme sort is taking place in the moment of the consultation has been added to the interface of the request of the data. In that sense, the permissions of data to be transmitted in case of scientific studies or actual consultations for second opinions are also added in the questionnaires, and also, the corresponding indications in the application for the doctors to input at the time of the requesting.

---

[8] This questionnaire is not part of VPP and has been created only for the purposes of the trials and the evaluation of the platform.

4.4 Discussion

One of the key aspects to consider in the future development of ICT hospitals' services is the EHR. Though not universal, EHR allows the digital management of health information and medical procedures, including telemedicine. Currently, interoperability between different EHR platforms has raised significant issues [20]. Moreover, the development of further specialised digital services may require some efforts to guarantee transparency of telemedicine transactions between hospitals and also, between patients and hospitals. An ideal EHR should contain, in the first place, the informed consent properly filled out, a copy of the resignation letter which must be completed even in case of patient death, and the hospital discharge form, which must be filled up through the IT application, which should be in compliance with national and regional regulations. All results of the provided services, including telemedicine, remote monitoring and specialist consultations, all therapies prescribed and administered, internal/external transfers of the patient within the different hospital's operating units and integrated graphics of hospital stay and of intensive areas must be recorded. Furthermore, medical assessments pre-sedation, pre-anaesthetic, pre-surgery (in cases where such procedures are foreseen) and surgical procedures performed shall be documented in the electronic surgical register, and a copy of the surgical report should be attached to the health record.

The VPP trial in the hospitals had involved the telemedicine and teleconsulting services but this kind of eHealth services are only a limited range of electronics' medical services. The evolution of the technical aspect of VPP will follow three major roads. The first is to expand the enforcement on the only exchange of EHR documents to the medical information exchanged orally and with video in telemedicine and teleconsultation; the second is to cover other eHealth services, such as consultation of EHR by the internal staff of the hospitals and by the patient himself or to all those electronic medical devices; the last way is to expand the enforcement to devices not specifically medical but which contain information comparable to sensitive data (e.g., smartwatch, fit band/fitness tracker, smartphone, etc.). The data subjects upon their registration receive their credentials and after answering a questionnaire, a PLA is generated for each organisation, which could be problematic as services adopt VPP. To tackle this problem we foresee the use of common credentials for every service, e.g., the social security number. However, regarding the multiple PLAs, we will investigate how to improve *PLA portability* between different installations of VPPs.

The main issue related to the integration of VPP with EHR lies in the fact that there is no standardised approach in Europe in the development of EHRs. For example, the situation of the Italian EHR is managed at regional level and the situation is fragmented [6]. European health organisations at all levels should be able to provide online services, i.e. teleconsultation, e-prescription, e-referral, telemonitoring and telecare, but these are not mutually compatible. These services are expected to increase accessibility to healthcare, appropriateness and quality of care, and decrease direct and indirect costs associated with care.

5   Conclusions

This paper presents a platform-supported approach for privacy management of citizens' data regarding its management and use. Data subjects can then safely share their data with organisations in order to take advantage of the e-services they provide. The agreement between data controllers and subjects regarding the use of data is conceptualised in a PLA, which is elicited through clear and non-technical questionnaires. This allows PAs, using our approach, to increase transparency and trust in their services.

From social perspective, VPP aims to raise data subjects' awareness regarding the value of their data through enhanced visualisation elements, and information that can be exploited of the determination of data subjects' privacy preferences. This way, and as previously explained, transparency and trust will increase the number of users using e-services. Data controllers can benefit from VPP, since they can manage personal data in an accountable and transparent way, and also provide data subjects with the option of controlling their privacy settings, regarding personal data they are obliged to share. Monitoring how personal data is used after it has been provided to data controllers is one of the main functionalities of VPP, provided by the Web Framework, making VPP play a critical role in the maximisation of transparency and accountability regarding activities of data controllers related to data subjects' personal data.

From technical perspective, VPP integrates a set of software engineering methodologies and tools across different levels, from the elicitation of users' privacy requirements to the enforcement of privacy policies during run-time, and different perspectives, from data evaluation to privacy assurance. Such integration provides a clear advantage over existing software engineering approaches and tools, since it enables a holistic analysis of both data controllers and data subjects' privacy preferences. To the best of our knowledge, VPP is the only approach in the literature that is able to identify and analyse privacy and security threats of data controllers' IT systems and to also allow data subject to declare their privacy preferences.

VPP represents a useful tool that can support the verification of data controllers' compliance with the GDPR. Future work includes the enhancement of tools for policies and law compliance, in order to allow data controllers to check their compliance with the GDPR and also, how to implement it in their systems. This will have a big impact on data controllers as, in this way, they will be able not only to provide privacy enforcement for the data subjects, but also they can use VPP for making them adhere to the GDPR, ensuring data subjects that their data is protected, according policies at organisational, country or European level. Finally, even this work focuses on requirements stemming from GDPR, approach or parts of it are applicable to systems and services under different legislation.

Further development of VPP can lead to mobile applications that data subjects can use to check and define their privacy preferences, access to statistics on the use of their data, notifications, etc. As the market of mobile applications is growing by year, our approach would be the best complement for the cloud environment and will facilitate data subjects in controlling their data and data controllers in improving their transparency. VPP integration in EHR, such as the SMART[9], which focuses on and supports the development of mobile apps integrated with EHR systems, is also part of possible future work.

Finally, another future work of VPP concerns the Industrial Data Space [21], which is a virtual data space for the secure exchange of data in business ecosystems, for creating and using smart services and innovative business processes, while at the same time ensuring digital sovereignty of data owners. The Medical Data Space is a domain-specific instantiation in the Medical Domain to address the particular challenges and requirements that arise in this domain. To address the data privacy concerns in this context, results and tools from VPP are going to be used. For example, the Industrial Data Space will offer privacy-relevant data analysis services, including an anonymisation service, where the tools and techniques on model-based privacy and security analysis from VPP will be used to determine that the desired level of privacy has been reached.

Acknowledgement. This research was supported by the Visual Privacy Management in User Centric Open Environments (VisiOn) project, supported by the EU Horizon 2020 programme, Grant Agreement No. 653642.

References

1. European commission: Directive 95/46/ec of the european parliament and of the council. http://eur-lex.europa.eu/legal-content/EN/TXT/?uri=CELEX: 31995L0046. Accessed 14 Jun 2017
2. European commission: Directive 2002/58/ec of the European parliament and of the council, July 2002. http://ec.europa.eu/justice/data-protection/law/files/recast_ 20091219_en.pdf. Accessed 14 Jun 2017
3. European commission: Proposal for a regulation of the european parliament and of the council, January 2012. http://eur-lex.europa.eu/legal-content/en/ALL/? uri=CELEX:52012PC0011. Accessed 14 Jun 2017
4. European commission: Eurobarometer 431 - data protection report. Technical report (2015)
5. European parliament: Regulation (eu) 2016/679 of the european parliament and of the coucil of 27 April 2016 on the protection of natural persons with regard to the processing of personal data and on the free movement of such data, and repealing directive 95/46/ec (general data protection regulation) (2016). http://eur-lex.europa.eu/legal-content/EN/TXT/PDF/? uri=CELEX:32016R0679&from=en. Accessed 14 Jun 2017
6. Forum-pa - osservatori digital innovation del politecnico di milano: Che cos'è il fascicolo sanitario elettronico e come utilizzarlo, December 2016
7. Colombo, P., Ferrari, E.: Towards a modeling and analysis framework for privacy-aware systems. In: 2012 International Conference on Privacy, Security, Risk and Trust (PASSAT), and 2012 International Conference on Social Computing (Social-Com), pp. 81–90. IEEE (2012)

---

[9] https://smarthealthit.org/an-app-platform-for-healthcare/about/.

8. CSA: Privacy level agreement outline for the sale of cloud services in the European Union. Technical report, Cloud Security Alliance, Privacy Level Agreement Working Group, February 2013

9. DErrico, M., Pearson, S.: Towards a formalised representation for the technical enforcement of privacy level agreements. In: 2015 IEEE International Conference on Cloud Engineering (IC2E), pp. 422–427. IEEE (2015)

10. Drogkaris, P., Gritzalis, S., Lambrinoudakis, C.: Employing privacy policies and preferences in modern e-government environments. Int. J. Electr. Governance 6(2), 101–116 (2013)

11. Earp, J., Anton, A., Jarvinen, O.: A social, technical, and legal framework for privacy management and policies. In: AMCIS 2002 Proceedings, p. 89 (2002)

12. Ebrahim, Z., Irani, Z.: e-Government adoption: architecture and barriers. Bus. Process Manage. J. 11(5), 589–611 (2005)

13. Farzandipour, M., Sadoughi, F., Ahmadi, M., Karimi, I.: Security requirements and solutions in electronic health records: lessons learned from a comparative study. J. Med. Syst. 34(4), 629–642 (2010)

14. Fernández-Alemán, J.L., Señor, I.C., Lozoya, P.Á.O., Toval, A.: Security and privacy in electronic health records: a systematic literature review. J. Biomed. Inform. 46(3), 541–562 (2013)

15. Greenhalgh, T., Hinder, S., Stramer, K., Bratan, T., Russell, J.: Adoption, non-adoption, and abandonment of a personal electronic health record: case study of healthspace. BMJ 341, c5814 (2010)

16. ISO/IEC: 27000:2016 information technology - security techniques - information security management systems - overview and vocabulary. Technical report (2016)

17. Jürjens, J.: Secure information flow for concurrent processes. In: Palamidessi, C. (ed.) CONCUR 2000. LNCS, vol. 1877, pp. 395–409. Springer, Heidelberg (2000). doi:10.1007/3-540-44618-4_29

18. Kalloniatis, C., Kavakli, E., Gritzalis, S.: Addressing privacy requirements in system design: the PriS method. Requirements Eng. 13(3), 241–255 (2008)

19. Li, J.S., Zhou, T.S., Chu, J., Araki, K., Yoshihara, H.: Design and development of an international clinical data exchange system: the international layer function of the dolphin project. J. Am. Med. Inform. Assoc. 18(5), 683–689 (2011)

20. Mahfuth, A., Dhillon, J.S., Drus, S.M.: A systematic review on data security and patient privacy issues in electronic medical records. J. Theoret. Appl. Inform. Technol. 90(2), 106 (2016)

21. Otto, B., Auer, S., Cirullies, J., Jürjens, J., Menz, N., Schon, J., Wenzel, S.: Industrial data space: digital souvereignity over data. Technical report, Technical Report, Fraunhofer-Gesellschaft (2016)

22. Rezaeibagha, F., Win, K.T., Susilo, W.: A systematic literature review on security and privacy of electronic health record systems: technical perspectives. Health Inform. Manage. J. 44(3), 23–38 (2015)

23. Spiekermann, S., Cranor, L.F.: Engineering privacy. IEEE Trans. Software Eng. 35(1), 67–82 (2009)

24. (W3C), W.W.W.C.: Platform for privacy preferences (p3p) project (2016). https://www.w3.org/TR/P3P11/. Accessed 14 Jun 2017

Better Data Protection by Design Through Multicriteria Decision Making: On False Tradeoffs Between Privacy and Utility

Bettina Berendt[✉]

Department of Computer Science, KU Leuven, Leuven, Belgium
bettina.berendt@cs.kuleuven.be
https://people.cs.kuleuven.be/~bettina.berendt/

Abstract. Data Protection by Design (DPbD, also known as Privacy by Design) has received much attention in recent years as a method for building data protection into IT systems from the start. In the EU, DPbD will become mandatory from 2018 onwards under the GDPR. In earlier work, we emphasized the multi*disciplinary* nature of DPbD. The present paper builds on this to argue that DPbD also needs a multi*criteria* approach that goes beyond the traditional focus on (data) privacy (even if understood in its multiple meanings).

The paper is based on the results of a survey (n = 101) among employees of a large institution concerning the introduction of technology that tracks some of their behaviour. Even though a substantial portion of respondents are security/privacy researchers, concerns revolved strongly around social consequences of the technology change, usability issues, and transparency. The results taken together indicate that the decrease in privacy through data collection was associated with (a) an increase in accountability, (b) the blocking of non-authorized uses of resources, (c) a decrease in usability, (d) an altered perception of a communal space, (e) altered actions in the communal space, and (f) an increased salience of how decisions are made and communicated. These results call into question the models from computer science/data mining that posit a privacy-utility tradeoff. Instead, this paper argues, multicriteria notions of utility are needed, and this leads to design spaces in which less privacy may be associated with less utility rather than be compensated for by more utility, as the standard tradeoff models suggest. The paper concludes with an outlook on activities aimed at raising awareness and bringing the wider notion of DPbD into decision processes.

Keywords: Implementation aspects of "by design" and "by default" paradigms · Aspects of privacy impact and risk assessment · User studies · Privacy and utility modelling and decision making

1 Introduction

Data Protection by Design (DPbD) has received much attention in recent years as an approach for building data protection into IT systems from the start.

© Springer International Publishing AG 2017
E. Schweighofer et al. (Eds.): APF 2017, LNCS 10518, pp. 210–230, 2017.
DOI: 10.1007/978-3-319-67280-9_12

In the EU, DPbD will become mandatory from 2018 onwards under the General Data Protection Regulation (GDPR). In a panel at APF 2015, summarized and elaborated on in [21], we emphasized the need for multi*disciplinary* approaches to DPbD and illustrated this with conceptual and empirical examples.

A significant part of DPbD is the Data Protection Impact Assessment (DPIA) in which, among other things, the likely impacts of the planned technology on stakeholders' privacy are assessed. In multidisciplinary DPbD/DPIA, this notion of privacy (impacts) will be interpreted not only from a computational standpoint (where well-defined notions of data security and data confidentiality will be central), but based on a wider understanding of privacy including legal, sociological and psychological aspects. And in line with the GDPR requirement to implement appropriate technical and organisational measures to effect data protection, design solutions must be based on state-of-the-art methods for reducing unnecessary disclosures of personal data and/or avoiding unnecessary inference channels towards personal information.

The present paper reports on a survey that started from a multidisciplinary notion of privacy, but discovered in the answers a much richer set of concerns. This shows that DPbD also needs a multi*criteria* approach that goes beyond the traditional focus on data protection and privacy (even if understood in its multiple meanings).

In this context, it should be noted that the terms "data protection" and "privacy" are not defined uniformly and often used synonymously. Therefore, DPbD and DPIA are also often referred to as "Privacy by Design" and "Privacy Impact Assessment", e.g. [5,6,21]. In the survey described here, both terms were avoided. In the discussion, I will use the terms "data protection" in the sense of EU law and "privacy" in the general sense that "privacy can be violated by data processing", i.e. the (vague, but commonly used) concept at the intersection of the EU fundamental rights to privacy and to data protection. I return to a more differentiated notion of the two terms in the Conclusion.

The paper is organised as follows: Sect. 2 describes the case study and discusses its results. Section 3 investigates the implications, in particular of the exploratory analysis for risk-utility or privacy-utility tradeoffs in DPbD. Section 4 discusses limitations, and Sect. 5 summarises the conclusions and gives an outlook on future work. Related work is referenced throughout the text to enhance readability.

2 A Case Study: Tracking Coffee Consumption

2.1 Context

Organisational and Technological Context. The technology introduction took place in a computer-science department of a large research organization that is offering free coffee, tea and mineral water to staff in a room open to all on the top floor of their building. For a number of years, two industrial coffee machines have been serving hot drinks. They are operated and filled with raw materials by an external service provider. (Hot water could be obtained from these machines or a separate, household-size electric kettle, with tea bags available on the table. Most tea drinkers use the electric kettle.) A paper sign on the door to the staff cafeteria, and paper signs on the coffee machines, communicate that room and drinks are for staff and their guests only. Doors are open during business hours and accessible via personnel-card readers at other times.

In November 2016, personnel-card readers were installed on the two coffee machines. The measure was announced in an email from the Head of Unit and explained further in a second email, in answer to a question by a staff member. The emails stated that the only change would be the need to swipe the card before getting coffee, and that "[t]here are no plans to collect statistics on everybody's consumption, neither the type of consumption nor the frequency". The costs of coffee per year were mentioned, and the benefits of the department only having to pay for its members' coffee consumption.

The personnel cards are contactless cards that are identified by a card number, which in turn is linked to the personnel ID. A card swipe causes an authentication request to the central authentication server. Upon successful authentication (= the cardholder is authorized to operate the resource), an electric circuit is closed for a few seconds and thus allows the resource to function (= the door to unblock, the coffee machine to dispense a hot drink, ...). All authentication requests are logged with card ID, resource ID, and timestamp.

The authentication server manages and logs data concerning the close to 70,000 members of the whole organisation. The department investigated in the present study employs 239 people, all of whom are authorised to consume coffee from the machines studied.

The cards grant access to a number of resources (originally doors and other gates) and have to be presented to a card reader to get food in the staff canteens. The recent deployment on coffee machines is in line with plans for employing the cards to control access to a wide range of other services (more doors, cupboards containing expensive equipment, ...). The organisation favours the deployment, for new purposes, of this form of access control because it is cheap (every member already has a card, the readers are cheap, and the authentication technology is in place anyway).

DPbD Considerations. The collected data are personal data, since they encode that a person identifiable via their card ID to their personnel ID, operated a certain resource at a certain time. (The card ID acts as a pseudonym.) The logged data encode the location and the fact of usage, i.e. *that* a drink was taken. Are they also sensitive data, i.e. special categories of data as per EU Data Protection Directive and GDPR? Food and drink choices are generally considered not to be sensitive data, although they may allow for inferences towards sensitive data, as the example of food preferences on airline flights shows[1] [13]. Other inferences are possible, for example from food/drink consumption to health status. In the current example, the evidence for this is weaker, first because "coffee consumption" and even "coffee addiction" are generally not considered true health risks.

---

[1] For example, halal/kosher food preference can be an indicator of religion.

Also, the card reader authentication does not lead to the logging of *what* drink the identifiable user chose (although some respondents believe that, see below); it could have been hot water or chocolate. Another possible type of inference is that the fact of using the coffee machine signals that the employee takes a break, but these inferences too are uncertain, since drinks are often taken specifically to accompany periods of intensive work, meetings, etc.

Motion profiles appear to be the most problematic type of inferences. With the planned increases in roll-out of card-reader authentication, these profiles can become increasingly fine-grained.

The introduction of such technology constitutes a potential application case for DPbD, since such data collection and processing falls under data protection law. The Article 29 Working Party observed [1, p. 4, original emphasis] "Data protection requirements apply to the monitoring and surveillance of workers whether in terms of email use, Internet access, video cameras or location data. *Any monitoring must be a proportionate* response by an employer to the risks it faces taking into account the legitimate privacy and other interests of workers. *Any personal data* held or used in the course of monitoring must be *adequate, relevant and not excessive for the purpose for which the monitoring is justified.* Any monitoring must be carried out in the least intrusive way possible." The possibility of relying on the employer's "legitimate interest" is emphasized in [7], and a more general regulatory analysis is given in [15].

A Good Case Study. Additional factors made this a good case study: "Coffee tracking", while a clear case of tracking, is perceived as neutral or even amusing by a majority of employees (as opposed to, say, a tracking of physician visits would be), and there is in general a high level of trust in the organisation and its data-protection integrity. This opened up a space in which people felt free to voice their concerns.

2.2 Research Questions

Staff members reacted in different ways to the introduction of the new technology, ranging from simply accepting the measure and bringing and swiping their cards to get coffee, via short discussions of possible reasons, to extended "hacker-humour" discussions of how to break the system. On the whole, it appeared that questions and dissatisfaction persisted even after a number of weeks, and this situation motivated the research.

The research was, in part, motivated by our work on Privacy/Data protection by design [21]. In addition, the question was what this change in technology and user interface of the coffee machines meant for privacy-related decision making in human-computer interaction.

Specifically, questions revolved around (1) the prerequisites for people to use PETs, in particular knowledge, beliefs and attitudes, in addition to or even before usability can improve technology acceptance, as posited in the step model of [18], and (2) the importance of social influences (as opposed to purely individual criteria such as cost-benefit analysis) on whether and how to use PETs, as posited by the ASPECT/ARCADE model of [17]. I was also interested in whether the knowledge about social effects can be leveraged for PETs technically via notions such as co-utility [10] and techniques such as collaborative distributed anonymisation [20], but decided to not foreground this complex construct.

The research questions were as follows:

- **(RQ1)** To what extent is the intent to use PETs dependent on prior knowledge of the underlying data collection technology?
- **(RQ2)** What are privacy-related decisions based on? In particular, to what extent is decision-making individual, and to what extent subject to social influences?
- **(RQ3)** Co-design: The new access control method constituted one design option. Would employees (as one stakeholder group) be able to generate more design options, and what would characterise these choices?

An additional motivation was to get an impression of attitudes and thoughts among employees, in order to understand the underlying current of discontent. This led to the practical questions

- **(PQ1)** Did employees know what personal data were collected, and did they care?
- **(PQ2)** Would they utilize an anonymization PET if it was available?

2.3 Method

A survey was created consisting of the following questions, all of which except (4) were open questions with free-form text answers (see Fig. 1 for an example):

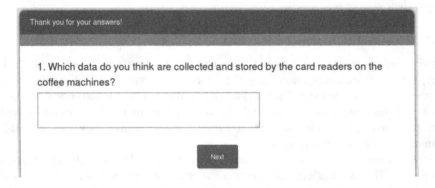

Fig. 1. Screenshot of the first survey question.

- **(Q1)** Which data do you think are collected and stored by the card readers on the coffee machines?
- **(Q2)** Do you think the purpose of barring unauthorized coffee-getting could also be attained with other data, or other means? Please explain briefly.

- **(Q3)** If there was a button "anonymised version of coffee-getting authentication" on the card reader, would you use it? Feel free to make any assumptions about the system and its technology, as long as you briefly explain these assumptions.[2]
- **(Q4)** Do you think your use of the coffee machines (including your use of the fictitious button of question 3) may influence how your colleagues use them? (choice between "no", "maybe", "yes")
- **(Q5)** If you checked "maybe" or "yes" in the previous question, please explain why. Feel free to make any assumptions about the system and its technology, as long as you briefly explain these assumptions.
- **(comments)** Would you like to make any other comments?

The survey was available (a) online at www.surveymonkey.com and (b) as an RTF file that could be printed out and forwarded to me anonymously. The invitation to participate in the survey was sent out on 30th November, containing the link and the file, via the email alias that reaches all 239 people working in the department (i.e. all the people who may and now, via their personnel cards, can use the coffee machines). The survey was described as part of a research project. Answers were collected anonymously. To reduce the chance of people participating multiple times, the survey used the surveymonkey option that restricts answers to one per device. No further measures against multiple answers were taken; however, given everybody's time constraints it appeared unlikely that people would take part in a survey multiple times.

2.4   Results and Discussion (1)

The survey was answered by 101 people, a response rate of 42%, within 2 days, with 1 paper and 100 online versions. One empty online result was not counted.[3] The free-form answers were analysed with a simple form of thematic-analysis coding [3].

The large majority of answers were thoughtful and respectful, and respondents also expressed, in the comments question, much positive feedback about the fact of the study and interest in the results. Some answers were short and/or expressed humour and irony, such as "I'd like to suggest a James Bond-style iris-scan for coffee privileges. It would be way cooler and in that way I don't have to worry about forgetting my card." or "I am in a coffee drinking competition with a colleague. We want authenticated personal stats!"

The questions were asked in an order designed to constrain answers as little as possible, by asking a question q dealing with only one out of several possible to another question p, only after p. Q1 asked about what *knowledge (or beliefs)* people had about the new technology that had been deployed. Q2 asked about

---

[2] The button was a fictitious PET, initially thought of as a version of distributed and possibly collaborative anonymisation [20], but open to interpretation by respondents.

[3] It is possible, but irrelevant for the results, that this person had first flipped through the online version, was blocked from re-taking it, and therefore filled in the paper version.

possible alternative technologies (or: *design* ideas). This question had to add a purpose (relative to Q1), without which the design question would have been meaningless, and it made a minimal assumption based on the official communication that had been made. Q3 could only be asked afterwards, since it asked about a specific instance of such technologies (anonymisation). Q4 was designed to explore an aspect that is characteristic of privacy and some PETs (including anonymisation PETs): social effects. With reference to PETs, it represented a further specialisation of Q3, and therefore had to be asked after it. Q5 was the request to elaborate on the multiple-choice answer to Q4.

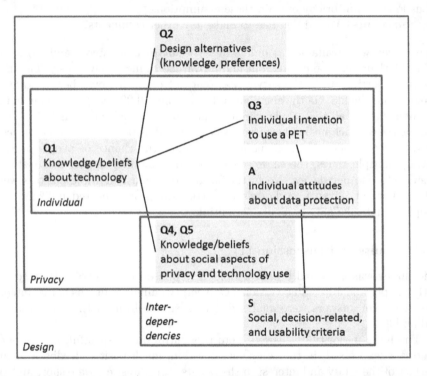

Fig. 2. Variables arising from the questions (Q1–Q5) and from the exploratory analysis (A, S), and their relationship to larger concepts. Lines between variables indicate the existence of dependencies.

For the purposes of discussing the results, a different order is more meaningful. Figure 2 shows a conceptual rendering of the decision aspects dealt with in the different questions. The analysis will cover variables describing individual knowledge/beliefs and intentions about technology and PETs, then variables that describe social knowledge/beliefs (and their intersection with privacy-related ones), and then design variables. A and S are variables defined in an exploratory phase of analysis (see Sect. 2.5).

Due to the open nature of the survey and the exploratory aspects of analysis, all data were analysed by descriptive statistics only. Inferential statistics are left for follow-up studies.

Q1. More than three quarters of respondents (rightly) believe that tracking takes place, but most do not know what is being tracked. 22.8% stated that no data were collected and stored. Only 26.7% gave the correct or near-correct answer that some user ID and the timestamp were being collected and stored. (Technically, only the card ID is logged, but of course this can be linked, via another database, to the user ID; therefore, these two answers were aggregated.) Another 26.7% thought that also the type of drink was being logged. 9.9% considered that aggregate consumption only, maybe with something else, was recorded and stored, and 3% suspected some other form of data.

Answers including the type of drink would be correct if the respondent understood the question differently: "which data are collected and stored through a card swipe", because the coffee machine does record the type of consumed drink, even if neither the card reader nor the authentication server logs have access to this kind of information.

The distribution of answers may indicate that the question, while correctly targeting data-protection concerns, was not optimally phrased, since technically there are three different devices that collect data (coffee machine, card reader, authentication server), and all three have different methods and durations of storing the collected data. In addition, from a data-protection viewpoint, yet another question is crucial: whether the data are collected and/or stored and/or analysed. One respondent noted the logical underspecification in the information that had been communicated: "The promise that there are no plans to collect statistics does not say there will not be plans in the future, and statistics are not logging so one can later still create statistics of the past." Regardless of these different possible misinterpretations, it is worthwhile noting that nearly a quarter of employees, against their presumably existing understanding of how a personnel-card reader works, (wrongly) interpreted the "promise of no statistics" as "no data collection".

Q3 was answered in the affirmative by 36.6% of respondents, and in the negative by 35.6%. 12.9% mentioned usability ("one more button to press") as a factor, with 9 of these 13 people regarding the extra effort as a deterrent. (4 would still use it.) 10.9% mentioned trust ("how would I be able to check?", "although I would not trust it"), although 8 of these 11 people would still use it.

Q1–Q3. There was a clear connection between the beliefs about data collection and intentions to use the proposed PET (see Fig. 3). Obviously, for someone who believes that no data are being collected, it would make no sense to invest extra effort to anonymise, and thus the majority of these respondents (69.5%) would not use the button. (The four people who believed no data collection to take place in Q1 but wanting to use an anonymisation button in Q3 may have changed their beliefs along the survey). 43% of those who believe some kind of user ID is collected (whether with or without timestamp and with or without other information) intended to use the anonymisation button, and only 27.7% did not intend to use it. Most of the remaining 29% skipped the question.

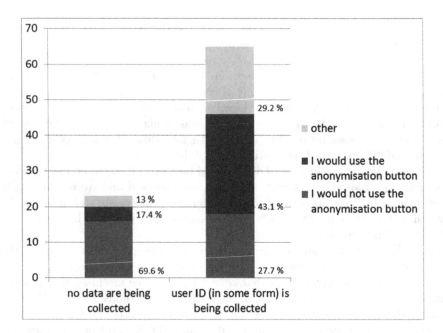

Fig. 3. Q1–Q3: knowledge/beliefs about data collection and intention to use the fictitious PET (numbers of respondents, percentages within the knowledge/belief group).

Q4 showed that nearly half of respondents (48.5%) believe that their use of the coffee machines has ("yes": 22.8%) or may have ("maybe": 25.7%) effects on other people. 34.7% explicitly believe that it does not have such effects ("no"). The remainder did not answer this question. The answers to question (5) showed that people had interpreted this question, as intended, with reference to coffee getting and data protection. Asked about the reasons why in question (5), only 1 person referred to k-anonymity (which had been the motivation for this question). 2 persons referred to effects of surveillance or chilling effects. Many more talked more explicitly about social influence and peer pressure, with 7 referring to influence via imparting knowledge (awareness or reflection) and 9 via imitation.

Q1–Q4. Both Q1 and Q4 ask about knowledge or beliefs, one about a technology (not a PET), the other about privacy and behaviour in general and specific PETs in particular. One may therefore expect that the answer distributions should be independent of each another. On the other hand, it could be the case that people who are more knowledgeable or reflective about privacy in general might also be the ones for whom it is more salient that a particular technology will collect data. There is (weak) support for the latter hypothesis: A majority (50.7%) of those who believe some form of user ID is collected, also think that their behaviour influences others, whereas this percentage is only 43.4% among the "no data are collected" respondents.

Q2. Respondents proposed many different design alternatives. Since some people offered various alternatives and others offered none, the following percentages do not add up to 100%. The most frequent answers were two: there is no, or no efficient, alternative (18.8%), and social control (24.8%). These can be considered, in the light of data collection, as two ends of the spectrum: "the problem of unauthorised coffee-getting exists (and the current amount of data needs to be collected)" and "the problem does not exist or is negligible (and the previous approach in which no data are collected, is sufficient)". 15.8% explicitly said that they did not believe the problem exists.

Other answers acknowledge that the problem exists, but take different approaches with respect to data collection:

- **without data:** lock the room (4.9%), warning sign (4%), security guard (5%), no plastic cups and no cups in the cafeteria (1%)
- **without personal data (collection and/or storage):** anonymous tokens (10.9%), typing a code (6.9%), only checking authorization (5%)
- **with less, or less fine-grained, personal data:** restrict access to the cafeteria with card readers, at all hours (12.8%), or restrict access to the coffee machines with card readers, but only outside office hours (8.9%).

Three people mentioned cameras and facial recognition, i.e. more personal data, and two others suggested an interesting variant: *deactivated* card readers or cameras. Three answers suggested that people wanted to reap advantages of data collection (personalization of the drinks).

In sum, these answers suggest that co-design with the affected employees could work, and work efficiently (50% of respondents came up with their design ideas in less than 6.5 min, and 79% in less than 15 min). Of course, some of these options may in fact have been considered, and the relative costs are not known, but the abundance of answers belies the simple acceptance by those 18.8% who considered the chosen option to be without an alternative.

Q1–Q2. There was also evidence that the beliefs about data collection were associated with the activity level and type of co-design. Figure 4 shows the distribution of the design groups over the "no data collected" resp. "some form of user ID collected" respondents. Not only are data-collecting technologies that collect fewer or no personal data more popular among the latter; they also propose reliance on social control (as a specific form of "no data" design) very often. Conversely, most of the "no data collected" belief group sees no alternative to the current technology.

With regard to the research and practical questions, the following results were obtained:

- **(PQ1)** Most employees knew they were being tracked, but there were many misconceptions about details, and around a third believed there was no data collection/analysis.
- **(PQ2) and (RQ1)** Only slightly more than a third would use the fictitious PET, an equal number would not use it, and the rest did not answer. Knowledge/beliefs about data collection were clearly associated with intention to use.

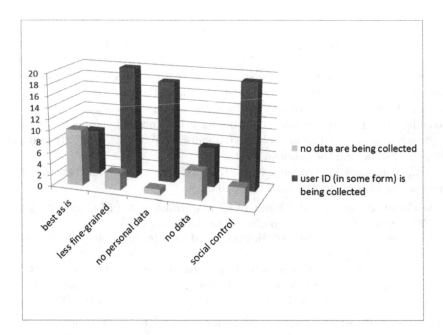

Fig. 4. Q1–Q2: knowledge/beliefs about data collection and proposals for design (numbers of respondents).

- **(RQ2)** Nearly half of users believe there are social effects.
- **(RQ3)** Users came up with many alternative proposals in a short time, with people who had correct knowledge/beliefs about tracking generating more and more privacy-friendly variants.

2.5   Results and Discussion (2): Exploratory Analysis

When coding the free-form answers to Q2, Q3 and Q5, further recurring themes were identified.

A. Some respondents explicitly described their *privacy attitudes*, both positively (e.g., "a severe privacy infringement") and negatively (e.g., "I don't feel protective of this data in the slightest"). Privacy attitudes could also be inferred from many answers to the five questions, but attitudes per se were not inquired about, so only explicit mentions were coded for this new variable. The resulting variable A can therefore be regarded as a lower bound on the numbers of respondents with positive pro-privacy or negative non-privacy-concerned attitudes.

A–Q3. As could be expected, respondents who expressed pro-privacy attitudes also said they would use the fictitious PET (14 yes, 2 no), while respondents who expressed that they did not care about protecting these data showed the reverse pattern (4 yes, 12 no).

S. There were *usability* comments, both about the fictitious additional PET (see results of Q3 above) and about the existing technology (the card readers). Some remarks were made about *accountability*, via references to charging for coffee consumption. Most of these were negative, but some were neutral (coded as positive below).

In addition, respondents talked widely about effects that had not been expected in this research. First, these were *altered perceptions of the communal space*. This occurred both as a description of why the new technology was rejected (e.g., "The department always have felt like a place where everybody tries to be as flexible as possible [...] It's sad that the department now seems to be willing to question this flexibility over the price of a few coffees."), and as a design alternative (e.g. "provid[e] minimal free service to [other members of the organisaton], be kind and open to non personnel, ..."). Other comments described *altered actions in the communal space* (e.g., "Yes, [there will be social effects: employees] will buy own coffee machine for the office. This will reduce the number of informal meetings in cafeteria"). The events also led to an *increased salience of how decisions are made and communicated*, with most comments claiming that there had been no or poor communication of the purpose of the new technology, and no evidence given of non-authorised coffee-getting.[4]

All S mentions identified concerns, i.e. that respondents cared about these values. Thus, for S (sub-)variables, "positive" means the expression of a disutility with respect to this criterion (e.g. for accountability: being charged for something that was previously free), whereas "negative" means the expression of a neutral or positive thought (e.g. that people would recognise the value of coffee).

The numbers of these comments are summarised in Table 1.

Table 1. Number of respondents with comments on A (explicitly expressed privacy attitudes) and on any of the other "social" criteria, summarised as S. Some totals of S are smaller than the column sum or row sum due to multiple criteria expressed by the same persons.

	A	Usability		Account-ability	Altered perception	Altered actions	Saliency of decision-making	S total
		(Present technology)	(Fictitious PET)					
Positive	17	11	13	5	11	13	8	32
Negative	18	0	0	2	1	1	0	4
Sum	35	11	13	7	12	14	8	33

---

[4] In reaction to this, decision makers said that observed cases had in fact been communicated, and asked whether it was their task to prove abuse – which indeed would be impossible without another form of surveillance technology.

A–S. In total, 55 respondents (55.4%) made comments about A, S, or both. Of these, about 1/3 each (22 and 20) talked about only A or only S, and 13 about both. A further analysis of polarity indicated a substitution relationship between "privacy" and "social" rationales: Of those who had not commented on A, 30% commented on S. This proportion sank to 17.6% among those who had commented on A positively (i.e. expressed that privacy was important to them), but it rose to 55.6% among those who had commented on A negatively (i.e. expressed that privacy was not important to them). One respondent expressed this explicitly: "Anonymity is not the point here", then explaining their concern about S topics.

3   Consequences for Risk/Privacy-Utility Models in DPbD

The high response rate of the survey in general, and the free-form answers in particular, indicated that many employees perceived significant risks and disutility through the introduction of the card-reader access control. This has to be considered in relation to the utility gained.

A standard approach to this decision situation follows [11] and models

- **utility** is the utility of data usage.
- **risk** is the disclosure risk (or, more generally, privacy risk) to those whose personal data are being collected.

It is generally assumed that the processing of a full data set has the most utility, but also the most risk, the processing of no data has no utility and no risk, and fewer or transformed (e.g. k-anonymised) data have intermediate levels of both. This produces the tradeoff "the more utility, the more risk". This is shown, schematically, by curve 1 in Fig. 5.

There is an alternative form of modelling, often used to describe and compare forms of privacy-preserving data mining/publishing. Here, the second component is a measure of (data) privacy, the inverse of risk, and the tradeoff is "the more privacy, the less utility" [2].

The *existence* of this claimed tradeoff is, in a sense, tautological: If an unconstrained optimisation (e.g. the accuracy of a classifier learned from a full dataset) is the definition of the "full" utility, then any constrained optimisation (e.g. caused by some data privacy measure threshold) *must* be smaller or equal, and is usually smaller than, the unconstrained optimum. The *amount* that has to be traded off, and the *shape* of the tradeoff curve, may however depend on the data transformation processes applied.

Utility and Privacy Risk in the Case Study: A First Model. Going back to the case study: What exactly are utility and risk?

The utility in the original tradeoff curves is "data utility": "the value of a given data release as an analytical resource – the key issue being whether

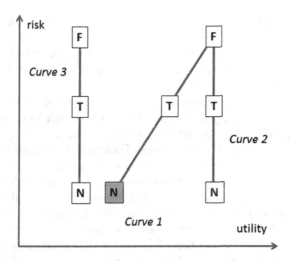

Fig. 5. Three schematic curves in risk-utility space. N = no personal data (with grey background: situation before start of data collection), F = full data, T = transformed data (e.g. k-anonymised).

the data represent whatever it is they are supposed to represent" [12, p. 135]. However, this notion accords a conceptual independence to the data and their function that they do not have in real-world contexts and applications.

From the perspective of contexts and applications, utility is linked to the purpose of data collection. This is linked to different factors. If a given factor is part of the purpose, then a technology that achieves this goal will create utility. If it is not part of the purpose, it will not create utility. Here:

- **authentication** only personnel members should be able to use the resource.
- **accountability**$_1$ of coffee consumers for their consumption.
- **accountability**$_2$ of the coffee supplier for invoiced amounts.
- **accountability**$_3$ of individuals or specified anonymity sets in cases of abuse, as when a theft has occurred and the persons in the room at the time are to be determined.[5]

The privacy risks are mainly the potential to create motion profiles, make inferences from them, and take action based on these inferences (see Sect. 2.1).

3.1   Risk-Utility Tradeoffs, DPbD, and Data Minimisation

What would it mean to apply DPbD in the present use case, or in extensions of this? On the one hand, a number of concerns that could be termed "classical PET concerns" would need to be taken into account: the security and encryption technology used for cards, for data transfer, and log storage, access control

---

[5] In the case study, the latter two were mentioned by administrative/management personnel involved in card-reader deployment, in a follow-up interview of the survey.

for the logs, separation of the logs from the mapping of pseudonyms to IDs, etc. However, as Schaar [19] has pointed out in a critique of a classical case of the failure of an ambitious PbD project, a focus on these technology-centric considerations may lead decision makers to neglect important data protection principles, in particular data minimisation.

Data minimisation depends on the purpose of data collection. In a nutshell, it asks whether a given purpose can also be achieved with less data. This question presupposes that data processing yields a certain utility (= by fulfilling the purpose) and generates certain risks. Therefore, I propose to regard data minimisation as casting DPbD as a question of design in a risk-utility space.

For illustration, some simple approaches will be discussed that depart from the current infrastructure and thus would impose only negligible extra costs. The costs of card and authentication-server infrastructure are sunk costs; and the deployment of different hardware was not considered an alternative and is therefore not considered further here. To measure the extent of the risks, a simple variant of k-anonymity is used. (Different measures, e.g. based on differential privacy, or taking into account the accuracy of inferences, are possible but would require more assumptions.)

Assume the purpose is only to prevent unauthorised use of the resource and accountability$_2$. An anonymisation of the logs whereby each user pseudonym is replaced by the constant "authorised user" or "unauthorised user" would suffice to serve this purpose with *no personal data*, thus leaving utility unaffected and reducing privacy risk to their starting level. (For the sake of simplicity of the argument, threats from stronger – and more costly – attacks involving for example physical observation and record linkage, are ignored.)[6]

If the purpose is also accountability$_1$, a follow-up question needs to ask whether in fact individuals are to be charged for their consumptions, or administrative units. In the latter case, a k-anonymisation of the logs whereby each authorised user's pseudonym is replaced by their respective unit ID would suffice to serve this purpose. Again, utility would remain unaffected, and privacy risk would be reduced to the level of k, with k the size of the smallest unit.

The distinction between individual and collective accountability [4] becomes more acute if accountability$_3$ is also a purpose. Various questions should be asked: Should and could this accountability be individual or collective (for example, it is conceivable that whole units take responsibility and are held liable in cases of theft)? Should such accountability be multi-step, i.e. the unit takes responsibility to the outside and imposes individual sanctions on the inside? Who should decide on this question?

For all forms of accountability, data are likely to be needed only for certain periods. Beyond that, they can (and therefore should) be deleted, an operation that will not affect utility but reduce privacy risks.

---

[6] This constraint on utility also illustrates the dependence of technical solutions' utility on purposes. The proposal "no plastic cups and no cups in the cafeteria" to Q2 would serve the purpose of barring non-authorised use, but not that of accountability$_2$. However, the existence of this purpose was likely unknown to respondents.

Best-case risk-utility values resulting from this thought experiment are shown, in schematic form, by curve 2 in Fig. 5, which indicates that there is no or a negligible tradeoff (negligible if the costs of data transformation are taken into account, no if they aren't).

3.2 Extending Risk-Utility Tradeoff Models by Multicriteria Decision-Making Modelling

However, as the exploratory analysis has shown, there is a third component here summarised as S. In the present study, the following additional factors of (dis)utility were found (cf. Sect. 2.5):

- usability
- altered perception of a communal space
- altered actions in the communal space
- increased salience of how decisions are made and communicated.

This can be modelled as an additional risk factor or an additional disutility factor. All else equal, this would shift curves upward (more risk) or to the left (less utility). Curve 3 in Fig. 5 uses the latter approach in order to not change the semantics of the risk.[7] It shows that in extreme cases, even with perfect PETs and data minimisation, the outcome could be worse than the starting point: Assume that authentication is data-minimal and secure, and no personal data are stored. As a result, utility with respect to the goals of authentication and accountability may increase, as explained in the previous section. However, this increase may be more than offset by a decrease in utility caused by losses in usability and perceptions of and actions in the communcal space. The increased salience of decision making may be considered positive for utility (to the extent that employee awareness and participation are desired) or as negative for utility (to the extent that such awareness is considered to lead to discontent for employees and/or work for management). These utilities and disutilities may be experienced by different stakeholders, but they can be aggregated into an organisation-wide utility measure. In sum, *any* choice along curve 3, which contains the available options with the new technology, would be inferior to the starting point, i.e. create less utility and the same or higher risk.

To avoid such inferior choices, DPbD should draw more strongly on multicriteria decision making: Data protection and privacy risks need to be measured but should be weighed against a notion of utility composed of the classical purpose-dependent utility and disutilities caused by usability and social implications.

---

[7] The semantics of the risk that are generally used in risk-utility models focus on an individuum-centric notion of privacy. The current focus on the risks of tracking using personal data (see Sect. 3) follows this approach. Certainly privacy is not only an individual but also a collective value, so some aspects of "altered perceptions of a communal space" could be modelled as an additional factor of privacy risk. However, it appears questionable to subsume also usability or the salience of decision making under "privacy risks".

4   Limitations and Lessons Learned

There were only two clearly negative comments on the survey, and these serve well as introductions to this section.

One respondent found the questions "silly, not precise enough, and highly biased".

I believe that silliness is a matter of perspective and will therefore disregard this. As explained above, the questions were on purpose underspecified and left much room for open, including unexpected, answers. It is true, however, that this openness also in some cases led to answers that were more difficult to interpret. So while openness allowed for exploration and the discovery of the variables A and S, and thereby led to the design ideas described in Sect. 3.2, the results should be validated in follow-up work in a confirmatory manner.

There was indeed some imprecision in phrasing, in particular with respect to Q1. This issue has been described in Sect. 2.3, and as argued there, this imprecision also had some unexpected advantages. Still, in follow-up work a compromise should be found between technical exactness and linguistic simplicity when describing technological functionality.

In this study, there were two main expressions or sources of bias.

The first relates to Q2. It implied that the card readers have the purpose of barring unauthorised coffee-getting. In fact, this was an *interpretation* of the communication to employees, which had not talked about purpose(s), but highlighted the benefit to the department of not having to pay for outsiders' coffee consumption (which had never been authorised, but previously could not be avoided). This interpretation led to the notion of "unauthorised coffee-getting" in Q2.

The phrasing of question (2) may suggest that this be the sole purpose. This was not the case (even if other purposes had not been communicated). While the phrasing of Q2 was legitimate in the context of Q2 (whose purpose was indeed to obtain design alternatives for this purpose), the phrasing may have influenced the answers to the questions following it. In follow-up work, the order of questions should be considered very carefully, and questions that may prime certain concepts may be placed later.

The second source of bias was made apparent by the results themselves, in particular in the exploratory analysis. The research and survey questions were formulated on a background of a long personal history of privacy research, and this may have led to a certain *déformation professionelle*. As Gürses and Diaz [14] observe, one always needs to ask who formulated the privacy problem: the "experts" or the "users". As they point out, privacy/security experts tend to perceive problems of institutional privacy, usually the collection and processing of data by powerful corporations or governments, whereas users tend to focus more on social privacy, the question of who among their peers should know what. In [9], we have proposed this question of "who defines the privacy problem" as one of five key self-reflective questions that privacy researchers should ask themselves to improve the quality and transparency of their work. The results of the present study suggest that part of the bias of the "expert" is, already prior to questions such as institutional or social privacy, to cast every problem as a privacy problem. While the present users' concerns about S topics often revolved around *social* consequences of technology, these were not limited, or even expressly not about, *social privacy*. When they were about privacy, they revolved around institutional privacy. Viewed over all users, there seemed to be a substitution effect of institutional privacy concerns versus social non-privacy concerns. Thus, the present study suggests an additional self-reflective question: "who defines the problem, and is it really (only) a privacy problem?".

The second critical remark from respondents was that "[t]his survey looks much like unnecessary criticism on the department's decision to install these card readers." As remarks from other respondents, referred to above as increased saliency of decision-making, show, many respondents voiced criticism of this decision. However, in the light of the De Hert and Gutwirth [8] analysis of data protection as a transparency tool towards the powerful (data controllers and processors)[8], it needs to be asked when such criticism is "unnecessary" and when it is not. Other respondents regarded the very existence of criticism as positive: "The critical reception of the card readers on our coffee machines is actually a good sign. One can't expect (junior) scientists to be good and uncritical at the same time." The survey itself led to some concrete measures for improving the transparency of decision making (so far, a voluntary self-commitment of the employee representative to communicate results of decision making more widely).

5   Summary, General Conclusions, and Future Work

The results of the case study validate models of complex individual decision-making in privacy-related questions, in particular the importance of social influences posited by the ASPECT/ARCADE model of [17]. They also validate the necessity of a number of prerequisites for people to use PETs, in particular knowledge, beliefs and attitudes, in addition to or even before usability can improve technology acceptance, as posited in the step model of [18].

The opinion, widespread among respondents, that privacy operates also via social effects can be interpreted, with some caution, as an understanding that "my privacy utility influences yours, and vice versa", thus presenting some empirical support for PETs that are built on co-utility [10]. However, concrete instances such as collaborative distributed anonymisation [20] require more dedicated user-based evaluations. In a first user study [16], we found that while non-technical users in general understood the concept of k-anonymity and the notion of privacy that it can provide for them, it was less clear to them that to obtain such k-anonymity, they need to contribute to it. Thus, the study did not provide evidence that these users understood or appreciated the notion of co-utility applicable in the example application and architecture. That study, however, suffered from an example domain in which participants did not have

---

[8] complemented by privacy protection as an opacity tool towards the powerless (data subjects).

strong privacy preferences. Follow-up work will aim at designing a more convincing task, taking into account also the results of the present study.

Beyond supporting earlier research, the present results however call into question the models from computer science/data mining that posit a privacy-utility tradeoff, where utility is measured in a simplistic way that centers on the accuracy of the personal data and (if applicable) the models learned from these data. The results illustrate how social considerations, and considerations about – both their own and organisations' – decision-making and its transparency, are woven into people's reactions to technology. The perceived negative effects on social spaces can even outweigh perceived threats based on data processing and possible privacy violations. Therefore, multicriteria notions of utility are needed, and this leads to design spaces in which less privacy can be associated with less utility rather than be compensated for by more utility, as the standard tradeoff models suggest. From a legal standpoint, a multicriteria notion of utility already ties in well with the GDPRs stated goal that data protection be the protection of a wide range of individuals rights and freedoms, not only the rights to data protection and privacy. From a computational standpoint, however, more efforts are needed to embed multicriteria utility into DPbD.

In future work, we aim to use the insights gained for different phases of DPbD, in particular Impact Assessments and design itself. This includes creating practical guidelines for including these considerations into (a then extended) Impact Assessment, and testing these guidelines for understandability and effectiveness. As a first step, this can build on the PIA Guidelines we developed for teaching and training contexts [21]. In addition, organisational card-reader deployment will be studied in a more general, recently started project involving the present author and others.

Acknowledgements. I thank all respondents of the survey for their thought-inspiring answers, and all those involved in the "New Developments in data privacy" workshops 2016 for support and valuable ideas: the Cambridge University Isaac Newton Institute and Turing Gateway to Mathematics, the organisers Mark Elliot, Natalie Shlomo and Chris Skinner, and all participants. Ralf De Wolf has provided helpful comments an on earlier version of the text.

References

1. Article 29 Working Party (2001). Opinion 8/2001 on the Processing of Personal Data in the Employment Context. http://ec.europa.eu/justice/data-protection/article-29/documentation/opinion-recommendation/files/2001/wp48_en.pdf
2. Bertino, E., Lin, D., Jiang, W.: A survey of quantification of privacy preserving data mining algorithms. In: Aggarwal, C.C., Yu, P.S. (eds.) Privacy-preserving Data Mining: Models and Algorithms, pp. 181–200. Springer, New York (2008)
3. Boyatzis, R.: Transforming Qualitative Information: Thematic Analysis and Code Development. Sage, London (1998)
4. Bovens, M.: Analysing and Assessing Public Accountability. A Conceptual Framework. European Governance Papers (EUROGOV) No. C-06-01 (2006). http://www.connex-network.org/eurogov/pdf/egp-connex-C-06-01.pdf

5. Crespo García, A., et al.: PRIPARE. Privacy- and Security-by design Methodology Handbook (2016). http://pripareproject.eu/wp-content/uploads/2013/11/PRIPARE-Methodology-Handbook-Final-Feb-24-2016.pdf. Accessed 13 Apr 2017

6. Danezis, G., Domingo-Ferrer, J., Hansen, M., Hoepman, J.-H., Le Métayer, D., Tirtea, R., Schiffner, S.: Privacy and Data Protection by Design from Policy to Engineering. ENISA Report (2014). https://www.enisa.europa.eu/publications/privacy-and-data-protection-by-design. Accessed 13 Apr 2017

7. Data Protection Commissioner (undated). Guidance Note for Data Controllers on Location Data. https://www.dataprotection.ie/docs/Guidance-Note-for-Data-Controllers-on-Location-Data/1587.htm.   Accessed 13 Apr 2017

8. De Hert, P., Gutwirth, S.: Privacy, data protection and law enforcement. Opacity of the individual and transparency and power. In: Claes, E., Duff, A., Gutwirth, S. (eds.) Privacy and the Criminal Law, pp. 61–104. Intersentia, Antwerp (2006)

9. De Wolf, R., Vanderhoven, E., Berendt, B., Pierson, J., Schellens, T.: Self-reflection on privacy research in social networking sites. Behav. Inform. Technol. (2016). doi:10.1080/0144929X.2016.1242653

10. Domingo-Ferrer, J., Martínez, S., Sánchez, D., Soria-Comas, J.: Co-Utility: self-enforcing protocols for the mutual benefit of participants. Eng. Appl. AI **59**, 148–158 (2017)

11. Duncan, G.T., Keller-McNulty, S.A., Stokes, S.L.: Disclosure Risk vs. Data Utility: The R-U Confidentiality Map. National Institute of Statistical Sciences. Technical report Number 121 (2001). http://www.niss.org/sites/default/files/technicalreports/tr121.pdf. Accessed 13 Apr 2017

12. Elliot, M., Mackey, E., O'Hary, K., Tudor, C.: The Anonymisation Decision-Making Framework. Manchester, UK: UKAN (2016). http://ukanon.net/wp-content/uploads/2015/05/The-Anonymisation-Decision-making-Framework.pdf. Accessed 13 Apr 2017

13. European Union Agency For Fundamental Rights FRA. Twelve operational fundamental rights considerations for law enforcement when processing Passenger Name Record (PNR) data (2014). https://fra.europa.eu/sites/default/files/fra-2014-fundamental-rights-considerations-pnr-data-en.pdf. Accessed 13 Apr 2017

14. Gürses, S., Diaz, C.: Two tales of privacy in online social networks. IEEE Secur. Priv. **11**(3), 2937 (2013)

15. Hendrickx, F.: Protection of Workers' Personal Data in the European Union: Two Studies. http://ec.europa.eu/social/BlobServlet?docId=2507. Accessed 13 Apr 2017

16. Herelixka, E.: Experiencing a Privacy Enhancing Technology. An Exploratory User Study of Collaborative Anonymization. Masters Thesis. KU Leuven, Faculty of Science (2016)

17. Jameson, A., Berendt, B., Gabrielli, S., Cena, F., Gena, C., Vernero, F., Reinecke, K.: Choice architecture for Human-Computer Interaction. Found. Trends Hum. Comput. Inter. **7**(1–2), 1–235 (2014)

18. Renaud, K., Volkamer, M., Renkema-Padmos, A.: Why doesn't jane protect her privacy? In: De Cristofaro, E., Murdoch, S.J. (eds.) PETS 2014. LNCS, vol. 8555, pp. 244–262. Springer, Cham (2014). doi:10.1007/978-3-319-08506-7_13

19. Schaar, P.: Privacy by design. Identity Inform. Soc. **3**(2), 267–274 (2010)

20. Soria-Comas, J., Domingo-Ferrer, J.: Co-utile collaborative anonymization of microdata. In: Torra, V., Narukawa, Y. (eds.) MDAI 2015. LNCS, vol. 9321, pp. 192–206. Springer, Cham (2015). doi:10.1007/978-3-319-23240-9_16
21. Tsormpatzoudi, P., Berendt, B., Coudert, F.: Privacy by design: from research and policy to practice – the challenge of multi-disciplinarity. In: Berendt, B., Engel, T., Ikonomou, D., Le Métayer, D., Schiffner, S. (eds.) APF 2015. LNCS, vol. 9484, pp. 199–212. Springer, Cham (2016). doi:10.1007/978-3-319-31456-3_12

Author Index

Printed in the United States
By Bookmasters